ANTHONY POWELL

A Quintet, Sextet, and War

ANTHONY POWELL

A Quintet, Sextet, and War

⸻

JOHN RUSSELL

Indiana University Press
Bloomington & London

Permission to quote from the works of Anthony Powell
has been graciously granted by Mr. Powell and his
publishers, Little, Brown and Company of Boston and
William Heinemann Ltd. of London.

Published in Canada by Fitzhenry & Whiteside Limited, Don Mills,
Ontario
LIBRARY OF CONGRESS CATALOG CARD NUMBER: 71-126217
ISBN: 253-10410-6
Manufactured in the United States of America

to my parents

CONTENTS

AUTHOR'S NOTE

With the final trilogy of his long novel *The Music of Time* remaining to be completed, it is obvious that this study of Anthony Powell, like the study of any other practicing author, has to be provisional. Insofar as it is able, it attempts to give a comprehensive account of Anthony Powell's writing to date. This begins with a consideration of Mr. Powell's record as a man of letters. What he has said in a long career of reviewing (more recently in some interviews), and what can be deduced about him from his biography of John Aubrey, indicate the very stable and resourceful attitudes of a man who did not start so rapidly into the production of fiction—his first book appeared when he was twenty-five —but who came on the scene as a nearly fully equipped writer with that first book. In the thirties, though his reputation did not burgeon then, he was one of a handful of English writers producing work of the first rank. *The Music of Time* volumes have crystallized that reputation now.

A comparison between the early and late novels is one of the concerns of this study, because of the direction Powell took in his later style. His books are works of the imagination, and this can be felt with redoubled force because of linguistic achievements he has made of two quite different kinds. But while this stylistic distinction is very prominent, a good deal of uniformity is found to prevail in Powell's fictional output with respect to his characters, situations, and themes. He is an unpredictable writer, yet a writer in whom design predominates on the one hand, and characters live and surprise us on the other.

Acknowledgments are due to the editors of *The Kenyon Review* for reuse of material in Chapter Two, which first appeared there. I owe a special debt, for help and encouragement with the manuscript in various of its stages, to James Bryan of the University of North Carolina, and to James Hall of the University of Washington. That it did have various stages reminds me that it took a longer time to complete than I had reckoned on, and in this regard I want to thank, for their forbearance, my family.

A NOTE ON THE TEXTS

Page numbers following the citations from Anthony Powell's books refer to the uniform Heinemann edition of his works, which correspond to the American edition published by Little, Brown; except that Little, Brown publishes *Venusberg* and *Agents and Patients* in a combined edition. The American revised edition of *John Aubrey and His Friends* is published by Barnes and Noble. The revised edition of *John Aubrey,* the new editions of the five early novels, and the first editions of the nine *Music of Time* volumes, were those used for citation. The following is an abbreviation key to the books, with their original dates of publication, and where applicable, the dates of the new editions that were used.

AM	*Afternoon Men* (1931; new ed. 1952)
V	*Venusberg* (1932; new ed. 1955)
FV	*From a View to a Death* (1933; new ed. 1954)
AP	*Agents and Patients* (1936; new ed. 1955)
W	*What's Become of Waring* (1939; new ed. 1953)
JA	*John Aubrey and His Friends* (1948; rev. ed. 1963)
QU	*A Question of Upbringing* (1951)
BM	*A Buyer's Market* (1952)
AW	*The Acceptance World* (1955)
LM	*At Lady Molly's* (1957)
CR	*Casanova's Chinese Restaurant* (1960)
KO	*The Kindly Ones* (1962)
VB	*The Valley of Bones* (1964)
SA	*The Soldier's Art* (1966)
MP	*The Military Philosophers* (1968)

ANTHONY POWELL
A Quintet, Sextet, and War

1

Orthodox Originality

Anthony Powell, the son of a soldier, was born in London in 1905 and lives today in Somerset near the border of Wiltshire. A productive novelist since 1931, he has risen to preeminence since the first of nine volumes of *The Music of Time* appeared in 1951. Powell in his younger days was a Londoner immersed in various literary pursuits; he moved to the West Country at age forty-five, in the same year of the first installment of his long novel. The gravitation of tradition seems always to have worked on him; his ancestors originally moved toward Wiltshire from the other direction, Wales. He may not have been alluding to them when he mentioned the ancestors of John Aubrey settling the same county: "Like the families of Baskerville and St John; Bromwich, Button, and Herbert; Vaughan, *Powell,* Gethin, Beavan, and many another of Welsh or Cambro-Norman descent . . . they had come to settle in that country from the Marches of Wales" (JA 20-21); however, it is true that his own ancestry parallels Aubrey's. Some of these forebears of Powell appear in *The Dictionary of Welsh Biography,* a book that impressed him by "its striking panorama of a small nation, on the whole less prone to self-revelation than

1

the other Celtic peoples."[1] His own temperament runs true to the type. In over forty years of a career in letters, since he came down from Oxford to join the Duckworth firm in 1926, till the present day, when he contributes a bi-monthly review to the London *Daily Telegraph,* he has put little before the public that could be considered self-revealing.

Over those years Powell has written fifteen books and edited several others.* Duckworth's published his first novels while he was a member of the firm—*Afternoon Men* (1931), *Venusberg* (1932), *From a View to a Death* (1933) came out in rapid succession; then he married in 1934, and *Agents and Patients* (1936) is inscribed to his wife, Violet Georgiana, daughter of the fifth Earl of Longford.[2] He left publishing to become a script writer for Warner Brothers in 1936, and went the next year to try his hand, without any luck, in Hollywood. On his return to England he wrote a novel about the publishing world, *What's Become of Waring* (1939). He had already begun reviewing for the *Telegraph* in 1936, and after military service he resumed this career, first for *TLS* (1947–1952), then for *Punch* (where he served as literary editor, 1953–1958), returning at last to his niche in the pages of the *Telegraph*—another small cycle completed. And in all that time Powell has committed only two pieces of personal biography to print: a memoir about Eton and a clarification of his ancestry for the *Anglo-Welsh Review.*[3] (He has been interviewed half a dozen times, but no one has done so much as a thumbnail personal profile of him.)

I put early weight on this undemonstrativeness only to suggest a reserve of formidable dimension. If the direction taken by most of the writers of his generation—the Audens and Orwells and

---

*Besides the books he wrote which are the subject of this study, Powell edited the Barnard Letters 1778–1824 *(London, 1928),* Novels of High Society from the Victorian Age *(London, 1947),* and Aubrey's Brief Lives and Other Selected Writings *(London, 1949). He also supplied the Preface to* The Complete Firbank *(London, 1961); this most recent editorial contribution shows his return to early interests, for it was mainly at his instigation, when a young publisher's reader at Duckworth's, that that firm began bringing out Firbank's works in 1929.*

Isherwoods—was rebellious, and above all confessional, there remained men of Powell's own conservative bent (friends, in fact, and college mates) who would keep pace with those liberals and generate a like quantity of expressive heat from their own side of the scene. The writers I speak of—Evelyn Waugh and Graham Greene, for instance, in their travel books notably—were to respond to the between-war years with a personal verve ("disgusto" as a Waugh critic once called it[4]) which has kept them too from crowding Powell as a classical practitioner of the arts. Even Henry Green, whose determined detachment has paralleled Powell's own and whose *Party Going* of 1939 was once called the perfectly inapposite book of its day,[5] was to produce a scaled-down autobiography, *Pack My Bag*, a year later under pressure of the expectation that he would not survive the imminent bombing of Britain.

In place of the travel book or self-portrait that a restless friend might write between novels and under duress, Powell, in the years when the Second World War was threatening, decided to write the biography of John Aubrey. It was a characteristic choice for him. *John Aubrey and His Friends* (1948), worked on intermittently all through the war, when the "machinery for producing . . . a novel . . . simply wasn't working,"[6] indicates, like a weather vane, the homing tendency in Powell. When he said of Aubrey's historical instinct that "the present must become the past . . . before it could wholly command his attention," and when he observed Aubrey's "scarcely counting himself as one of the actors on the stage" (JA 11), he was describing eminently classical tendencies in himself which his novels bear out.

Moreover, the choice of working on a subject of the remote past, and an undynamic man at that, seems to be an act of faith for a man in uniform, as Powell was for six years. It indicates a way of setting in perspective even so cataclysmic a thing as the war, just as Aubrey pursued his antiquarian interests through the years of the English Civil War while remaining a staunch loyalist. (Aubrey's 1648 discovery of the megaliths at Avebury, for example, came during a fox-hunt which could have been something more than that, since "this notable gathering of Royalists" may have been hatching something in the King's service. Nevertheless,

Aubrey recorded his deserting that company for a while in order to dwell on "a more delightful indagation," the Avebury relics [JA 60–61].) Powell clarifies this act of faith when he contrasts the unbeleaguered Aubrey to earnest partisans of now-forgotten causes in the seventeenth century, for "by some vitality less unreal than theirs, he has remained alive" (JA 115). This is the vitality of reining in to keep perspective (as Aubrey actually reined in his horse on the dash through Avebury), of expending energy on what is already past, but transmittable and of value, regardless of what topical portents may be at hand. The classical point of view, in short, reduces the individual and his predicaments in importance, while valuing the role he can fill as "connector."

Halfway through the 1960s, as readers are aware, Powell came to the point in *The Music of Time* of describing England at war. If I have seemed to rush toward reference to it, this has been because, by his own account, the war has been the fulcrum of his life and that of writers of his generation. "I suppose the fact is, one emerged from the war rather a different person."[7] In his case the approach of war may have doubled in impendingness because of the fact that he was brought up an only child in a military family.

Following in the pattern of other sons of upper-middle-class and professional families, Powell went through the traditional educational stages of preparatory school, public school, and university. At Oxford especially, where he read history at Balliol, he became friends with artistically precocious young men who were on or beyond the verge of achievement while still undergraduates. Graham Greene, Evelyn Waugh, and Henry Green have been mentioned: other contemporaries were Cyril Connolly, Peter Quennell, Harold Acton, Robert Byron, John Betjeman, Alfred Duggan: all but the last two were to secure their literary reputations quickly—certainly before 1930. As Nick Jenkins, the narrator of *The Music of Time,* says of two acquaintances just down from the university: "I was almost startled by the ease with which both of them appeared able to write books in almost any quantity . . ." (BM 247.)

Ingenuously enough, Powell told a *New Yorker* interviewer that it was the very *ordinariness* of producing novels that was to send him in the same direction. "I was brought up to do ordinary things. My parents always insisted on that. . . . Everyone at Oxford was writing a novel. At Eton, my school, novel-writing was also an ordinary thing to do."[8] It is safer to adhere more closely to the literal statement when assessing what Powell means than one might where another writer is concerned. Irony in the last quoted passage could occur only if one threw a bridge across the sentences and decided that Powell's parents told him to conform and get his novel started. Taking the statements sentence by sentence, there is no irony. They do tend to point to a temperamental difference between Powell's Eton and Oxford associates and himself, granting the independent spirit necessary for undertaking literary careers. As his memoir of Eton reveals, he was somewhat differently placed in being responsive to the social and aesthetic revolutions of the twenties without being weaned, as were so many, from a soldierly respect for subordination and duty.

The first boy Powell remembered seeing at Eton was whistling "K-K-K-Katie," but from under a top hat and in posture exhibiting "the world-famous Eton-slouch"—a less regimental demeanor could not easily be imagined. And "This was the most sophisticated thing I had ever seen."[9] The exposure to sophistication "took," as shown by Anthony's joining the Etonian Art Society: Harold Acton in *Memoirs of an Aesthete* remembers him then as being "concerned with book illustrations, Regency costume and Lovat Fraser."[10] At the same time, Powell could value his own moderate advancement in the Officer Training Corps, where he became a sergeant, and he expressed unqualified admiration for the regular army adjutants detailed to the Corps.

What bears emphasis is the balance suggested in a young man from the first postwar generation, who would soon take up a career in the avant-garde world of letters without making the first sign of cultural rebellion that caused many another to write off whole segments of English tradition as unworthy of inspection. A quick reference to Proust and Kipling may be in order. Henry Green (who, while a co-member of the same Eton Art Society, had resigned from the OTC) was to remark of his and Powell's Oxford days that Proust's reputation was at a zenith matched only, for conspicuousness, by the nadir at which Kipling's rested.[11] It was a natural observation to make in the mid-1920s. Now for Powell, Proust claims first place among novelists; but Kipling has also always been one of his favorites—"A writer for whom I have enormous admiration. . . ."[12] It would be dangerous to generalize about polar opposites vying for influence in a writer, on the strength of a few expressed personal preferences—though Powell has written quite a lot about these two particular authors. He certainly does grant Kipling's "uncomfortable side," a sometimes egregious tastelessness. But one of the areas where he admires Kipling is in that writer's conviction of the value of action, *without the usual corollary of cavorting about physically himself.*[13]

This helps explain Powell's pursuit of a career in the arts unaccompanied by any denigration of the normal active world. It incidentally shows that he is misrepresented when called a satirist. He has ways of paying respect to that world, and the one time notably that he did so—when he went in the army to serve in his father's former unit, the Welch Regiment, and later in Intelligence—he gave over wholly his creative vocation. *As* a creative writer, he is much more like Proust than like Kipling; but a healthy tension comes in when one overlays Proustian sensibility with the Kiplingesque instinct for duty. Call it bias or call it instinct, the point is that Powell's inclination for subordination is a force that never would let a sheer and Shavian intelligence take command of and vitiate his work. He will even seek out the subordinative bent of a genius of indulgence *like* Proust, ending one review of the Frenchman's letters with this bland admonition: "National Servicemen should note that Proust asked (unsuccessfully) for his period of army training to be extended."[14]

Pairs of forces—to judge mostly from the patterns in his fiction—seem continuously at work in Powell's writing life to induce that balance I have been suggesting. With little documentation so far, but with the sense of the characters who seem to represent him being edged here and there by almost equalizing forces, I have wished to imply that temperament rather than willed choice lies at last responsible for the originality and classicism of his writing. "But you can't write about something that isn't, so to speak, in you already," he said once in an interview. He had already maintained that a calm state was required for expressing whatever was "in you already," and was picked up by the interviewer:

> INTERVIEWER: How does that state of "calmness" that you mentioned a moment ago figure here?
>
> POWELL: If you're straining too hard, you can't write. I used to play a game as a child in which you jumped little horses along a ribbon in a race. If you jerked the ribbon too hard, the horses fell down. If you didn't jerk it hard enough, somebody else won. That's rather like writing so far as effort is concerned. You got to give out just the right amount.[15]

This sense of working in the middle between forces comes refreshingly at a time when ordinarily (witness many recent *Paris Review* interviews) it is the full-tilt veering of romantics that commands the attention of the fiction reader. "The fact is, of course," Powell has said, "that we have all become so hopelessly steeped in Romanticism that it is hard for anyone to imagine any other point of view."[16] But in his novels, when dissipation seems one of the pulls exerted on his protagonists, a certain diffidence will work against it; if Love exerts a force, Duty will draw in the opposite direction. These facts are implicit in his early work; they become explicit in his later. In neither is there any romanticism. Even if he is to choose a title from Ezekiel, it will be a cool and clear-seen title, *The Valley of Bones,* and not an agonized *Can These Bones Live?*

A rather pertinent anecdote closes "The Wat'ry Glade," Powell's Eton memoir, which had spared much time for "sybaritic" reflections. On his last day there the Corps of officer trainees were turned out in full kit to go off for a final bivouac on Salisbury plain. But Anthony was ill that day, and had to follow the marching battalion to their train in a cab. "I brought up the rear, at the tail of the column, in an open victoria with my rifle between my knees and my equipment on the opposite seat."[17] I find the image keenly apropos: the sensed chagrin at being the tag-along, yet the duty-consciousness marked by attention to equipment, and most of all the touch of elegance ("in an open victoria")—this last supplying a relief from restiveness but perhaps unable to prevent an infusion of melancholy. These qualities cohere to define the young Etonian who has quite an eye for assessing tendencies.

Powell's early protagonists and his alter ego Nick Jenkins combine these properly poised yet unpropitious attitudes. Almost all of these characters have left behind them anything to do with the military (until Jenkins joins up by way of his reserve commission as war begins). Like Powell, his early protagonists have gone into the upper-bohemian world of art and letters (or fringes of it, like museum-curating and journalism). And in the main they display—it is their weakness but turns out to be Powell's strength—an instinct to protocol in dissipated circumstances, through which they permit themselves to be jockeyed, as though along a ribbon, keeping some balance. Later it will be seen as a sort of dance they do, one of the things that offers to confuse the rhythm being the advent of the will to power.

HUMOR AND THE EARLY NOVELS

Much as I have intended to present a "homing" view of Anthony Powell, the fact remains that his five novels from the thirties are about seemingly rootless Londoners, who may travel into the country or abroad, or make the rounds of London pubs and galleries, with no sense at all of homing determination clinging to them. And London, Powell says, was "where I spent all my adult life."[18]

The years of the late 1920s and early 30s were the years of depression, of the rise of -isms, and of wholesale social interloping. One gets the sense in Powell's novels (as in many others) that individuals are thrown on their own disordered resources, that the times are not ripe for continuing families (there are almost no children in Powell's fiction), that self-advertisement and the confidence game have become universal ploys, and that you can only tell a genuine soul from a fake one because the fake thinks faster and thus can get what he wants (and keep at least himself alive). In short, as a fraudulent nobleman says at the end of Powell's second book: "It is the sentimental who do most harm in this world

of ours. You are no doubt familiar with the works of Nietzsche?"
(V 183). The times were not propitious for those who had leanings
toward subordination.

On the other hand, the problem at stake for a beginning writer
was that of testing immediate experience in its own context. As a
result, Powell's sense of the verdict of time was more or less held
in abeyance in his early books, which are essentially graphic in
impact. In *The Music of Time* he would be going back to the days
of his young manhood, but his books of the thirties are *about* the
thirties.

A word of caution is necessary, however, so as not to underrate
his historical sense. All five of his early titles derive from sources
between the seventeenth and nineteenth centuries, duly cited in
epigraphs. *Afternoon Men* comes from Robert Burton; *Venusberg*
from Baedeker; *From a View to a Death* from the nineteenth-
century song "John Peel"; *Agents and Patients* from Wesley; and
What's Become of Waring from Browning. These derivations fore-
warn us that the past is not to be shunted out of sight as we try to
take the measure of these novels. Nevertheless, their mode of operation is spatial rather than temporal as far as their way of present-
ing material is concerned.*

This spatial effect registered on the critic who gave Powell's
novels the most thorough consideration they were to receive in the
thirties. In *Twilight on Parnassus*, G. U. Ellis brought up another
pair of literary opposites in his remark that Powell "learned from
Hemingway in manner, and from Wyndham Lewis in aim."[19] By
mentioning Lewis, that great advancer of the spatial as opposed to
the temporal in the arts, Ellis attested the rigid external objectivity
aimed at by Powell as he began writing; the restrained manner of
Hemingway, in the meantime, forestalled that weakness for decla-
mation which was Lewis's greatest fault. (Powell's own favorite
word for this is "buttonholing.")

A toned-down brand of satire could have been the result. But

---

*The discussion of Powell's early and late styles, in Chapter Three below,
will illustrate at some length this spatial mode and the style which dis-
places it.*

as the actions in the early books went from the aimless to the futile, towing much laughter in their wakes, the carry-over of methods from Lewis and Hemingway was to leave characters hung in the air, so to speak, only because Powell had pitched onto some resources of writing discipline. One man had an eagle eye that would never misrepresent a thing out of sentiment; the other knew when and how to stop elaborating. To claim influence beyond these areas would be wrong. If the laconic early prose could show that Powell was alert to what was going on in the novel form, it is more important to see that his early books are books of well-guarded feeling —this more than anything else. As he once said, reflecting on the time when he began writing novels,

> When you're that age—I suppose I was about twenty-four when I began writing [Afternoon Men]—I think you can write in a much more, as it were, lyrical kind of way. It comes out—you haven't thought out what things are like—it's all feeling, really, which I'm sure really a novel should be. The older you grow, although you get to know more, and how to deal with things, I think you're apt to lose this feeling—though you may develop other capabilities. The great gift when you're young is this simple, all-observing ability, which is very difficult to preserve as you get older.[20]

I daresay that such a convinced recollection that "feeling came first" would surprise some admirers of Powell's early books, to many of whom the best thing of all is that those books are so funny. With their concentration on bogus people and affairs, they understandably have caused some to admire early-Powell as splendid counterattack fiction. It would be easy to instance, let us say, that Michael Arlen's 1924 novel *The Green Hat* was made too much of with its glorified barflies and nymphomaniacs, and that one could sense retaliation in Powell's *Afternoon Men* as the same London milieu is cross-examined and found flatulent. Or one could recall that Duckworth, Powell's own firm, was still publishing Elinor Glyn's notorious *Three Weeks* when *Venusberg* came out and exposed the trumped-up passion of all that Englishman-abroad-learns-about-love nonsense. But more important than anything like the mock-bohemian milieux in Powell's first two offerings is the fact that they stay close to the nerves of their two leading males (called Atwater and Lushington), men of the impeccable taste of Powell himself and unmistakable forerunners of Nick Jenkins in *The Music of Time.*

These main characters are ungrotesque, and this is a crucial matter; for if the earliest work is to be elevated to the stature of the latest, more than a talent for bizarre characterization will have to be found in it. The novels are most important when they fulfill the criterion laid down by Francis Wyndham, who called Powell a "corrector of clichés," and then went on to say of *The Music of Time,* "Again and again . . . one comes across some received idea . . . that has hitherto been treated conventionally by even the most sophisticated of novelists, at last *got right.*"[21] This would be Powell's own criterion, and the first novels must be judged by it. A disclaimer he once made underlines the point: "I'm not a comic writer, I'm simply a novelist."[22]

Though the laughable minor characters in each book might seem to get in the way of applying the criterion, compensations are at work to keep the books from becoming zany. First, a word about these grotesques. One coming fresh from the early fiction might find his memory filled with cretins and dwarfs, large-headed young men and rabbit-toothed young women, middle-aged people who have scrubbed floors to lose weight, and, in every novel, old people who have gone through the fracturing of life since the first war and now serve as broken road signs pointing to the futures of the young. But any such catalogue is misrepresentative, because even the oddest characters are given the consideration of a second look. V. S. Pritchett made this point very well, and connected it to "a stolid native melancholy" in Powell "that is terrifyingly full-blooded"—his habit, that is, of coming back and showing that a character is alive for all his idiocy.[23] Almost, perhaps, to check himself from reconsidering, Powell keeps certain "cases" offstage throughout a novel. "He has no roof to his mouth, has he?" (V 13)— but this is said of someone we never meet.

There is still a certain catalogue effect that remains undeniable and transmits its measure of grotesqueness.* Why, then, such an ample supply of the bogus? The answer lies with the protagonists —here is where a Lewis-like rigor (trained on himself, one wonders?) results in character-codes different from those of Hemingway. What Powell provides is a protagonist able to single out the right kind of man or woman but unable to join him or her, so that no farewell to the inauthentic can be made. This is why, when even the most negative alliances are made in the early books, the humor keeps rounding toward pathos. So in *Venusberg*, when Lushington cannot remain in love with a genuinely fine woman, but instead returns to an obviously second-rate mistress, sadness is the strongest feeling at the end. Reviewing this book twenty years after its original edition, and observing its honesty of emotion as reflected across that span, Anthony West took a view of Powell's humor which tallies with the author's own: lyrical impulse was behind things. The humor, said West, "is used as an acid to burn the sentimentality and evasiveness off the story of a very painful love affair."[24]

In *The Music of Time*, where evolutions go in slow motion and a musing, reconsidering style holds outrageous material in check, humor more patently operates in the service of realism. Hence, it has seemed to me important to make these remarks with respect to the five early books. They do in fact complete, in short dashes, the same long thematic run that is sighted on through the first sextet of *The Music of Time*.

There is a kind of curve involved, and the third early volume, *From a View to a Death,* begins to mark out the curve. Power-seekers now take up the baton and throw much more exertion into the action. The first two books had had their inconclusive actions framed into no less than seventy scenes, because their leading males had been so aimless. In *From a View to a Death* and *Agents and*

---

*This is important, for individual descriptions sacrifice hyperbole to precision nearly every time. Here, from the first book, is an exhibitionist arriving at a dinner party: "They heard Wauchop arrive and gather impetus by beginning to chuckle half-way up the stairs, so that he came into the room with the full force of a roar of laughter behind him" (AM 68). There is not a trace of exaggeration here: the fun (or horror) lies exclusively in the realism.

Patients the chapters (and the machinations) become more extended, the protagonists cruder, and the angle of narration panoramic (getting away from the foot-dragging central figure). We go from London to the English countryside in *From a View*, following the artist Zouch, bent on crashing county society; and from London to continental capitals and back, in *Agents and Patients*, as a dull young man, Blore-Smith, is given a fleecing along with an initiation into some low-ish forms of high life.

As manners break down in these books and the first flares of the power-motif begin to burn, one terrible highlight balks comedy consistently (though *Agents and Patients* is much less grave than *From a View*). This is that characters have become mutable, touched as they are by "the will to power." Unlike Atwater and Lushington of the first stories, the new characters really are tempted away from beaten paths. But instead of exercising power, they play into its hands. This is because Powell comes to take a more or less sanguine view of natural power: something that cannot be had for the asking, though it may well be thrown away.

The power-wish remains in *What's Become of Waring*, but there is a toning-down as a mystical motif is blent in. This occurs because, technically, the panoramic point of view shuts down and Powell passes all experience through the medium of a narrator. (It marks his first trying-out of the mode of *The Music of Time*, first-person narration.) A book about the London publishing world —where power-collisions produce very little literature—*Waring* is also provided with some real "mediums" whose séances bear on the action occultly. What the powerful do is thus modified by a new emphasis on the mysteries of coincidence.[25]

The turn taken in *Waring* leads to a judgment made by Kingsley Amis of the postwar novels. Amis had noticed Powell's sense that "things only happen when they are somehow appropriate," which led him to find Powell "approaching the edge of quietism. . . ."[26] In *Afternoon Men* and *Venusberg* there was no sign of his leaning this way; but by 1939 and *What's Become of Waring* the sign had been made. Powell touched the edge of quietism as the hero of *Waring*, Captain Hudson, was helped back to his former fiancée during a crisis at a séance, neither having planned to be there, both resigned to a separation that would not be patched up if either of them had to take the step to patch it.

It is probably no accident that Powell made this, his mellowest book, end with things put right in the life of a soldier—though one who has been on a literary hunt (tracking the writer called Waring). It is certainly no accident that things do turn right because Hudson is able to revert to type. He had nearly strayed outside his own nature, but checked himself, as it were, in mid-stride. Instead of becoming a potentially public literary figure, he packs up for the camel corps; but soldiering in fact suits him. Reversion to type indicates a progression in Powell from the point he had reached in *Agents and Patients* and *From a View to a Death*. In not becoming altered, Captain Hudson earns an assurance about his own identity—even though the crux of the novel has been the discovery that the man and writer he emulated, T. T. Waring, was a fraud.

In these later thirties' novels, Powell's protagonists make a fair assortment: a stolid military type (Hudson), a rich nincompoop (Blore-Smith), a thug of an artist (Zouch). He knows them thoroughly but seems to *be* Atwater and to *be* Lushington. And while he sights the very clear dangers of radical change with the later group, one feels that as he started he wished his first two heroes *would* change. The wish relates to their being neither activists like Zouch nor even acted upon like Blore-Smith. They simply drift. Their problem, made clear through their love affairs, is that they lack the capacity for grief and therefore have no capacity for loyalty. I should say that the whole motive for Powell's writing starts from a division—earlier called a balance, but that is the healthy hindsight view of it—between an instinct for loyalty and an intelligence so reserved that it foils that instinct. *The Music of Time*, by the way, supplies a substitute for grief that can induce loyalty: patience. Its first sextet, covering the same ground as the thirties' quintet, puts forward the tentative proposition that character grows through a formal "dance" to a more illumined sense of itself—and of others too—if only it does not rush.

"I suppose no man can violate his nature," Emerson said in "Self-Reliance," then went on: "A character is like an acrostic or Alexandrian stanza [i.e. palindrome];—read it forward, backward, or across, it still spells the same thing. . . . Character teaches above our wills."[27] When Powell called one of the sections in *Afternoon Men* "Palindrome," he could not have held the Emersonian view, for his palindromic characterization of Atwater was a regretful one. His later view does accord with Emerson's—with this classical exception: the *formality* of biding one's time would not be valued by the Transcendentalist. In *The Music of Time* the narrator's considered way of going through paces and stages will even allow some capacity for grief—a kind of intelligent inlet for it, in lieu of the more immediate apprehension of it. But nether Nick Jenkins nor Powell's first two heroes are thrown into anything approaching agony in the 1920s and 1930s when they are in early manhood.

TECHNIQUE AND "THE MUSIC OF TIME"

It is an odd fact that Powell completed his book on John Aubrey in 1946 but did not publish it till 1948. While the reason stemmed from nothing more than postwar logistics problems, the fact seems emblematic of the plodding quality which the book deliberately, so it would seem, does not shake free from. It might be putting too strong a construction on things to say that the biography was re-teaching him how to write; all the same, when he began *The Music of Time* in the year *John Aubrey* was published, "It needed a different kind of effort."[28] Perhaps one could say that from now on he would go through creative labor rather than creative expression, if such a distinction can be made. Thought and experience fill in where feeling once dominated and decided. An altogether greater density characterizes the new style, nearly always sacrificing momentum to clarification. This meticulousness had entered Powell's style very obviously in *John Aubrey and His Friends*.

Momentum is one thing the Aubrey book lacks. This is perhaps because of the respect Powell had for the "actualness" of the people he was considering—as *and His Friends* may indicate. Thus, in naming an Aubrey correspondent, Powell begins, "Andrew Paschall (who had lived in Erasmus's rooms at Queens', Cambridge) . . ." (JA 193). The entry will have nothing to do with Erasmus or Cambridge. Yet strangely enough this kind of chance and inconsequential fact achieves a presence, an aliveness, for these names from the past—by association with names from the further-off past! But this is not necessarily Powell's intention; it is more, in this unlaconic book, a *tic*. A few lines further in the paragraph, when the name of another friend bobs up, Powell inserts an Aubrey parenthesis: "Sir Jonas Moore ('sciatica he cured it, by boiling his buttock') . . ." (JA 193). The question of Moore's health will not figure in the entry.

Parentheses and dashes, side quotations and proper nouns become the redundant features of the *Aubrey* pages, while affecting momentum somewhat less sharply, colons and semicolons, temporal cross-references and categorical asides slow up *The Music of Time*. In yet one more parenthesis, Powell had noted how Aubrey "was for ever pursued by afterthoughts" (JA 180), and critics have seized on the relevance of the phrase to the habit of Powell's narrator, Nick.[29]

In the first trilogy—*A Question of Upbringing* (1951), *A Buyer's Market* (1952), and *The Acceptance World* (1955)—Nick Jenkins puts up more or less dignified bars around his private life, yet finds himself drifting toward a merger with a girl, Jean Duport, another man's wife. The years covered are the twenties (public school and university years) on through the Slump year of 1932. By the second trilogy—*At Lady Molly's* (1957), *Casanova's Chinese Restaurant* (1960), and *The Kindly Ones* (1962)—this affair has ended, and Nick becomes more publicly involved with a circle of friends and particularly the aristocratic Tolland family, into which he marries. The dates cover the mid-thirties—the time of the Abdication and the Spanish Civil War—with the last volume flashing back to World War I before bringing the sextet to a conclusion at the commencement of World War II. Nick's private life then sinks further from view with the novels dealing with the war, *The Valley of Bones* (1964), *The Soldier's Art* (1966), and *The Military Philosophers* (1968). But by "public" a moment ago I did not mean that the events of the later thirties catch Nick up in action: rather, his independence becomes compromised by inevitable entanglements. Marriage is a natural cause of this, but Nick barely describes his own in any intimate way: the idea is that maturity has made his guarded sense of separateness (thematic in the first trilogy) yield before the oft-confirmed insight (in the second and third) that he is more like others and they are like him. Alluding to this discovery before he makes it, he says in the middle of the first trilogy that "As time goes on, of course, these supposedly different worlds, in fact, draw closer, if not to each other, then to some pattern common to all . . ." (BM 159). In the thirties' novels, the characters themselves were not preoccupied with pattern. This was imposed from without. They had been well-made novels, carefully rounded off (one reason their lyricism may have gone undetected)—short dashes completed "in form." But now with this open concern for patterns "common to all," and the sense that the design is gradually getting clearer, one finds all of the volumes of *The Music of Time,* even those that end trilogies, taking the form of beautifully lengthened preludes.

A slow appreciation of character, and an awareness in himself that this growing appreciation must question too rapid diagnosis or prognosis, account for the prelude effect of *The Music of Time* volumes. By the end of the first sextet, Nick Jenkins can say with confidence that "In human life, the individual ultimately dominates every situation, however disordered, sometimes for better, sometimes for worse." (KO 61). But as James Hall has pointed out, Nick has had to make reassessments all along the way before supporting such conclusions. There are two kinds of reassessment. First are the categories that prove untenable when Nick tries to "place" people—these he has to get rid of. Comparing Powell and Henry Green as attackers of the concept of category itself, Hall remarks that Green does this by scenting the originality of his characters intuitively. "Powell does something similar from the opposite side. He comes on people from their remoteness, not their immediacy. His characters appear first through the maze of category . . . and only gradually take on their own definite existences."[30] The second form of re-checking, curiously enough, has to do with Nick's awareness of the growth of his own intelligence; it has a slowing-down effect on his life which he understands must be cast off when and if certain real crises are to be contested. It is as if Powell has discovered that "the individual dominates," and has even learned to ease off on the very intelligence which can make such discoveries. Thus intelligence does not get in the way when the cue for individual decision at last arrives. As Nick says at the time of his engagement: "Of this crisis in my life, I remember chiefly a sense of tremendous inevitability, a feeling that . . . too much reflection would be out of place" (LM 203).*

How Powell's "afterthought" method slows down characterization may be understood by examining the descriptions of a pair of eccentrics, introduced respectively in the books that start the first two trilogies. Powell catches them both as they hesitate to enter a room. (Either description could be contrasted with that given above, page 12 n., of an old-style entry.) The first is Uncle Giles, about to intrude on Nick and a friend at their school; the second, Erridge, Earl of Warminster, about to intrude on Nick and a friend who happens to be borrowing the Earl's cottage. Both have knocked, and this is what we are given:

[Giles]

The hinge creaked, and, as the door began to open, a face, deprecatory and enquiring, peered through the narrow space released between the door and the wall. . . . He delayed entry for a brief period, pressing the edge of the door against his head, the other side of which touched the wall: rigid, as if imprisoned in a cruel trap specially designed to catch him and his like: some ingenious snare, savage in mechanism, though at the same time calculated to preserve from injury the skin of such rare creatures.   (QU 14–15)

[Erridge]

It seemed at first surprising that such an unkempt figure should have announced himself by knocking so gently, but it now ap-

---

*Nick's understanding of his own behavior-patterns, James Hall says, "raises a new set of problems which novelists have been slow to explore. A person who understands his emotional patterns and their development does not respond to new situations as he 'naturally' would." With this, Powell has proved psychologically "so orthodox that he is unorthodox." (The Tragic Comedians, pp. 129–130.)

peared that he was overcome with diffidence. At least this seemed to be his state, for he stood for a moment or two on the threshold of the room, clearly intending to enter, but unable to make the definitive movement required which would heave him into what must have appeared the closed community of Quiggin and myself. I forgot at the time that this inability to penetrate a room is a particular form of hesitation to be associated with persons in whom an extreme egoism is dominant: the acceptance of someone else's place or dwelling possibly implying some distasteful abnegation of the newcomer's rights or position.

(LM 112–113)

Stylistically there is some small difference between the passages, the first moving toward metaphor because it is more exhaustively descriptive. It remains on the "caught" man, while the second speculates on just what sort of motion is "required" to get the man into the room. In other words the first description has a *phenomenal* aspect and the second, so to speak, an implied recollection of other occasions of having observed people entering rooms. The second moves away from exotic shock and toward stored knowledge: as Nick says, he "forgot" the egoism that such hesitancy signifies. When the older Nick in this second passage says "I forgot" we can notice his riding herd on his *own* reactions, and, as we shall see, his decision of how much he is going to tolerate this nobleman's egoism is going to have an effect on no less an event than Nick's marriage.

"My theory is that if you've got your characters right, they move logically forward," Powell once said: getting Giles and Erridge right means *not* letting them move logically forward through those doors.[31] Only on the grounds of aptness will the slow-motion style elicit its own sort of appreciation.

In *The Music of Time* there are well over a hundred characters who are treated with this same respect—which is not to say only in slow-motion. Allusions to the arts, for example, afford good going for Powell, and while some allusions (such as that to Poussin's *A Dance to the Music of Time,* which opens the book and gives it its title) lend themselves to being "worked up," it remains true that he can accomplish a stroke of characterization through a single proper noun. Thus, in a procession in Hyde Park, the fatuity of the aged novelist St. John Clarke will be caught through a description of his "unenclosed" white hair, "lifted high, like an elderly Struwwelpeter's, in the stiff breeze that was beginning to blow through the branches" (AW 129–130). But if the hair makes the man—and there is a fairly mythic aptness to the notion—then one of the disguised heroes of *The Music of Time,* a vague-headed World War I veteran named Jeavons, will display "dark, shiny hair, in which there was a touch of red, rolling away from his forehead like the stone locks of a sculpted head of Caracalla" (LM 22). That gravity plays with Clarke's hair but not with Jeavons's is one thing; that the former's is white while the latter's suggests some apparently cellular form of human endurance is another; suffice it to say that Powell's allusions will be backed by appositeness that can be searched into as, say, Eliot's can. Caracalla was an emperor of the *pax romana* who had warlike attributes: Jeavons is not misaligned with him, and will at the end of the sextet be described as being quite "at home within [war's] icy grasp" (KO 235).[32]

The coincidences by which Powell's army of characters cross Nick's and one another's paths generate most of the novel's action. Evelyn Waugh, who once demurred about the credibility of such "seemingly haphazard conjunctions of human life," later left a short record of his own and Powell's path-crossings, by way of recantation, concluding that "It is one of Tony's achievements to record this interplay which, I think, is essentially English."[33] While the patterns of this cross-movement are grained in the characters' lives, Powell has admitted that, from the writer's own standpoint, "you haven't always got your characters alive and vigorous, and that does mean an enormous amount of arranging, and—how shall I put it—contriving that the patterns and situations shall work out properly. I think a great deal of writing is in doing that. That, I suppose, is what's called art, isn't it?"[34]

A scene from the third trilogy illustrates how he is able to "arrange" a fairly incredible situation. In this case the problem is to get Nick's sister-in-law Priscilla into a restaurant where her estranged husband Chips Lovell has just been talking to Nick and some of his friends. Lovell departs, a deeply hurt man as Nick discovers, but we don't think of Priscilla as being within miles of the place. To bring her in at this point is almost unthinkably difficult, yet necessary to the theme. Powell makes two resorts to get the thing done: first to a present and then to an absent character. The character on the spot is Audrey Maclintick, who is badgering Nick's friend Moreland, who was once in love with Priscilla Lovell. The character not present is Peter Templer, who is equipped with hard-won knowledge in the field of women's affairs.

Moreland has been complaining about his stagnation in the war, and Mrs. Maclintick has been undercutting each speech. When this happens for the third time, Powell makes his move.

> "Oh, don't go on about the old days so," said Mrs Maclintick. "You make me feel a hundred. Try and live in the present for a change. For instance, it might interest you to know that a one-time girl friend of yours is about to sit down at a table over there."
>
> We looked in the direction she had indicated by jerking her head. It was perfectly true. Priscilla Lovell and an officer in battle-dress were being shown to a table not far from our own. The officer was Odo Stevens [her paramour]. For a moment they were occupied with a waiter, so that a brief suspension of time was offered to consider how best to deal with this encounter, superlatively embarrassing, certainly soon unavoidable. At first it struck me as a piece of quite undeserved, almost incredible ill chance that they should turn up like this; but, on consideration, especially in the light of what Lovell himself had told me, there was nothing specially odd about it. Probably Stevens was on leave. This was an obvious enough place to dine, though certainly not one to choose if you wanted to be discreet.
>
> "Adulterers are always asking the courts for discretion," Peter Templer used to say, "when, as a rule, discretion is the last thing they've been generous with themselves." (SA 123–124)

We have then a paragraph of typical reconsideration by Nick, flanked by dialogue that is viable in the extension it gives the characters of Mrs. Maclintick and Templer. Thus is Priscilla brought into the room. Since all coincidences, in and out of fiction, can offer nothing in themselves to give them verity, it is probably the peripheral trappings that steal in to color the picture right anyhow. Here, a little reflection on how a Hardy or a Dickens would have done the thing ought to send one back to "That's what's called art" approvingly.

This scene brings up names which are household words to *Music of Time* readers. So strategic is this that the recursion to Peter Templer marks a double ability in *The Music of Time,* that leads to a last series of remarks on technique.

First, with a simple "used to say," Powell is able to abdicate time and place, and frequently, with a wedge of dialogue like this, he will set a whole scene back in time for several pages without any sense of dislocation. And he can move forward, too: every one of the first six volumes contains a moment when he alludes forward to the war. But all of these are easy modulations, never causing sharp or symbolic breaks in the text. "I know of no writer," Norman Shrapnel has said, "who uses the time-skid with such brilliant ease and seeming naturalness, putting the cumbersome old 'flashback,' we would hope, in the lumber-room for good."[35]

Second, Peter Templer's remark is an example of the aphoristic afterthought that brings definitiveness to a passage. Those aphorisms with the most snap to them are modestly put into the mouths of Nick's friends—certainly not into his own. If, returning from a cremation, he hears his friend Barnby say that "Funerals make one's mind drift in the direction of moral relaxation" (BM 252), he does not realize that he himself will be in the bed of the dead man's female lodger in half an hour's time; but he does afterwards reflect on the strange timeliness of such an action. And from this sort of thing come his own aphoristic pronouncements—less pungent and direct than those of Templer, Barnby, Stringham, Moreland, or even those Tweedledum and Tweedledee intellectuals, J. G. Quiggin and Mark Members.*

All these aphorists are clearly distinguished: Templer is racy; Barnby, self-possessed as though his sayings were self-evident; Charles Stringham,

Nick often produces the sort of aphorism represented by the following pair, taken from the last two books of the first sextet.

> In the end most things in life—perhaps all things—turn out to be appropriate.   (CR 2)

> One passes through the world knowing few, if any, of the important things about even the people with whom one has been from time to time in the closest intimacy.   (KO 217)

And from these two aphorisms in particular, a syllogism could be worked out to approximate Powell's view of time. This is due to Nick's characteristic hesitancies—"most things in life—perhaps all things," and "few, if any, of the important things." *All* things in life would be proved appropriate if we discovered we knew *nothing* of any real import about other people: that would be the syllogism, and toward it *The Music of Time* always moves. Meanwhile, hedge as he may with "perhaps" and "if," of this Powell is certain: *most* things in life turn out to be appropriate because we know *few* important things about people around us.

Powell's view of the operation of time is, in other words, mystical. If we did know the important things about people around us, we would better understand the patterns repeating themselves in their lives and joining them with others. After all—to take coincidental meetings that so often surprise us in life or Nick in the book—no individual is ever surprised about his *own* particular whereabouts at any given time. And Powell's view would be that the rhythms, habits, and schedules in our lives have even more

---

amazing for choosing slight redundancies and banalities, with raised eyebrows, so as not to be caught in the posture of a pundit. Hugh Moreland is trenchant, antithetical, and poignant. But nothing could illustrate the tremendous control and aphoristic validity in Powell more than to mention that he introduces bad *apothegms by way of Quiggin and Members. But not their own. They are fond of retailing for fun the ponderosities of St. John Clarke. "St. J. always says there is 'nothing sadder than a happy marriage,'" says Quiggin, and Members reports the novelist's passé witticism about some dinner, which had "'only two dramatic features—the wine was a farce and the food a tragedy'" (AW 117, 121).*

intrinsic relevance to our deep selves. A measure of the change
that comes into his later work—whereas the hazard of men changing their identity bothered him in his early books—would be his
basic accord with lines from Arnold that speak of permanently
grounded identity. They sum up the poem "The Buried Life":

> Fate, which foresaw
> How frivolous a baby man would be—
> By what distractions he would be possessed,
> How he would pour himself in every strife,
> And well-nigh change his own identity—
> That it might keep from his capricious play
> His genuine self, and force him to obey
> Even in his own despite his being's law,
> Bade through the deep recesses of our breast
> The unregarded river of our life
> Pursue with indiscernible flow its way. . . .[36]

Yet emphatically Powell would disavow the cry in that same poem
that "The same heart beats in every human breast!" (That is
where romantic coercion begins, and the observed's pattern is
forced to bear a resemblance to the author's own.)

The word "pattern" itself presupposes repetition; any point *in*
a pattern implies inevitable causation, since what can be marked
as recurrent can be inferred to have undercurrents of similar productive forces. Thus while caprice appears to be trying to keep
things in flux, the reflective mind finds something inexorable
about what it contemplates. But this is in reference to the fates of
individuals. When Nick tells his brother-in-law, "Everything
alters, yet does remain the same" (SA 110), he is speaking of how
this truism is driven home to oneself personally, regardless of one's
willingness to admit that change is the essence of life.

"Inevitable causation." In terms of the modern novel, this could
have a suspicious ring. But to sum up one might say that Powell
is so sensitive to the concatenation of causes of an act that he
is left struck by the magic that all these should at last meet in
confluence. This is not the same as determinism for the simple
reason that the determinist would aspire to enumerate causes in

a positivistic way, whereas Powell, while able to suggest so many contributing factors, continually resorts to generalization so as to imply that the strands are at last unaccountable. (But the patterns that he perceives still imply their presence.) And moreover, with his conviction that the last secrets reside in character, he keeps alert for psychic causality along with or meshing with other causalities. A *quantitative* difference is involved, Powell registering the sense of the measureless possibilities of little accruing causes, striking or glancing against different people in different ways because the *people* are different: and in the end the casual cannot be separated from the causal, as though one were forever spelling one of those words wrong while employing the other. The latest and least likely inputs to an action will have been just as important as long-pending ones; and these latest inputs usually have a concrete uniqueness about them, showing that whatever the possibilities may have been, the finality of a situation has been dependent on a timely arrival of some force that will set the die one way for good.

When Francis Wyndham summed up Powell's estimate of life "as a series of possibilities rather than events,"[37] he hit on one of the reasons everything "does remain the same." The "possibilitarian"—and that is a coinage of one of Powell's favorite novelists, Robert Musil—is always thinking of alternatives to what might have happened, but then strikes a concessive posture. He concedes that he has not been able to anticipate the surprising adjuncts to situations that turn them a certain way, and prove both indispensable and fitting. When in the last war novel the fascinating Widmerpool tells Nick that he intends shortly to "go red," Nick the possibilitarian wonders whether this is a political statement— or perhaps a declaration of some obscure sexual intention. Either could be possible, but now Nick will have to get the evidence of some concrete catalyst to "prove out" the possibility. However, what Widmerpool means is that he hopes to be promoted and to be putting up the red tabs of a full colonel. Suddenly the whole scheme of causality has shifted, and everything is seen to have depended not on some moral phase of Widmerpool but rather on his extraordinary predilection for picking up military jargon ("going red"). Thus the long view, the historical view so to speak, can find patterns repeated such as a man's marrying, serving in the army, begetting heirs; but there is also the close view, which elicits the similarity of extraordinariness. Nick's aphorism to this effect in *The Acceptance World* was that "All human beings, driven as they are at different speeds by the same Furies, are at close range equally extraordinary" (AW 85). Powell's classical concept of character, reduced to homeliest terms, amounts to the idea that everybody is in the same boat only because all boats are different and there are no grounds for comparison.

The paradox that results is that the more uncategorized the characters of *The Music of Time* become, and the more the first-person narrator recognizes them as containing the same non-self-surprising vagaries as himself, the more the pattern of *The Music of Time* needs to be charted as that of a single life (in spite of the immense claims made for the book's social documentation). The second paradox is that only through such opaque art can a host of readers, analogically and one by one, abstract from the patterns of Nick's life the suggestion of patterns in their own.

"Life is full of internal dramas, instantaneous and sensational, played to an audience of one" (LM 43). That aphorism of Nick's again shades toward the solipsism of someone like Emerson.[38] The will power involved in Powell as novelist is different though, for, something like Arnold when he gave up poetry, Powell forever *trains* himself on others. I would hope that the foregoing discussion of technique would bear this out—and that the slow-motion accretion of details, the gradated aphorisms, the allusions, the time-shifts could be seen to bear the marks of high originality, after the fact, so to speak. It would be originality not pursued for its own sake, but resulting from a way of writing that keeps dredging up standards for comparison so that patterns might be deduced. Sometimes Powell is like an archaeologist going over some pretty unexciting stretches of ground. That is not necessarily to be regarded as a fault, in an age when the average novelist resorts to almost any device so as not to run the risk of being remote and inviting yawns. Some of Powell's readers sometimes undoubtedly yawn. With remoteness of approach a factor common to all these methods, the judgment of Jocelyn Brooke seems to me borne out: that

> his technique as a novelist is based largely on a process of de- liberate rejection: his originality lies not so much in what he does, as in what he manages to avoid doing. He eschews all the time-honoured tricks of the novelist, all those stock devices of suspense, comic relief, romantic descriptive passages, etc., to which even the best writers are wont to resort occasionally. This technique of rejection seems to me an important innovation, comparable with the experiments of Joyce and Eliot.[39]

POWELL, PROUST, AND CLASSICISM

Marcel Proust has an airtight view of time in comparison to Powell's. The most mechanical way to explain the difference would be to say that real time exists outside of Powell's characters and inside of Proust's: or in other words that, looking outside for signs of time's interference with characters' lives, Powell con- tinually confirms but cannot lay claim to knowledge of the mys- tery, whereas Proust's narrator in the last sequences of *Remem- brance of Things Past* avers that real time exists within himself. Poussin's painting of *A Dance to the Music of Time,* with time represented as influencing the circling dancers from outside their group, seems warranty enough that Powell will never come to the Proustian position—essentially a position of *control*—giving rise to a decided philosophical theory. Recapturing at the end of the novel the sound of a bell, announcing years before—Swann's de- parture from his house, Proust's narrator concludes that "It must be, then, that this tinkling was still there and . . . I could recapture it, go back to it, merely by descending more deeply within myself. It was this conception of time as incarnate, of past years as still close held within us, which I was now determined to bring out into such bold relief in my book."[40]

Since Proust and Powell do both believe in the idea of hazard, there remains some philosophical connection between them. Proust had been able to make such ringing assertions as those just quoted ("merely by descending," "such bold relief") because of a tumbling series of chance recapturings of the past, and had from first to last in his novel denied the possibility of regaining essential moments through action of the will.[41] Yet the incredibly powerful emphasis on capturing (consider the imprisoning of Albertine) as well as recapturing makes Proust in the end not comparable to Powell, regardless of affinities which exist. The heights and depths to which "Marcel" soars and sinks make his case an altogether more special one than Nick Jenkins's, and nowhere in *The Music of Time* will one ever find counterparts to "O mighty attitudes of Man and Woman . . ." or "The death of Swann!" or "Magical power of literature!"[42] It is because the hieratic quality is utterly absent in Powell.

One can even find this hieratic pitch in the language of Proust when his narrator is being very precise about his feelings rather than giving vent to them. Here is a reflection coming shortly after Albertine has deserted him: "All those so pleasant moments which nothing would ever restore to me again, I cannot indeed say that what made me feel the loss of them was despair."[43] To define the rhetorical species to which that sentence belongs, one would have to employ some such term as "anterior appositive"—the point being that even as Proust negates despair he jacks the sentence around and into periodic form. The whole "carry" of the sentence thus forces the narrator's voice to a higher register. And while this is but a sentence it would not be going too far to say that at times Proust's paragraphs call to mind the high-strung prose of, say, Poe or Faulkner.

Of course there are scores of portraits in Proust that are comparatively free from this heightening, and when Powell does finally pretend to quote from *Remembrance of Things Past* in his ninth volume, the long, complex sentences that describe a certain Prince Odoacer do resemble Powell's own pedigreed and analytic descriptions. This is the longest "quotation" in *The Music of Time,* by the way, running to 500 words in only four sentences (MP 119–120).* Later in *The Military Philosophers,*

Powell usually quotes accurately from literary works, but has resorted to some other intriguing inventions, such as when he fakes a quotation from Pepys's Diary (LM 11), and another from Byron's letters (VB 171).

Powell's clear sense of moving in the traces of Proust comes across as Major Nick Jenkins passes through Cabourg, the seaside town Proust had called Balbec. The incident was highly appropriate in that Nick had prowled around "Marcel's" own Grand Hotel without realizing where he was. Only later did the recognition rush upon him that Balbec was where he had just been. This was a triumph for Marcel Proust, in short. It confirmed Proust's conviction that the keenest experiences, when they do come, must come marred. Nick had to acknowledge "a faint sense of disappointment . . . in its way suitably Proustian too: a reminder of the eternal failure of human life to respond a hundred per cent; to rise to the greatest heights without allowing at the same time some suggestion . . . that things could have been even better" (MP 168).

Above all else, however, the reader understands the self-preoccupation of the narrator in *Remembrance of Things Past,* despite the memorable portraits, despite the phenomenological clarity of that book. It is understandable because transports alone, rather than "notable adventures" like Nick's, continue to mark the secret quest of the narrator. He is almost always palpitating, almost always chasing phantoms, no matter what he knows. Hence his emotional life can only be assuaged when he absconds with one of those moments, caught from the past but interacting with the present, which carry the recipient "entirely outside of time" (the corollary of discovering he has time inside him).[44] It is after such transports that Proust's narrator loses all his artistic sluggishness, by the way, when we find him ruthless about such claims on him as society or even friendship.* Powell, quite to the contrary,

---

Friendship, says Proust, "is a delusion, because, for whatever moral reasons he may do it, the artist who gives up an hour of work for an hour's conversation with a friend knows that he is sacrificing a reality for something which is non-existent. . . ." (Remembrance of Things Past, II, 998.) *Through his best friend Saint-Loup the narrator had long before realized the same obstructiveness: "In the life which a friend like this provided for me, I seemed to myself to be comfortably preserved from solitude, nobly desirous of sacrificing myself for him, in fact quite incapable of realising myself."* (Ibid., I, 680.) *Compare Powell on Aubrey: "Friendship was the essential basis of his life"* (JA 268).

will serve notice of credit due, not to the artistic gift, say, of Nick's friend Moreland—and he is a genuine artist—but rather to Moreland's "true compassion for [his friend] Maclintick's circumstances," which brought Moreland to the other's house on a certain desperate occasion. Powell's understatement at this time comes as close as he will ever come to a Proustian accolade: "It was an act of friendship of some magnitude" (CR 206).

In an essay on Powell, Gene W. Ruoff indicated why Proust affirmed the "free act of the artist," something Powell does not do. It was because Proust's mature life was set off *against* the source-experience of his art: his childhood experience at Combray.[45] Nothing could compare to that ideal past world. Proust in fact understands before his experiment why he will not succeed in capturing Albertine: it is because of "a sort of ruled line that my character must follow," namely, "that it was my fate to pursue only phantoms, creatures whose reality existed to a great extent in my imagination. . . ."[46] In *The Music of Time,* the most Proustian situation is Nick's affair with Jean Duport. But there Nick's character follows a line toward clarity, and even if the fullest clarity arrives only after the affair (Proust's arriving in advance), it is nevertheless true that Nick experiences sure moments during it—as when he says, "There is always a real and an imaginary person you are in love with; sometimes you love one best, sometimes the other. At that moment it was the real one I loved" (AW 79). (Compare Proust: ". . . I have been shaken by my love affairs, I have lived them, I have felt them: never have I succeeded in arriving at the stage of seeing or thinking them."[47]) Not only is Nick by comparison unromantic, but through just this sort of openness to new ramifications he never needs to bear a grudge against the present; neither is he led to make of art the sacrosanct converter of his experience, artist though he is. With this classical ability to cut his losses, Nick may seem too different altogether from "Marcel" to warrant a Powell-Proust comparison, except for one fact: Proust's narrator is a romantic *treated* classically.

In order to affirm the classicism of Proust one might bring up a writer who does resemble him but falls over on the side of self-esteem and thus into a key error, what Powell has called "the romanticism of action."[48] I have in mind Lawrence Durrell, who disclaims relationship with Proust in his preface to *Balthazar*, and claims a classical intention there as well—both erroneously. Durrell, like Proust, is remorseless in investigating love, and is even more like Proust in the hieratic approach to experience justified by the direct turning over of that experience into art. As in Proust the narrator in Durrell will affirm of his quest that "I know that the key I am trying to turn is in myself."[49] (As we shall see, the climax of the first half of *The Music of Time* will depend upon the turning of a key that is outside Powell's narrator, requiring communication between him and someone else. See below, page 174.)

But the fact that *Remembrance of Things Past* and *The Alexandrian Quartet* are in the last analysis novels about the making of novels does not permit the license which Durrell takes (and Proust declines) in the continual arrogation, to the narrator and other key characters, of qualities binding them more and more into a select and precious group. Particularly will Durrell's Darley throw a ring around himself and others, like Pursewarden and Clea, by arrogating ceaselessly to them and himself the title of "artists"—and if it is men of action that are to be described, again there will be room made for that not-to-be-rivalled savor. Let Narouz break a horse and we will be asked to believe that "Nothing could finally tire that powerful body—not even the orgasm he had experienced in long savage battle."[50]

Darley in other words runs perilously close to self- and group-infatuation, as the worked-up underwater climax of *Clea* reveals. Hacking away madly at the transfixed hand of Clea, Darley discovers that "It was as if I were for the first time confronting myself —or perhaps an alter ego shaped after a man of action I had never realised, recognised."[51] Once ashore, as Balthazar sets about attending to that hand, Darley is faint with despair. "But again this unknown alter ego whose voice came from far away helped me to adjust a tourniquet, roll a pencil in it and hand it to him."[52] And there are similar do-or-die situations which show that the hieratic principle can be a compromising one. A patchier work is simply the result, showing the danger of a self-confessedly classical attempt turning romantic. Escaping to the past, where Darley escaped into unbelievable action, "Marcel" figures as much the lesser escapist, because (like Nick) he does belong, in Proust's words, among "those people whose self-analysis outweighs their self-esteem."[53] But as a romantic he needs special sustenance where Nick does not.

Setting off the would-be classicism of a writer like Durrell against the real thing in Proust has been done of course with the intent of illuminating Powell. The cult of experience gets in the way of classical production. Durrell's oracular novelist Purse-warden lays the following axiom down once as "the first impera-tive of the artist, namely, create and starve."[54] Reacting to that imperative (for George Orwell had brought it to Powell by way of George Gissing), Powell was to write that

> The test was, of course, "Have you starved?" That was what Gissing used to ask; that was the approach so congenial to Orwell. But you might just as well inquire: "Have you eaten oysters and drunk champagne?" "Have you been in a cavalry charge?" "Have you ever cornered the pepper market?" . . . Certain experiences may intensify the characteristics of a nov-elist; they cannot do more than that. They certainly cannot, in themselves, make him great.[55]

Powell distrusts the idea of going through some utter form of experience in order to quicken the imagination. In reviews he re-peatedly registers impatience with the same experiential fallacy. He quotes from Huxley's *Doors of Perception*—"Art, I suppose, is only for beginners, or else for those resolute dead-enders who [are] content with the *ersatz*"—and, conceding that it would be nice to see the world as Falstaff or Joe Louis sees it, can only observe that Huxley under mescalin remains, alas, Huxley.[56] He said Orwell had the same problem, always driving himself into forms of life "in some odd way artificial. Perhaps this was because he rarely allowed himself to like things for their own sake." Then Powell struck deeper by perceiving that Orwell wanted material things, at all costs, to "yield up their secrets," or these would get the better of him.[57]

What he seems to be indicating is the leading and paradoxical error of romantics: that the wishers after experience, those who profess they want to empathize and know others from the inside out, forever stumble on their own most covert wish, not to become others but to make others become them. Proust avoided this error, and Powell avoids it. Powell distrusts any assumption, in art or politics, that would consider likeness between individuals to be so great as to make them assimilable to any single intelligence. "It is in his intense realization of the individual that Proust excels," he has said, "and his examination of the human heart must constitute a formidable confutation of any collectivist view of mankind."[58] Compare the views of some of the Alexandrian denizens for a contrast: Pursewarden's notion that "In the end . . . everything will be found to be true of everybody," or Capodistria's that "The world is a biological phenomenon which will only come to an end when every single man has had all the women, every woman all the men."[59]

Summing up the classicist's view, we may say that genuine perception takes differentness into account, and is crossed with a power-wish once it ceases to do so; that dissatisfaction with the world is one of the symptoms of this warped feeling, promoting the wish to go through self-annihilating "doors of perception"; and that the identity-hunt ("the key is in myself") is only another symptom of this restlessness. Historically, Powell's interest in the seventeenth century can be related to the fact that individualism had arrived but had not yet become infected with the kind of self-obsession here under discussion. That began to be salient in the later eighteenth century. Reviewing *The Diary of John Evelyn,* Powell remarked that the inquisitive seventeenth century had made possible "the appearance of the individual from the mists of the Middle Ages and the violence of the earlier Renaissance. . . ."[60] But passing on to *The Private Diaries of Stendhal,* he pointed up how "complicated considerations of sentiment [were] making themselves felt. Stendhal is in a positive fever, hung between the spheres of Power and Feeling."[61] Darley's lung-bursting discovery that he is a man of action can stand as the simulacrum for all have-it-both-ways men ever since.

It may be noted in passing that the Renaissance criterion of the man of parts becomes mimicked rather than recovered through the modern fatuousness about the super-realized self. Episcopal bishops wanting to pass as mediums, attorney generals wanting to be ace climbers of Canadian mountains, magazine editors who put themselves through the regimen of professional athletes, movie stars who want to direct a nation's policy—all confuse the worlds of imagination and of action. Self-consciousness is the problem: not the capacity for thought and action, but the compulsion for gauging oneself in one, then another of those roles. Given this welter of self-consciousness, the difficulty for the novelist of objectifying his material, even when not writing autobiographically, comes up. Powell is content to acknowledge the split between active and reflective types. He has illustrated his sense of the muddling on this score, often found in fiction, through remarks about Graham Greene's Scobie and Scott Fitzgerald's Gatsby. Greene's men of action, says Powell, are galvanized "into the shape of reflective men, and [supplied] with the trappings of a comparatively intellectual mental equipment"—"but one of the remarkable achievements of [Fitzgerald] is that . . . Gatsby's personality is quite untainted by that air of being a literary person with which novelists are so often apt to endow their men of action or perpetrators of violence."[62] The inference of the writer's imposing himself on his creations ought to be self-evident.

One of the virtues of the remote approach of *The Music of Time* is that its narrator gradually discovers an identity by not searching for one. The identity-hunt has become such a bane to the modern novel that the whole problem of cultivating an individualistic style has become suspect. Where Virginia Woolf led an attack against Bennett in the twenties for his coarse externalizing of life, in 1960 a writer like Pamela Hansford Johnson (the wife of C. P. Snow) will lead an attack against Virginia Woolf's internalizing of life. "What shrivelled away was any contact between man and society."[63] Thus the widespread attempt, in the recent English novel, to escape the isolating effect of self-exploratory prose. The non-individualistic, craftsmanlike prose of someone like Angus Wilson—who comes between Powell's generation and that of the younger British novelists—has become the model for the whole new anti-style aspired to by the "New University Wits," as William Van O'Connor has called them. The concluding chapter of O'Connor's book of that title deals with these writers' reservations about style:

> Virginia Woolf's metaphors and elegantly phrased observations are appropriate to characters deeply concerned with their own feelings and looking into their own consciousness. They would be inappropriate in novels taking off a Jim Dixon when drunk or getting into a fight with someone trying to take his girl away from him. . . . The age of experiment appears to be over. A new style has emerged. . . . In fiction it aspires to be a non-style. It is a style nonetheless, because it is trying to get beneath sham and pretentiousness.[64]

David Lodge, taking up this issue in *Language of Fiction,* is less willing than O'Connor to see a gain in this changeover. He sums up the now-familiar "modern"-"contemporary" controversy: "The contemporary tends to have a fairly simple faith in the competence of ordinary prose discourse to represent 'life'; the modern feels the need to employ an elaborate linguistic craft to fix and identify the uniqueness of every individual experience."[65] And giving a very fair view of the linguistic resources of Kingsley Amis, he indicates the strain on a wary writer who dares not affect the style of "modern" individualism because it would be unfaithful to the chopped-down no-nonsense view that he takes of himself and that his characters (insofar as they represent him) take of themselves. Now the *performances* of Amis, Wain, Braine, and others seem pegged on the premise that experimentation with language must nowadays prove a detriment to the novel form, which must save itself from a kind of centrifugal destruction through the return of its practitioners to some plain standard of fairly informal English. Yet while Wain feels that Powell has produced "possibly the most unreadable work of our time," Amis and Braine have unhesitatingly declared that Powell is the most important living English novelist.[66] The extremes here are interesting, Wain's being understandable in that Powell *is* the most conspicuous "modern" as regards risk and originality in our day. But the fact that the others praise without emulating points to the autonomy of art at last. The factors of temperament, gift, and background all enter in; in the case of the younger novelists, a "grouping" has resulted, whereas, as I tried to show at the start, Powell's sensibilities have been kept in balance because of the *lack* of a pull any movement could ever claim on him, from his time at Eton till the war. Even a certain sluggishness and ruefulness may be counted in the estimate, characteristics he seemed to regret in his first two novels (even as late as *The Kindly Ones,* in a pantomime of the seven deadly sins he will have Nick Jenkins portray Sloth).

It may be that the expressive form of the aesthetic writers of the generation before Powell's did need checking, over the middle years of this century, but Powell has not been an adherent of most of these anyhow. He has an aversion for Lawrence and Bloomsbury, and says of Joyce, "He is not classical enough for my taste."[67] Proust, yes, he praises, and his own language does gravitate toward the formal, as Proust's does. Nonetheless, it is the premise of this study that in the novel, an individualistic style and manner, despite the lengths to which experiment may have gone in this century, are still the necessary concomitants of modern classical art. This may sound a paradox, but my own strongest feeling about the word "classical" itself is that it accounts for, is forever cognizant of, differentness: and that the differentness of one man from another is not only an inviolate fact but one that, whenever registered, will be registered via a *medium* of differentness—the specialness of that complex of thoughts and feelings combined in a single man, the artist at work.

When David Lodge made the point that "Most great classical literature was attached to a metaphysical system of some kind,"

he enumerated some attempts made since the Romantic movement to replace these systems by writers individually, such as

> Wordsworth's Nature, Shelley's Neo-platonism, Eliot's Tradi-
> tion, Yeats's System, Lawrence's Dark gods. But in a sense all
> these solutions are working hypotheses which do not demand
> categorical assent from the reader. Transcending these hypothe-
> ses in almost every case is a belief in art itself as a substitute for
> metaphysics, a belief which reached its apex in the great mod-
> erns. Such a belief permits a para-metaphysical use of language
> —the recovery, through such devices as symbolism, irony, am-
> biguity, and paradox, of areas of experience ruled out by posi-
> tivism. . . .[68]

In Powell's case, the private orthodoxy to which he turns and on
which his art is grafted is History. Since he is not a symbolist, not
primarily an ironist, and driving always through ambiguity over
the course of time toward clarity, it might be said that the para-
doxes (or unpredictabilities) of Coincidence serve as his gauge
for the repeatedness (verifiable by history) of human situations,
regardless of change. There is implied a great respect for the
myths art can delineate, but they are myths based *on* something,
some thinking and recertifying check made on experience through
the study of things after they have happened. It might be called
not art for art's sake but art for history's sake. As far, then, as his
language is concerned, its tenuousness and slow-motion protract-
edness (in *The Music of Time*) are the instinctive medium for a
mind making slow appraisals. An admirer like Kingsley Amis
could not possibly emulate Powell not only because of the fact
that the "contemporary" novelist mistrusts the "modern" novelist's aesthetic dedication which separates him from the present
world, but also because the immediate concern with contemporary
society would clash with a writer like Powell's consuming interest
in the recently past world. And this consuming interest I would
account for in the end through temperament. (If in one of Kingsley Amis's novels, *I Like It Here,* we are presented with a writer
who cannot be an experimenter because he cannot tolerate an

aesthetic approach to life, distrusting it as a pose, it is also true that in another novel, *Lucky Jim,* we are presented with a historian who cannot take himself seriously because he does not trust history.)

Powell trusts history and goes far back to ally himself with beliefs of men of antiquity. The nearly literal belief in the punishing "furies," by means of whom he closes out the first sextet, is a case in point. His openness to the possibility of psychic causation is another. Though he did, as an outsider, attend meetings of the Society of Psychical Research in London in the thirties, his approach here is a rational one: simply that judgment must perpetually be reserved, there being too much unexplained in phenomenal experience for any "realist" ever to be able to close the book on the subject with impunity. Of Aubrey's notorious superstitions he once wrote, "Aubrey believed in witches, supernatural occurrences, and astrology. To dismiss as mere rubbish the first two of these, in the light of anthropological enquiry and the examination of poltergeist phenomena, for example, is no longer so enlightened as might once have been supposed . . ." (JA 66). His sense of the past is a third case in point. He once said of this sense that it was "like being musical or playing a good hand at cards . . . one of those gifts granted to some and withheld from others. . . ."[69] One could scarcely find a stronger indication of his own temperament in this regard than in his words concerning Rose Macaulay's *Pleasure of Ruins:*

> There may be those who do not share in the melancholy delight of ruins. . . . Ruins are a challenge to individual egotism, especially to the life of action, just as they are inevitably monuments to the decay of human effort. All the same, their attraction cannot be entirely explained by moralizing. There is something inherently beautiful in ruined shapes.[70]

There is a fourth gift, less likely to induce melancholy or a falling back on myth and a questioning of how things fit: Powell's instinct for detecting the bogus in life and art. My favorite example comes from a review he made of a biography of Lindbergh (for one is as apt to find his attention turned to such a popular matter as that, or say to Elsa Maxwell's *I Married the World,* as one is to find him reviewing books on genealogy or the Bayeux Tapestry or the history of military uniforms). Quoting the biographer's reconstruction of a train ride the young Lindbergh once took across the prairies, with its awed phrases about "the boy's eager gaze" and "a land that remembered glaciers," Powell became nettled and said, "But why should the reader be subjected to such appalling slush? All we want to know at this stage is the origin of the Lindbergh family."[71]

With or without a guiding faith in history, the work of an artist must still demonstrate the shaping power of its author's imagination. In his early work, as I have said, Powell permitted his historical vision to become occluded, and produced scenic, temporally arrested books. That these books are extremely carefully constructed has been attested to by many critics (some actually argue that they have been too well made). After considering in the next chapter the way Powell works his early stories out, and then taking up the matter of the radical style shift his work undergoes, we shall thenceforward be concentrating on *The Music of Time.* With these volumes, and the intrusion of history by various means—first-person recall, time-skids and allusions, patient delineations of background—there has been a tendency among critics to wonder whether an inevitable looseness or bagginess has inhered in the fabric. But now that he has three-quarters of the novel completed—and with all due consideration for the fact that no last word can be imagined now—I think Powell has given us quite enough to go on toward demonstrating that his structural powers are enormous. An admirer of his, Bernard Bergonzi, has said recently that "Because of his lack of mythic or obsessive preoccupations Powell's fiction is less clearly patterned or structured than Waugh's."[72] Waugh is of course a careful constructor, yet with due respect to him I think Bergonzi's judgment has to be reversed. Elusive and lifelike as *The Music of Time* remains, its crowning achievement is architechtonic: the feel for myth—and the talent for merging it with historic realism and moral insight—is that strong in Powell.

2

Quintet From The Thirties

LANES OF PROTOCOL, TORQUES OF POWER

In the summer of 1963 Powell was in an enviable position. The six volumes that made up the first half of *The Music of Time* were in the hands of readers. He had just sent off the manuscript for *The Valley of Bones,* a new beginning for him because this book brought his fiction in touch with the war. The record of the between-war years now complete, the hitch in the belt had been taken up (or let out) with the first book of the new sextet. Before its appearance, however, Powell had the opportunity to look back over his older work in another way: he went to London that summer to watch the rehearsals of the play adapted from his first book, *Afternoon Men,* and shortly before this, over the B. B. C., had come a dramatization of his second book, *Venusberg.*

That adapters should dramatize these novels thirty years after they appeared attests to the stir made by *The Music of Time* but also to their own durability. In a way, *Afternoon Men* and *Venusberg* lent themselves better to dramatic adaptation than the novels which immediately followed them because they were not exploring a power-theme, but instead came closer in form to

40

comedies of manners. Their protagonists, Atwater and Lushington, are polite listeners like Nick Jenkins. Since both novels are
told from their point of view, and they will not remain for long
in situations where their behavior-code is violated, flagrant behavior does not have much real room in which to expand. A good
example occurs in *Venusberg* when Madame Mavrin, who is
Lushington's mistress, in a moment of petulance speaks rudely to
her husband. Lushington takes the older man's part when Mavrin
leaves the room:

> "Let one thing be clearly understood. I will not have you
> speaking to your husband in that way."
> "And why not?"
> "Because you should show him some respect. He is a very
> clever man indeed and you speak to him as if he were a school-
> boy."   (V 104)

A humorous scruple, yes, coming from the man who is doing the
cuckolding. But so well-mannered are Lushington and Atwater
that their very scrupulousness rather calls in question the comedy-
of-manners designator, for they have lived their way into their
roles too far for light comedy.

Though the novels' plots are stylized—*Afternoon Men* is about
party-going, *Venusberg,* a sojourn on the continent—the love affairs are not. Lushington and Atwater could not be classed with,
say, Huxley's cross-mating intellectuals, since they want to drift
away from their intellectualism and toward people who are life-
rather than mind-oriented, like Susan Nunnery, a girl Atwater
meets in making the rounds of London parties. "She was separate,"
Powell says; and no sooner does Atwater meet her than he becomes "filled with a feeling of intense irresponsibility towards all
human creatures" (AM 24, 28). The reaction is harsh because Atwater is so observant—he is marked by a quizzicalness almost
pathetically strong. It makes him tend to realize that the girl Susan
cannot be caught by the likes of him.

Self-knowledge is Lushington's weakness, too, frustrating him
in a different way because he has touched the essential life of a
woman. He is afterward beset by the knowledge that he will leave

her. Lushington is a newspaperman, on assignment to the capital
of a Baltic country not long a sovereign state and still tingling with
the memory of having been a Russian province. (Powell's long
visit to Finland in 1925 seems to have helped provide the setting.[1])
At this almost unreal place he is tested on two sides: on the soft
new side of his love for Ortrud Mavrin, a professor's wife, and on
the old firm side of his decorum. In this last he is shown to be fit:
once, for example, Frau Mavrin's son tears the ribbon off his hat.
"It's all right," Lushington says. "No one will notice that the
ribbon is not sewn on if I put it round the hat to go home in. I
can easily wear it like that as far as the hotel" (V 113–114). But
no further, the thought strikes us: and a scene which might have
been funny works toward pathos, partly because the man has
tried not to be bothered by the hat yet all but tells Ortrud that he
cannot leave it be. He was in the apartment because she had said
she could not say goodbye to him properly in the street. The
abyss between what she means by "properly" and what Lushington would mean is great enough to show why the real abyss of
the North Sea will be between them before long. She may be a
Catherine Barkley, but if he were to dive as Frederick Henry did
in *A Farewell to Arms*, it would be to swim off in lanes laid down
by protocol.

While structural comments are to follow in this chapter, on
each early novel in its turn, it may be well to mention Lushington's last meeting with Madame Mavrin, at a state ball, to indicate
the nearest approach he makes to the position of Frederick Henry.
He has made his way over to Ortrud and she smiles at him, "making him think that perhaps he would give up his job on the paper
and try to find a post on the spot, a waiter's or something of the sort
where it would not be necessary to learn much of the language" (V
158). He is on the verge of Hemingway's river here, but two words
will forever prevent him from plunging. The one is "perhaps"—a
qualifier showing the grip he has on his own reactions. The other
is "post"—the public servant's flashing thought. The sentence
seems to me the most painful in the book. It is not simply that he
lacks the courage to accept a waiter's job; it is that there is no such
thing as a waiter's post.

That Ortrud Mavrin, for her part, is worth equating with Catherine Barkley is clear from the first moment we see her, for Powell was gratuitous then and said, "her eyes showed that at some time in the past she had been hurt and made to suffer" (V 20–21). This is part of a technique, restricted to these first two books, of emphasizing his early heroes' failure to become agonized by setting off against them characters who have indeed suffered. In *Venusberg*, the Central Europeans knew what anguish was. In *Afternoon Men*, Europeans are not so available, but Jews are. It is Verelst, a Jew who fought in World War I, who aims straight for Susan Nunnery and makes off with her. Late in the novel, just before she goes away with Verelst, we see Susan through Atwater's eyes, listening to Verelst tell a story:

> Only he looked as if it would hurt him if she did not hear every word that he was saying to her. When you were close to him you could see that he had a pain, an agony, at the back of his eyes, but whether it was a racial appanage or something acquired . . . Atwater could not make up his mind.   (AM 127)

Verelst's move-all-obstacles sort of passion is unavailable to Atwater and Lushington. Thrown off balance by love, and having nothing like his experience, they regain equilibrium through their daily rounds of bon mots, of knowing the kinds of wines to order or faces and figures to pass judgment on. They are settling for the life of connoisseurs because they are too much aware of how awkward the demands of passion and loyalty can become. Yet while remaining fastidious, they know this to be a second-best arrangement. The sadness lies in the fact that they don't deceive themselves, yet can't snap the monotony of their "afternoon" lives.

As a matter of fact, Dostoevsky's famous comment, "to be hyperconscious is a disease,"[2] applies to these men. Although it may occur to the reader that their moments of pain-and-clarity are all too familiar in existentialist literature, there is this difference: Lushington and Atwater are not *driven* like existentialist heroes. They are afternoon men, not underground men. Their social adroitness holds them far from rebellion; they neither go underground (no prisons, no ghettos, no asylums or hospitals for them), nor do they operate as confidence men within society. The closest approach they make to the lacerated or isolated state of the underground man comes about through casual imagery, as when Lushington takes in a quick local impression on his way out of the newspaper building: "Lushington went down the stairs, which were of stone like those of a prison or lunatic asylum and were, in effect, used to some considerable extent by persons of a criminal tendency or mentally deranged" (V2). Even though they have institutional jobs, they are dissociated from the civil servants of Kafka or Dostoevsky or Camus because they have nothing at all against the paper or the museum or the country they serve. In short, for all their connoisseurship and good manners, they have no egos.

Egos, on the other hand, are in plentiful supply among the leading characters in Powell's next three books. They too may get involved in love affairs but these are side issues and we have three-way male clashes predominating in each story. Within these three-cornered relationships lines of force are set up as follows:

a) In *From a View to a Death* a county landowner named Passenger takes on two opponents individually and bests them: the city-raider Zouch and the poaching-neighbor Fosdick;

b) In *Agents and Patients* two poor confidence men, Maltravers and Chipchase, team up to take in hand a rich victim, Blore-Smith;

c) In *What's Become of Waring* an unnamed narrator, who works in the publishing house of Hugh Judkins, plays off against that man a literary protégé, Captain Hudson.

What is new about this group of three novels is that there is real exercise of will among the central characters—most often, an unbalanced over-exercise of it, causing confusing torques of force to produce results beyond those that were anticipated.

Captain Hudson's reversion to type at the last séance in *Waring*, where he finds his girl again, helps make *Waring* Powell's mellowest book. Not entirely mellow, however: there has been plenty to exacerbate Hugh Judkins, the London publisher who has tried to change his celibate nature and been made ridiculous in the course of the narrative. Hugh actually flies into a rage at the last séance and is on the point of attacking the medium, when "An exterior force put a sudden end to this situation. The door of the drawing-room opened and the maid said: 'Captain Hudson'" (W 231).

Hudson had not planned to go to the séance and was only there to pick friends up; Hugh Judkins had planned to go and to cry out in the middle of it against all such abominations, having now become a reformer. And Hudson is the force that breaks up Hugh's tirade. By this fifth novel, Powell's view has come to be that the man who does not *want* power *has* it. Hudson represents unintentional force. Connections can be made to the two preceding novels to show how this view of power evolved.

From a View to a Death and *Agents and Patients* diverge, the one toward tragedy and the other toward farce. The near-tragic fate of Zouch, killed for his pains during his changeover from bearded artist to country squire, runs contrary to the "progress" of Blore-Smith from young man vested in Midlands money to miscast bohemian. So sharp is this contrast that Zouch is an agent-turned-patient, Blore-Smith, a patient turned into an agent. (An "agent" is one whose will accomplishes his wish; a "patient," one acted upon by circumstance—or by agents.)

Zouch has dominated his novel, though he is shaky as an artist and sensitive about his poor breeding. In his book-long visit to a country house, he squirms repeatedly as his hosts come near to seeing through him. But he is brave enough to be there and have imperious people on his hands, and finally attempts to marry into this county family. Blore-Smith, in the other novel, has put himself *into* the hands of some sharpers so that he can learn about life. He is a bewildered university graduate reading law in London so as "to have something definite to tell people when they questioned him about himself" (AP 6). For him, as for Zouch, the tables turn: he eludes the sharpers in the end, while Zouch bores forward to his death.

We tend to smirk at Blore-Smith's silly gain, but the waste of Zouch's life is rending. And this is true even though, watching

Zouch's power-play, we come to desire his fall. On the other side, we want Blore-Smith to succeed. Yet, as he performs his first agent's action and breaks the hold of his former manipulators, we are unaccountably let down. In his final scene, an invitation to St. Tropez from a homosexual colonel completes this transformation from patient to agent: Blore-Smith will now become financial parasite instead of host. But this Colonel Teape is a fate worse than death. Teape is the equivalent of Mr. Todd, to whom Tony Last had to read Dickens for the rest of his life. We do not care. Let Blore-Smith go. On the other hand, a very special final chapter in *From a View* has been unmistakably fashioned to make us weep for Zouch.

With Zouch getting more sympathy than the fuddled Blore-Smith, we seem left with a double view of power. Powell would seem to trust power when it is native but to distrust it when it is willed. The desire to mutate one's nature seems, therefore, the grievance that helps account for the different tones of these novels. If a man changes his nature and dies for it, he is worth tears; if he breaks out of a natural "patient's" status, he will have gained only an ersatz power, worth catcalls.

Mentioning Teape a moment ago makes me reflect that earlier I had spoken of the reconsideration given minor characters, a tendency which is general enough to reduce the comic and increase the tragicomic effect of the early novels. Now Teape is virtually an "offstage" character who gets no second look, but it is necessary to add that unreclaimable figures like him do come into these novels, at least one in each, for thorough inspection. Some of them appear to foreshadow the famous Widmerpool of *The Music of Time* (though he gets tremendous reconsideration). The ones that Powell places in commanding positions I shall call "messenger" figures. Their names will come up in the structural comments to follow, so they may be singled out now. In the order of the appearance of the thirties' quintet, they are Fotheringham, Bobel, Fischbein, Schlumbermayer, and Lipfield. Names like these sound pejorative enough even before they are attached to characters. All are "messengers" because they signal, as it were, the negative moral pole of each book. And the major characters will be judged by what affiliations they have with these five.

In a less symbolic way, Powell compensates for much of the comic stage-business (or the offstage voices) by aligning the novels emotionally by means of the women. It may do well to look at them for a moment collectively, for one of Powell's real marks of achievement as a young writer, as has been well said, was his "astonishing maturity of approach both to the problems of love and sex which preoccupy most young novelists, and to the feminine protagonists who exemplify such problems. . . ."[3]

In all five books, the leading male character is involved with two women, one clearly superior to the other—more winsome, generous, passionate, or self-sufficient. Above all, in their various ways, the girls who could be called heroines do not give way to self-pity. Either the others do (like Mary Passenger in *From a View*), or else these others make sure they are never in a position to need to pity themselves. In the first four books, the leading male loses or gives up the better girl and becomes a pawn of the lesser. With Captain Hudson of *What's Become of Waring,* the pattern reverses, which is why—along with the turn taken in the power-theme—*Waring* is Powell's most heartening early work.

Susan Nunnery and Ortrud Mavrin have been mentioned as life-oriented heroines; the distinction Powell makes between them and their rivals is harrowing. In *From a View to a Death,* the distinction is not so marked; but one is made, nevertheless, between Joanna Brandon, a girl Zouch compromises, and Mary Passenger, who becomes his fiancée.

Fastened home by a derelict mother, Joanna has only read about life until the exciting Zouch sweeps her nearly off her feet. But not quite—and as a result she is the emotional center of the novel. She does not at first succumb to Zouch's practiced advances—at an inn where they have attended a party—but later she is disgusted with her primness. "Her conduct had been of the very kind which in theory [she reads D. H. Lawrence] she most despised" (FV 124). She has the chance to rectify this primness. Joanna stays the night at Passenger Court after a pageant held there, and Zouch sleeps with her.

The surprisingness of the scene marks one of Powell's attributes as a novelist, for Zouch—of all things—is tender. But betray her he does, in a day's time: having made his conquest, he is reawakened to the presence of Mary Passenger and soon they are engaged. (How this one had champed at the bit can be seen through her description of the "beastly, beastly, beastly" cocktail party they had all gone to—beastly meaning Zouch had left her unattended [FV 123].) The complexity lies in the genuine sexual exchange between Zouch and Joanna, which Powell suggests rather than insists on. But the young man chooses greedily the next day, and makes a variation of the mistake all the early protagonists of Powell make—in Zouch's case, a fatal one.

Blore-Smith's exploits in *Agents and Patients,* running toward incompetence where Zouch's ran the other way, are much more provokingly funny. His program for seeing life has involved his paying for trips to Paris (to get his psyche straight) and to Berlin (to get a taste of the film world: for he is financing a free-lance film for one con-man while paying another for psychiatric treatment). In Germany, he goes off with as beautiful a woman as appears in a Powell novel, Mrs. Mendoza. But Maltravers and Chipchase, the manipulators who have brought him to that country, know he will remain a patient as long as Mrs. Mendoza will have him near her. Maltravers says, "After living with Mendie for a week he will be more in need of treatment than ever. After a fortnight we shall be able to dictate unconditional terms" (AP 158).

The other woman in this novel is Maltravers' wife Sarah, a racing-car enthusiast who at first smacks slightly of a character out of Nathanael West. But, as with Joanna Brandon, Powell reclaims her and she becomes—though not so poignantly—the emotional center of *her* novel. (For what it is worth, she and Maltravers represent the only married couple in Powell's early fiction. Though there could be no possible resemblance, it is still interesting that this was the book Powell dedicated to his wife, the first one written after his marriage.) Appealing as she is when asked to be Blore-Smith's mistress ("Sarah in her surprise allowed a large amount of water to be spilt on the carpet" [AP 115]), she is even more fetching when on her balance and able to make someone else do the spilling. Here is her response to Schlumbermayer, who has told her a certain Frenchman who takes drugs will be coming to visit him:

> "Have you laid in a stock of poppy and mandragora and all the drowsy syrups of the world?"
> Schlumbermayer laughed so much that he spilt his coffee all down the front of his coat. Then he stopped laughing and looked disturbed.   (AP 161–162)

Blore-Smith went out of his depth even to think about a girl as bright as this. To jump about for Mrs. Mendoza becomes *his* second-best settlement to the recurring Powell triangle.

The meting-out of woman medicine continues in *Waring*, but with softened effects. Roberta Payne, a beautiful journalist, imperils Captain Hudson when he and she have to go over material for a biography of the noted writer T. T. Waring. Roberta causes Hudson to break off his engagement and then, in no time, to split with her, too. She cannot understand why he was bothered when she went off on a cruise with another man. (This was Hugh Judkins, and that cruise was his undoing: Roberta delivered nothing in return for the ticket he'd bought her.) Nor does it cross her mind that Hudson may have broken up with his fiancée out of conscience.

By the fifth Powell novel, this sort of conscience *has* become odd. The beauty is that Beryl Pimley, the fiancée, is just as straitlaced; yet she and Hudson are fundamentally intense, approached for rugged individuality only by the characters who die in *Venusberg*. This is the triumph of the commonplace with a vengeance.

Powell's technique with Beryl is the same as it had been with Sarah and Joanna—that of giving an unsympathetic first view. On meeting Beryl, the narrator says, "Like so many girls whose lot has been to lead dull lives, her manner implied that all men were her slaves" (W 54). By the end, Beryl's character has replaced that early archness of manner, one quality in particular clinching things. Having discovered that T. T. Waring is not only a plagiarist but her own bad-actor brother (something Hudson dreaded to tell her), she wants to get this news to Hudson without any thought of using it to start up with him again. "She did not seem specially surprised to find that her brother was T. T. Waring. Authorship is only impressive to those in the book business. All she wanted was that Hudson should benefit by the information" (W 205).

Beryl's solicitude is her main quality here, but a choice aside comes in the middle sentence. She is not impressed (and is not depressed, either) about her brother's plagiarism. Literature is not that important. And when, as a result of the séance, she is reunited with Hudson—when they marry and he, fed up with literature, returns to the army career that suits him—the note of self-loyalty strikes for both of them. It is a quietist note, true, but one that muffles for good the claims of talkers and charmers and purveyors of information—as though Powell had thrown a blanket across every last literary poseur to allow one of his novels to end with something to rejoice over.

"AFTERNOON MEN"

Characters "got right" have been the strong point of Powell's fiction, but he is also a master of technique and always has been. This can be seen immediately in the first two novels, for though the protagonists are similar the structural principles are different. Where Powell made three labeled divisions in *Afternoon Men* bear on Atwater's changeless milieu, he caused the unlabeled divisions of *Venusberg* to depend on Lushington's personal contacts. So a "recoiling" as opposed to an "expanding" structure evolved, which can be shown by indicating how the imagery in *Afternoon Men* works: associated often with the sub-characters, it keeps deflecting back to Atwater's condition. Imagery does not operate in similar fashion in *Venusberg*.

"Montage," "Perihelion," and "Palindrome" are the section headings in *Afternoon Men*. Because of the montage, and despite the perihelion (that point on Atwater's track when he passes closest to his "sun," Susan), a palindrome has been ordained and the book could as well be read backward as forward.* The borrowing of the epigraph from *The Anatomy of Melancholy* does the same fixating work and to it the key images are related:

> . . . as if they had heard that enchanted horn of Astolpho, that English duke in Ariosto, which never sounded but all his auditors were mad, and for fear ready to make away with themselves . . . they are a company of giddy-heads, afternoon men. . . .

From this we should be led to expect some theme of madness. The particular form of it portrayed by Powell seems to descend because two sounds of the maddening horn have been heard too long by these carousers of the twenties, who are different from the ones in Waugh and Huxley. Far from being excessive plungers, Powell's afternoon men are afraid of being *shortchanged* or *poisoned*. It is along these lines of concern with pocketbook and health that he develops two image patterns that will feed into the madness vortex.

Many minor characters, but particularly Atwater's friend Pringle, carry forward the two motifs. Pringle is an untalented artist who wins his way into the reader's sympathy by the very blatancy of his self-promoting, as when he cheats a fellow-artist in shove-halfpenny. Another time, when he catches his mistress Harriet Twining on a sofa with this same man, Pringle determines to drown himself—changing his mind in deep water. Then, having walked in on a nearly distraught parcel of friends who have brought his clothes from the beach, he is made to leap to colossal comic scale by telling them he hopes they were careful of his wrist watch.

---

*The essential meaning of "montage," since the first novel is highly scenic, would be that we are afforded fade-ins and fade-outs of scenes without transition, of Atwater at parties, at his museum office, at a bohemian club or gallery, and so on. However, Susan Nunnery is the one different visitant to these haunts, and there is another sort of montage effect on his first seeing her: she gives the impression of a portrait against a false background, "where the values are those of two different pictures and the figure seems to have been superimposed" (AM 24).

As for health (the un-drowning episode fits here), the novel opens this way:

> "When do you take it?" said Atwater.
> Pringle said: "You're supposed to take it after every meal, but I only take it after breakfast and dinner. I find that enough."
>
> (AM 1)

When parties work their havoc on Atwater (who does not, like Pringle, fortify himself with medicine), and he answers a greeting at his museum office with "I had some lobster last night. I may have poisoned myself," Powell keeps it going as his colleague responds, "Those shooting pains in my back have returned" (AM 34). Thus the scabrous montage grows. At the start of "Perihelion" it seems checked, as Atwater tells someone, with Susan at his side, "I have my life before me" (AM 88). But halfway through, things have become so bad that one of his friends facetiously suggests marriage (small chance of that). The themes are fused in this scene which lasts but half a page, quoted here:

> Barlow said: "If it's really poisoning your life, why not ask her to marry you? . . . The other thing to do would be to get the museum to advance you a quarter's salary and take her down to Brighton for the week-end. . . ."
> Atwater said: "Brighton air gives me a liver."
> "Then you'll have to marry her," said Barlow. "Having old Nunnery for a father-in-law would make the trouble and expense almost worth while."   (AM 123)

This old Nunnery is an afternoon man emeritus, dreaming of parties and money at the top of one of the most evil-smelling staircases in literature. Fotheringham, the abysmal "messenger" figure, points this out. In a pub one day he delivers the novel's message in three bursts. To start with, he disburdens himself of the longest sentence Powell has written to date, a lament on the way of life of the afternoon men. Then he pops this philosophical chestnut: "But there must be something beyond all this sex business" (AM 63). And, at last, he pronounces on Susan's father, arch-partygoer of the earlier generation, a brilliant man "whose mind has become a complete blank. . . . You can imagine what good company he is. . . . All the brains and understanding there and never the least danger that they are going to become a nuisance" (AM 64).

So madness is now onstage with a vengeance, its street-barker Fotheringham, its completed specimen old Nunnery, its causes the nervous expenditure of money and health, the ultimate goal (which health- and money-preservation seem ever about to guarantee) success with that knowledgeable sexual cadre of women who drive men mad. (There is a mad archaeologist in this book named Crutch, who in a walk-on appearance wants to buy the lewd images under Atwater's curatorship. Observe the madness-sex-money-health interplay.) Hence Powell's first description of a woman alludes to what finally transforms these weakened men into dolts. Harriet Twining "had fair hair and a darkish skin, so that men often went quite crazy when they saw her . . ." (AM 4). The largest dolt she achieves is Pringle, whom she will cause to wade into the sea in the "Palindrome" section. The moulting Atwater (visiting them as his Susan roams other territory) will copulate with Harriet while Pringle is in the water, and they will all have trouble, after the rescue of Pringle, coping with the temptation to undertip the rescue-man.

Something very depressing about the Pringle episode is that while he walks nude and unconventional into the sea, Harriet and Atwater watch from a cliff above and then, unstirred, turn rather conventionally to each other. (Atwater is not at—water but a—twater.) And it is the fact that Atwater notices her good grooming that causes him to make an advance on her. His makeup requires a girl to pass muster before anything can happen emotionally to him. Can it be argued that even his love for Susan is vitiated, because she passes muster so well? One way or the other, Atwater's re-entanglement with these others makes it little wonder that the cadences of the book's only other long sentence, Fotheringham's lament (AM 61–62), are recalled at the last as Atwater's mind goes looping off in Joycean prose. He has found that Susan has been taken to America by Verelst. He is roaming the streets with some of Nunnery's port in his stomach (a gift of Fotheringham), his mind running out 100-word sentences of remorse on "the time he had wasted when she had not been with him and the other time, that now seemed the only time when he had been alive at all. . . . Or was it that filthy port that made him feel so ill?" (AM 215–216). The last sentence roots up the theme, and Powell doubles on it by having Atwater pass a man who hooks him with an umbrella. It is Fotheringham, and he needs ten bob.

The novel now ends. "Perihelion" had not finished so factitiously. Perhaps a more forgivable madness was at work then, for, in a kind of coda, Powell stresses climate, just after Atwater's farewell evening with Susan. The coda begins, "In this meridian of London summer it was melancholy . . ." (AM 145). We have not previously been made aware that we are in mid-summer. "Only mad dogs and Englishmen . . ." as the saying goes. Powell may intend to elicit commiseration here—even inanimate things are affected at summer's meridian. He had taken early care in describing the museum office, so as to set up the conclusion to "Perihelion." It comes with a view of Atwater in the office; "smuts" have come into the room to lie "all over Atwater's desk and his papers"—permitting this focus as the novel's one truly sad section ends: "The heat made the papers on the desk curl into spiral shapes and blisters came out on the walls' buff distemper" (AM 145–146).

''VENUSBERG''

In *Venusberg* there is more of a sense of the inevitability of the characters' fates than in *Afternoon Men,* because more of them are genuine—are "good soldiers" in the sense that Ford's title character was. If the destruction that comes on some of them has seemed inevitable, one might expect the effects to rub off on survivors, and this does happen to a degree. So much, in fact, does character rather than motif determine structure in *Venusberg* that Powell has accomplished a kind of six-hands-round in his deployment of people in a novel which he has quartered for their accommodation. (The number could be expanded to eight or ten to take in minor figures—the emphasis would be on the even number and the sense of pairing off.)

The principals who complete Powell's main scheme, along with

Lushington, are the two women in his life, Ortrud and Lucy (an English actress, once his mistress but now cooled to him), two counts named Scherbatcheff and Bobel, and Da Costa, Lushington's old friend, temporarily of the English legation at the Baltic capital, but not a professional diplomat.

Da Costa could easily be the finest character in Powell's early fiction, wholly winning, more than charming though fidgety to the point of capsizing, a man his own (and certainly no afternoon) man. He is not intrigued by women, and, since Lucy back in England has a passion for him, Lushington has to explain that "He gets on without them [women]. Some men can. It has been done" (V 13). Da Costa, that is, won't play the emulate game, and when we recall poor, hollow Fotheringham wondering how "there must be something beyond all this sex business," we may appreciate why Da Costa is a pretty much untrammeled human being.

Exactly at the first quarter-pole of the book, Powell has Lushington adjusting to Da Costa's presence, "slowly getting to work like the warming up of an engine . . ." (V 48). Other special descriptions are reserved for this man, as for instance his strange ability to resist the meddlesomeness of his manservant. "It was a process comparable to the pouring of liquid on to an inverted vessel. The whole room would be messed up with Pope's personality and Da Costa alone would remain untouched" (V 81). He is a person to anchor to; and there are others (like Ortrud), but Lushington doesn't want his anchor to hold, once having heaved it.

In Da Costa's flat the two friends stand looking through double windows at the Baltic, Powell indicating that "The two surfaces of glass were faulty in the middle, so that the spires of the Lutheran churches seemed to have broken away from their swollen bases as they narrowed up" (V 42). There is an application here to the moral separation of the two men. In his study of Powell, Robert Morris has noted that of the six principal characters, three —Da Costa, Ortrud, and Scherbatcheff—live respectively "in the High Town," on "one of the higher floors," "on the top floor" (V 42, 63, 94).[4] This carries significance as we shall see.

Ending with the reunion with Da Costa, this first quarter has centered on Lushington's painful situation with Lucy; the second traces the steps in his new love for Ortrud, but it also ends on the note of comradeship. In the novel's most haunting scene and centerpiece, Lushington accompanies Count Scherbatcheff to the desolate apartment block where this nobleman's relatives live, refugees from Bolshevik Russia. These are actually his grandmother's quarters. Lushington had learned from Scherbatcheff that the grandmother was once thrown from a bridge by Social-Democrats, and on another occasion had been informed, "You are English. In England you do not make scenes. But my grandmother does not try to control herself. She screams. She throws herself on the floor" (V 61). Small wonder then that at the midway point, when Lushington meets her and she misunderstands (she thinks he's another sleeper brought to the overcrowded flat)—small wonder he fears he will be ejected "neck and crop" until, the situation explained, a very beautiful, simple hospitality is extended him in that sad place.

Scherbatcheff, though he is a sick man, seems a comic character —but this is because of Lushington's noncommittal attitude toward him. Earlier, on the ship where they met, we had seen him cut an ace of spades, having sworn that in the game of life he often threw "the zero." His opposite number, Count Bobel, had then piped up in a counter-key: "I am the King of Hearts. That is my representative card. It bespeaks my character. You agree, all of you?" (V 23). Lushington reacted to neither one of them, the doomed man nor the fraud. He preserves this attitude even when, in the central scene, Scherbatcheff tells of his secret longing for Ortrud, an emotion that touches off the book's third movement. Ortrud would respond to no Russian, we have learned. Meanwhile, Lushington's own affair with her has begun to make him restive, and with his diplomatic friends he goes into the country for a spell of skiing. They are joined by Scherbatcheff, who has been ordered out of the city because of his health and is first encountered wearing his overcoat in an overheated chalet.

Scherbatcheff has been worked into a situation directly opposite to Lushington's. The European remains loyal to his feeling for a woman, but unsatisfied; the Englishman is sexually (but disloyally) satisfied. Da Costa, too, like Scherbatcheff a self-loyal man, has been chafing in his attaché's role and has brought up his pet subject of taking a try at archaeology. Ortrud has also been chafing—not because the bonds of the affair are restricting but because she is willing to give more than all to Lushington and finds his commitments split. "And then one day," we read, "Count Scherbatcheff died" (V 140). It is the beginning of a chapter that gets ready, sounds a death-gong, for the book's last turn. The novel had reached a thematic climax on the preceding pages when Lushington, the skiing excursion over, met his test and was able to muster every last resource to preserve his social address. In passing this social test, though, Lushington forfeited his ties with non-emulators, real people.

The voluptuary Count Bobel, with a sleigh waiting outside, had been mistakenly sent up to Lushington's hotel room, accompanied by two women of the town, only minutes before the English legation chief Bellamy would be arriving with his wife. At Bobel's entrance, "Lushington, remembering that he was in his shirt sleeves, took up his tail-coat and began to struggle into it" (V 136) —a spasm of some interest, this, for Bobel's girls are recognizably unsavory. Bobel is not a man to be levered about easily, the girls have begun to settle down in the room, emergency is romping through Lushington's bones, and for the first and only time in the novel he breaks decorum and performs a positive action:

> Lushington took Count Bobel by the lapel of his coat and led him into the corner of the room.
> "Count Bobel, I must speak to you plainly. It was a misunderstanding that they showed you up here. I am busy. I must inform you that the door opposite leads to my bedroom." . . .
> "You mean, Mr. Lushington—"
> "Exactly." . . .
> Count Bobel fell into an arm-chair and began to roar with falsetto laughter. He said:
> "You English! You English! When shall I become accustomed to your way? But why did you not say so at once? And I myself was so slow that I thought you were putting your clothes on. Never for one moment did I guess that you were taking them off. You are cunning, *mon cher.*"   (V 137-138)

Enabled by this to elbow all three out his door, Lushington saves himself unendurable shame before the eyes of his country-men the Bellamys, who are at that moment riding the lift to his floor.

Powell's stroke of genius in the scene, however, occurred be-fore this moment of truth, when he worked in a version of rats leaving the sinking ship. Two other knocks had come on the door before all this. Ortrud had come up unannounced, only to find Lushington unwilling, unable perhaps, to make an eleventh-hour excuse to the insipid Bellamys. Ortrud left with a small slam of the door. But came another knock. It was Da Costa—"I was passing and saw a light in your sitting-room . . ." (V 133).

Da Costa bolts on hearing that Bellamy, his supervisor, is due there. Shoptalk appalls him. But the novel has begun its death-dive. The next chapter reports Scherbatcheff's death, and when, in the scene after that, Professor Mavrin says his wife has fallen in love with Da Costa, he proves wrong in fact but right in Pow-ell's structural logic.

The quarters of *Venusberg* are struck by scenes with Da Costa, Scherbatcheff, Bobel, and Lucy. The drift is ugly. The fraudulent Bobel, lecher and face-cream salesman, fitly represents those whose first concern is to keep well-oiled the "machinery of the body," to use his phrase. But Lucy and Lushington rank with him, and the three are set against Scherbatcheff, Ortrud, and Da Costa respec-tively. Nothing but contrasts appear when you look at them by twos; what is less evident is that nothing but similarities appear when you look at them in columns. A key fact about the one column of characters is that they are shown indissolubly linked with their families—the Scherbatcheffs being salient, but Ortrud, for instance, being torn between her husband and son and Lush-ington. Ranging the others against these, we find them unattached —Lushington drifting, Lucy divorced, Bobel not even identifiable as to nationality. But if it be objected that we will naturally find residents of the Baltic capital with their families about them, we can quickly perceive Powell's drift by turning to Da Costa, a non-resident. Why did Da Costa choose *this* post after deciding to leave England? "The idea was fostered by his elder brother, who was married and had several children and who had once been called the most popular man in Throgmorton Street" (V 6). The dryness of the last phrase notwithstanding, Powell has done something to admit Da Costa to the "family" column.

The sense of subordination I credited Powell with in the first chapter, also the exacerbations of going counter to it, should be clear here. When Lushington registered at his hotel in the Low Town, it might be added that the clerk had asked him the profession of his mother's father—"I don't know it"—and the date of his parents' marriage—"I can't remember" (V 40–41). As droll on their side as the reference to Da Costa's brother, these fragments still work slyly in edging Lushington toward no-man's-land. (Powell the genealogist would have known those answers.)

Whatever it is about Da Costa—that sense he has that things are wrong, that his skin doesn't fit—he has been made more sober by Scherbatcheff's death and is found by Lushington haunting a fossil room in a museum. He is killed a few days later, and Frau Mavrin dies in the drosky with him, when chance Bolshevik shots aimed at a political leader hit these two as they are going home from a state ball.

The three authentics are now dead, and Lushington soon leaves the city by steamer. It is only fitting that he will find that other "beauty specialist," Count Bobel, in the dining-saloon and share a cabin with him. It is a pity that the Count does not have in his valise a cosmetic that would obliterate the birthmark soon to depress Lushington, on the last page, when he is with Lucy. They are in a place by the Thames and he recognizes the man with the birthmark as being from his newspaper. His retreat from the Baltic has not spared him daily contacts with marked people after all.

"FROM A VIEW TO A DEATH"

"He liked women but never put them before his work" (FV 6). The sentence refers to Zouch; his hack-work as an artist is meant. but even more his sense of operating as a superman. And the motto could apply to all three power-novels of the thirties (as it could not to *Afternoon Men and Venusberg*). So in the later trio, males—three men in each—take precedence as far as conflicts are concerned, a distinction that is worth remembering as we turn to them.

All the action in *From a View to a Death* revolves about the country town whose seat is Passenger Court, where Zouch, down from Chelsea, imbibes the flavor of country living. It galls the household's head, Mr. Passenger, that Zouch is sponging on him, and so the two begin to grapple—sociably, but in earnest. Zouch wins the first round in a scene placed in the middle of the novel. Passenger has the last laugh—indeed all the last laughs, for he also wages and wins another battle with a formidable town resident, Major Fosdick. The attrition of Passenger's birds, caused by Fosdick's poaching, keeps the novel shifting, when not following Zouch, between the Fosdicks' house in town (where they keep two outlandish sons) and Passenger Court (where the daughters, Mary and Betty, are not quite so bizarre). The mothers in these households prove able to visualize gainful marriages for their young; but Fosdick and Passenger retreat all the time to reverie, having found that only nausea can attend even passing thoughts of their offspring.

Danger beckons one of these men. The escape route Fosdick has chosen comes to involve his locked dressing room and transvestism —and if we wanted a symbol of Powell's theme about changing one's nature we could find it here, watching Fosdick getting into his sequin dress and picture hat. The aberration ruins the Major, for Passenger catches him at it, and the title *From a View to a Death* then leaps forward like a cannon into battery to bear on Fosdick's disaster. (Though he does not die, they cart him off to an asylum.)

The title comes from the poignant lines about foxhunting in "John Peel": "From a find to a check, from a check to a view,/ From a view to a death in the morning." They apply most directly to Zouch, and in little provide an insight into the novel's structure. For Zouch is the city fox hunted and killed in this novel.

Its first quarter amounts to a find: Mary Passenger's finding of

Zouch, his presence by invitation there, and the mutual recognition between supermen that a chase is on.

The check occurs with the words that end the first quarter, "He wondered what part had been cast in the pageant for Joanna" (FV 56), the girl with the invalid mother. As plans go forward in the next movement for the two main scheduled events—a cocktail party at the *Fox and Hounds* and the seventeenth-century pageant at Passenger Court—Zouch makes contact with Joanna. Then in the third quarter his two moments with her arrive, when he first frightens her at the inn but later finds her adorably ready for him the night of the pageant.

Why this all amounts to a "check" is that Passenger's quarry has here got blurred. Zouch as a threat to his daughter's hand has not materialized. But the third part ends with Miss Passenger, so unexpended for so long, suddenly engaged to the artist. As a sop to her father, Mary exacts two pledges from Zouch: he will ride to hounds when he returns in the fall, and he will shave his beard. With this last the title moves into battery again. "Fox in the bush," it used to be said in Brooklyn, when a beard was spotted. Zouch's beard had kept him isolate in the sense of that slogan, rather than lending force to his life. But now he does a rash thing. Shaving, he breaks cover and is viewed. Death is the next step. His obliging would-be father-in-law has him mounted for a hunt on a dangerous horse. Yet Zouch had averred he could ride. The horse bolts, throws Zouch, and breaks his neck.

For more than any other reason, though, Zouch hiding behind his beard has become palatable through three-quarters of a novel because so much hostility has beaten up against him. The master of the hunt is of course the dangerous one, but the entire Passenger household (except Mary) dislike him. Nor is Passenger, a stupid man, to be admired for anything at all to do with driving Zouch from cover, and this is a last reason for an upsurge of pathos on behalf of the man. For in the middle of the novel Passenger could have broken through the "check" and sent Zouch packing— could have had his view and a bloodless triumph. It was this great scene that lent Zouch what turned out to be fatal borrowed time.

When the scene occurs the novel is far enough along for us to understand that the younger superman, using the approach of calculating ingratiator, can hardly stand up against the man in his castle who can afford a direct, brusque approach to power. But Passenger's power potential is apt to become suspended because he is brought to a standstill by the unusual. (This is why his victory over Fosdick, with whom he shook hands "with all the restraint in the world" [FV 185] while that man was in woman's clothes, is not a clean and complete one.) In the central scene, he and Zouch are approaching the big house over Passenger's fields when they see a formation of city hikers converging on them. Among the group are a man named Fischbein and his girl, who know Arthur Zouch to the core: Chelsea pouncing in on him unexpected. Now, as Fischbein spouts intimate facts about Zouch, the artist's seamy past unfolds for Passenger's ears. But the landowner seems to have chosen this time to lay down laws about hedge-breaking to Fischbein's girl.

Passenger has simply been stunned by the apparition of these people. Hence Powell had hamstrung him with a superb thrust as soon as the marchers were spotted:

> "Hikers" [said Zouch].
> "Hikers?" said Mr. Passenger. *"Hikaz?"*
> The word was evidently unfamiliar to him and he pronounced it as if it belonged to some oriental language.
>   (FV 95–96)

From this idiotic point on Passenger can take nothing in, and his visitor escapes hideous exposure. The mid-point now touched, though, and Zouch's escape having been so narrow, we learn that "In retrospect the encounter with Fischbein had produced a strong effect upon him. *He had made up his mind to change his way of life*" (FV 108; my italics). Some of the inevitability of tragedy, if not its heroism, has made its way into the book.

The one thing Zouch had was natural power over women. When he traded on this, misjudging what he could acquire, when he told himself, "The will to power should teach him how to ride" (FV 145), his instincts betrayed him. After Zouch's death, Powell turns the tables on those who had apparently seen through Zouch: he has the flippant elder Passenger girl, Betty, hunting in an unspeakable manner for her father's hidden cigars, which she wants to smoke, and he has one of the townees hear a thing or two from Fischbein. But when Fischbein reports that Zouch was no hand with horses *or women either,* the dead man has to be redeemed by the reader. This amounts to a silent demand of Powell's, no matter how reluctant the reader may be. One place the mind of many readers may go is to the bedroom where Zouch wakes, disengages himself from sleeping Joanna, and goes quietly to the window. "He looked out of it towards the fields, at this hour unnaturally close to the house. The morning light brought them up just beyond the lawn. The grey, mysterious English fields" (FV 138). The check is over; these are fields the fox will run across soon. If only he had put women before his work.

"AGENTS AND PATIENTS"

With so many patients in the provinces, and agents infesting the city to which Powell now returns, *Agents and Patients* and *From a View* become contervalent books. Notice how two descriptions, purportedly doing the same work, underline the difference. Here from the earlier novel is a provincial character, one of Major Fosdick's sons, pedalling his bicycle through town, his life pinched in at either end: "Senile decay seemed already to have laid its hand on him while he was still in the grip of arrested development. Prematurely young, second childhood had [already] come to him . . ." (FV 37). But there is a less hopeless way of putting this. Here is an art entrepreneur from the later book, Reggie Frott, "looking more than ever himself, an intemperate little boy of twelve years old or, alternatively, an octogenarian jockey . . ." (AP 19). They are both young men, these two, but where one is on a treadmill the other has elasticity, and so does the metaphor now, because he can live by his wits.

However, there is a rub. The setting of Powell's fourth book is the depression, and as a result of this, the natural agents single-track their will-power, using it to extract money. Thus the patients, who have the money, are potential agents themselves. This "reversibility" causes a special sort of crisis, when an agent waters at the knees, to become endemic to this novel of the depression.

To protect themselves, true operators develop a sang-froid style of living, complete with brow-beetlings and decisive gestures of all sorts. A symbol of them all is a side-street exhibitionist in the first pages, a sword-wielding, car-shaking ape-man who belabors a crony all trussed up, but who makes us wince as he turns to direct wheedling of the crowd—"Why, I've been doing this turn for fifteen years and if it wasn't a fine decent entertainment would I be doing it to this day, I ask you, ladies and gentlemen?" (AP 8) —exemplifying how, when style vacates, agents become patients.

Along with Blore-Smith, though not his counselors yet, the journalist Chipchase and the scenario-writer Maltravers watch the ape-man from the crowd. They remain bland. Maltravers does go over the scene later, summing it up to his wife Sarah as a symbol of their marriage. "I lie on the ground gagged and chained and you prod me with a sword" (AP 15). But this is to catch him on the verge of patient-status, not there. Though he and Chipchase both have inherited a paranoia attendant, Powell says, on journalism, they do hold snug to their roles.

As with Regan and Goneril, there is a difference. Chipchase is a sidler; Maltravers, a spurter-forward. (This last produces contact with Blore-Smith in the first place, as Maltravers runs him down in his sports car.) At the end of the first chapter, Chipchase has taken Blore-Smith on for psychoanalysis and Maltravers has pledged him to finance his forthcoming psychological film. Congratulating one another, they are able to leave parenthetical such real problems as Maltravers' concern over his wife and an ugly little race-driver. (Chipchase overcomes physical jolts as Maltravers does matrimonial ones.)

Out of this sort of thing comes the book's greatest irony—that a man with a really constitutional handicap emerges as agent par excellence. Gaston, noble Frenchman and drug addict, is not spurred by the will to power, but he has spontaneity—which gets surcharged when "supplies" run low. He does need money and is being entertained at the estate of Schlumbermayer, who is bargaining for Gaston's art collection. Volatile as Gaston is, he needs diverting, and so Maltravers and Chipchase have been invited to take an impromptu film out at the Broadacres estate. These two want to re-control Blore-Smith, however, who at this late date has broken from them. They are able to hale the young man off to a Chinese dinner, on the pretext of discussing the film with Schlumbermayer. But at the dinner Gaston goes out of control.

This raging scene is formative as far as Blore-Smith's life is concerned. It enables him later to steal a car at Broadacres and make his escape from his tormentors. All because, as Gaston goes berserk, "For the first time . . . Maltravers and Chipchase, like Frankenstein, seemed unable to control this creature of their own contriving" (AP 178).

But Chipchase and Maltravers do overtake Gaston after he has run from the restaurant, and before that Maltravers had the presence of mind to tell Schlumbermayer and Blore-Smith to repair to his own flat where Sarah would admit them. These two remain captives, in other words. Schlumbermayer is indeed the arch-patient in the novel, and this scene ends with heavy derision of the inert pair consuming their food.

The middle four sections of the novel, their action culminating in this restaurant scene, have gone fairly predictably: Blore-Smith's introduction to vice in Paris, followed in London by his inane effort to seduce Sarah Maltravers; some more carousing in Germany, followed by a purgatory under Mrs. Mendoza back in England. The control exerted by the two rogues, snapped now at last as far as overt power is concerned, has prompted Robert Morris to see in Powell's arrangement a parallel to the temptation of Adam. Not only does Morris find supporting evidence—for example, one of the Berlin nightclubs is the Eden Bar—but he is right in not being heavy-handed about the allusions. He knows they are not fully serious. All the same he is led to raise "those more emphatic questions which *Agents and Patients,* no matter how teasingly, asks. Should experience be sought? At what price? Are dynamic reversals of psyche . . . to be preferred [or postponed]?"[5] The answer to these questions is implicit in all of Powell, and can be arrived at confidently if one remembers his distrust of the cult of experience. The answer is that dynamic reversals of the psyche are to be, in the best interests of any character, postponed. Colonel Teape's capture of Blore-Smith at the end is clear enough in import: Blore-Smith should never have got into any of this business. And anyway, Powell's is a simple classical position. In our day, one can find it in a writer like Wyndham Lewis, who influenced these early books. As Geoffrey Wagner says, "Lewis' work is a retraction from, rather than a mingling in, experience."[6] Or one could go all the way back to the Renaissance and find Roger Ascham citing Erasmus: *"Erasmus* the honor of learning of all oure time, saide wiselie that experience is the common scholehouse of foles, and ill men: Men, of witte and honestie,   be otherwise instructed."[7]

From the restaurant episode on through the sixth and final section of *Agents and Patients,* things roll along in deceptively lighthearted slapstick. An art dealer flies into Schlumbermayer's pasture to buy Gaston's art objects right under Schlumbermayer's nose. The gorgeous Mrs. Mendoza is present and by now has fallen for Gaston. In the course of a wild scramble arising out of competition for Mendie, Gaston hijacks both her and the waiting plane and flies off to France before the eyes of everyone. During the melee Blore-Smith gets up nerve to steal the car. And Maltravers and Chipchase have caught the whole thing on film.

There is nothing cruel in all this, but it has been a cruel book all the same. Mainly because it has had a Berlin interlude. Chipchase took Blore-Smith there, to join Maltravers who was doing some spot film work. And power-moves there were as gross as the "Gross Gott!" that came out of the mouth of a dwarf movie director, "whose right arm ended in a hook" (AP 126). Powell placed dwarfs all around, in fact, tubercular Nazis among them. Those grudgingly allowed full stature seldom wore garments correspondent to their sex. Germany in 1932 must have seemed hideous to Powell, who coarsened these scenes in *Agents and Patients* in a way not matched elsewhere in his work. In one episode a waiter named Adolf, on his evening off, muscles in among hotel guests to chastise a stunted fellow-waiter, finally spilling the man to the floor in a frenzy of "night-off" self-assertion. (Christopher Isherwood, in his *Berlin Stories* of the same date, invariably saw Germans large, whether as hateful body-worshipping Nazis or as "powerfully built youths wearing hammer-and-sickle armlets";[8]   but Powell saw runts.)

The resulting furore causes even durable Mrs. Mendoza's nerves to break. Nothing short of utter Teutonic squalor could have caused her to bolt from the continent with Blore-Smith as escort. Before forming plans, she and he took respite at a café:

> Because the café was raised above the level of the street it was out of reach of the beggars, who were unable here, as at other cafés and restaurants, to approach and stand close up to the tables with bowed heads. This architectural exemption was advantageous. Berlin beggars, neatly dressed for the most part in gloves and plus-fours, would remain immote for lengthy periods, distressing but somehow repellent from the limitations and Germanness of their methods. Like all their countrymen they were hopelessly technique-bound.   (AP 144)

Though a Kurt Weill could have been found there too at the time, Powell had to turn a blind eye on this terrible town. His fury precludes compassion.

It would be improper to wonder whether the German section of *Agents and Patients* cauterized any wound Powell may have had. It is enough to hear Mrs. Mendoza say she wished she could have been born a man. "I could have learnt Greek. . . . The Greeks knew how to live. If they heard music they danced . . . if they came to blue sea they swam in it. They were natural, beautiful, free" (AP 144–145). Her longing casts back to the phrase from a Wesley sermon that gave the novel its title. *"He that is not free is not an* Agent, *but a* Patient." It is quite out of the ordinary to find sentiments like Mrs. Mendoza's working up to the level of speech in a Powell novel. One wonders whether the relief at last to come in *Waring* owes anything to them.

''WHAT'S BECOME OF WARING''

Agents and Patients tended to guffaw at meaningful structure, but Powell made *What's Become of Waring*, like *Afternoon Men*, a three-part novel (nine chapters and a short tenth for epilogue). *Waring* describes the London book world and touches also on the interest in spiritualism in the thirties. The fusion of book- and séance-worlds grows out of Hugh Judkins' scoffing flirtation with the occult. The leading author on the Judkins firm's list is T. T. Waring, a man the publishers have not met, who writes travel books well dosed with spartan philosophy. On the night the newspapers announce the death of T. T. Waring, the letters "Tee Tee" squeak out from the voicebox of a medium. (Had he read the papers? No one will ever know.) That Alec Pimley, impersonator of Waring, has caused the "death" to be broadcast does not really matter. A warning about the *imminent* death of the writer might be involved, and in the epilogue chapter Alec Pimley is indeed reported dead. Alec's first go at plagiarism came at the expense of his grandfather, who had modestly published a book on Ceylon without affixing his name. Not till the end of the novel is the plagiarism traced to Alec, so that Waring is considered to have been an actual person through most of the action.

The search for T. T. Waring information then becomes the mainspring of the book. Captain Hudson is tapped as biographer because Powell's narrator, a reader for Judkins and Judkins, finds that Hudson revered Waring's travelogues and that the captain can write as well.

The novel's structure becomes determined when Roberta Payne, a journalist who was engaged to Waring *alias* Robinson in France, puts her doctored information up for sale. The second movement starts with her name; she is to put Hudson and Judkins through a third of a novel of trial-by-woman. Another man becomes implicated, the narrator, but this inveterate listener (Powell's last prototype for Nick Jenkins) becomes a confederate of Roberta's rather than a victim.

That this dispassionate narrator is writing a book called *Stendhal: and Some Thoughts on Violence* turns out to be instructive. His close-mouthed attitude becomes itself associated with power—notably when he keeps concealed from Hudson that the Robinson they frequently hear about is T. T. Waring. "He could be told at a later date why he had been made to hear all this about Robinson" (W 89). Where Atwater and Lushington were exempt from a power-taint, this later version of them is not. (His tendency to withhold information will be expiated in *The Music of Time*.)

A big scene caps the middle section of the novel, with the narrator caught in its wake. Hudson has to escort his fiancée

Beryl Pimley to a military ball and needs the narrator to fill in as escort for Beryl's sister. The only inducement Hudson can offer is that his friend will see Lipfield (the "messenger," and a prototype of the famous Widmerpool) in full Territorial regalia.

Before the ball Hudson is short-tempered with the Pimley women—an odd thing, since he supposedly loves Beryl and has always been attentive to her and her family. All this is cleared up when Lipfield's party, and the novel's moment of moments, arrive. Among Lipfield's group is Hugh Judkins, escorting Roberta Payne—who keeps looking round the ballroom. This seems puzzling until the narrator hears a voice behind him say, "Well, I'm damned!"

> It was Hudson. He had come back and was standing beside me. I looked round at him. He was staring at Roberta. And then all at once the explanation of why Roberta had seemed to search round the room when she arrived was made clear. She wanted to see Hudson because he was in love with her. That was why she had allowed Hugh to bring her to the dance. Roberta saw Hudson gaping at her and waved. He went across and took her hand. . . .
> "I thought you—" said Hugh.
> She did not hear him. He was left grinning irritably at the place where she had been standing. Lipfield, whose appearance in mess-kit fully justified Hudson's promise of a spectacle worth any hardship, took my arm.   (W 125–126)

With these sentences Powell has caught the essences of his three leading males. The coup de grâce is the last sentence, showing the narrator's mind pulled away from the two men to whom he should owe some allegiance. But meanwhile his body is being towed off by Lipfield. Once again: guilt-by-association—as Powell had managed it with Blore-Smith and Schlumbermayer at a Chinese restaurant, with Lushington and Bobel on a Baltic steamer. Our narrator, after all is put right at the final séance, will be left to dine with . . . Lipfield.

And now Roberta will betray Hudson by sailing off to Scandinavia. Hugh Judkins takes her on this trip, but gets nothing out of her for his pains and that is why he grows so choleric in the last pages. Hudson meanwhile, struck down by the "betrayal," plunges anew into the pursuit of Waring. Thus Roberta's maneuver brings on the novel's last third, and with it the last letdown—the trail to Waring ending at a manure heap, from poor Hudson's point of view. A friend of the narrator's, residing at Toulon, has the two biography-hunters visit him and provides the last plot-link when a volume he owns proves the source of another crib by Waring. Now Hudson abandons the biography. At which point he meets Waring. It is Beryl's brother Alec, married to an old dowager. Tying onto this rich woman was the reason for his decision to bury that other-self T. T. Waring.

Alec breaks from the smouldering Hudson by hoisting anchor and fleeing St. Etienne in a storm that drowns him and his wife, we are to gather at the end. Hudson remains stuck not so much because of the imposture but because the impostor was Beryl's brother. He cannot bring himself to reopen communications with her, being rather like Conrad's Marlow hiding the secret of Kurtz from the fair beloved. Powell refuses to satirize this attitude.* Beryl will show her own strength though, as we have seen. Before the day is saved, however, the narrator is dragged in as an equal underminer of Captain Hudson. His Toulon host causes him to admit as much when Hudson leaves them. How did the man get so far in the dumps, the host asks.

> "T. T. Waring and Roberta Payne."
> "And yourself."
> "I suppose so."   (W 180)

---

*Robert Morris, observing that Hudson had sworn he would "give some-thing" to meet Waring, says that "What he 'gives' is a part of his own identity, perhaps the most important part since it holds his romantic vision of the world." (The Novels of Anthony Powell, p. 93.) This is not alto-gether true, for while his Waring-attachment was a sign of his romanticism, this is the very best thing for him to shuffle off (it takes some "giving," yes). Still, his Marlow-like sensitiveness to Beryl's feelings shows his basic charac-ter has not been modified, and a reduction rather than a stripping-away of his romanticism has resulted. One might say he matriculates—gets rid of some infatuations but is not ready to apply the results of disillusionment randomly on all sides. In this he is like Captain Rowland Gwatkin of Powell's first war novel.

This is why, at an early but most mystical moment in the novel, the old Pimley grandfather, catching sight of the narrator, had garbled out the syllables "Al . . . ec. . . ." This turns out more hauntingly appropriate than the goings on at any of the séances.

Falling asleep as the book ends, the unnamed narrator has a catalogue of its personages run through his head, all of whom, he reflects, "wanted power." Alec and Roberta belong at the top of his list. He turns out like them. (So also in Browning's poem "Waring," from which we get this title, is the narrator linked with the wanderer Waring, whose face was "So hungry for acknowledgment / Like mine!"[9]) But absent from the list are Beryl and Tiger Hudson; and a modest provision of power comes to them, where it is not sought. Meanwhile, for the narrator there remains the Stendhal chapter that has lain fallow three years, going under the title "Laughter is Power." Or perhaps this does not remain, for he is back in advertising again, and may perhaps be able *to* laugh (as he never does in the novel). Hugh Judkins is back at schoolmastering again and it appears this was what he was cut out for. The urge to coerce has seemed to loom as the giant fault of those crashing the book world, and the old placid grandfather Pimley seemed the right one to detect resemblances among marginal creatures in that world. For had he not published anonymously, and allowed his truant grandson to take support from him in every way, right down to plagiarism? That old Pimley was a captain himself, father of a general, in fact, is an added Powell touch. We should be wrong to suspect in Powell any wholesale deference to the military—Colonel Teape and Major Fosdick provide reminders enough on that score—but of course soldiers were his own antecedents. He would become one shortly after *Waring,* and would stop writing novels then, for twelve years. This may not have been owing, but does seem appropriate, to what *Waring* revealed about what many writers wanted. In *The Valley of Bones,* Nick Jenkins would say that "Whatever inner processes are required for writing novels, so far as I myself was concerned, war now utterly inhibited" (VB 113). This was "morally inescapable"—that was his phrase.

$\cdots\bullet\!\!\!\!\!\!\!\raisebox{0.3ex}{$\cdot$}\!\!\!\mathbf{3}\;\mathbf{I}\!\!\raisebox{0.3ex}{$\cdot$}\!\!\!\!\!\!\bullet\cdots$

Two Distinctive Styles

SOME SATIRIC SHADINGS

Readers familiar with both stages of Powell's career would undoubtedly attest to the denser prose style of *The Music of Time,* and would probably connect this with the more intricate detailing of social declensions in the long novel. One thing these same readers would probably admit, though, is that the early and late styles have some meeting places. Generally, the more satiric a cast Powell makes, the more an early passage and a later passage will tend to resemble each other. Though this is not the most important thing about his writing, he does often assay to get things down with icy clarity (as Nick Jenkins once said he felt he could do after a party in *A Buyer's Market*). The secret of this side of his style is its lapidary precision: the construction of segmented, heavily stopped sentences where each detail is in a sense formally burned into place, the next then undertaken. Here for example is his first description of a seduction (from *Afternoon Men*):

> Slowly, but very deliberately, the brooding edifice of seduction, creaking and incongruous, came into being, a vast Heath Robinson mechanism, dually controlled by them and lumbering gloomily down vistas of triteness.   (AM 83)

72

From *A Buyer's Market,* a passing description of an Oxford don turns satiric through the same cumulative method. Nick sees him from the rear, in his evening dress,

> the crumpled tails of which hung down almost to its wearer's heels, giving him the appearance of a music-hall comedian, or conjuror of burlesque, whose baggy Charlie Chaplin trousers, threatening descent to the ground at any moment, would probably reveal red flannel, grotesquely spotted, or some otherwise traditionally comic, underclothes, or lack of them, beneath.
>
> (BM 109–110)

In these descriptions the pitch is kept high throughout, so that we get the archness of a continued mild exaggeration. Hence the trousers threaten to descend "at any moment," and, in the first example, the contraption "comes into being" portentously. Also there are the proper-noun allusions ("Charlie Chaplin trousers," "a vast Heath Robinson mechanism"), docketing the subject for the reader and giving him a humorous advantage over it. Finally there is bathos, one vision moving off into "vistas of triteness," the other conjecturing at the end that under those Charlie Chaplin trousers there may be a bare behind.

Something interesting about the bathos is that it is typically gained through anti-climactic diction in the early books and through anti-climactic syntax in the later. The second method may mark an advance in being a little less sententious. A last reflex of syntax ("underclothes, or lack of them, beneath") gives the effect of a mind suddenly seeing a new comic possibility. The alternative is a mind which has seen the whole comic possibility all along.*

Some ironic styles could well be differentiated on the basis of such a concept. Swift, for example, made it a staple of his style to appear to add on the most maddening details casually, as in this from A Modest Proposal: "I have already computed the Charge of nursing a Beggar's Child . . . to be about two Shillings per Annum, Rags included. . . ." (Jonathan Swift, Irish Tracts and Sermons 1728–1733, ed. Herbert Davis [Oxford, 1955], p. 112.) The style of a satirist like Peacock, conversely, gives the sense of foreseeing the whole comic situation, and of relying on the pungent phrase to deliver it over

Periodic sentences, which by their nature cannot produce bathos through syntax, traditionally are the product of a mind that has thought out its emphases in advance. And in the early books Powell gets some of his best effects by ending periodic constructions with horribly bathetic phraseology. For instance, a sentence in *From a View to a Death* shifts some massive deadweight onto the last three words, as a silly man is interrupted by rain from disporting himself in front of a group rehearsing for a pageant:

> He too gazed into the sky for a few seconds, and then with a sweeping gesture conveying in its scope, rage, despair, thwarted ambition, contempt, defiance, disbelief in the goodness of human nature, and a stumbling hope in some pantheistic creed, he indicated the house with his unnaturally long forefinger.
>
> (FV 67)

We are in Peacock country with a description like this (it is even a country house that that forefinger is indicating). But—to turn to another instance of trouser-deflation in *The Music of Time*—the trailing relative clauses of the following sentence appear to have been formed as the eye was moving: and while the first pauses on the pretension to knowledge of the subject (a stuffy Frenchman), the second turns all to bathos by making him a clotheshorse:

> As he strolled back across the lawn towards the house, he stowed away his pipe, which he seemed to use as a kind of emblem of common sense, in the pocket of his black alpaca jacket, which he wore over fawn tussore trousers.   (QU 148)

The main clause dealing with the pipe comes early, and then the description of the apparel is tacked on. It is a typically loose sen-

---

entire. *Thus we are shown a character from* Crotchet Castle *"throwing himself back into a chair . . . with [a] premeditated design . . . but by miscalculating his impetus, he overbalanced his chair, and laid himself on the carpet in a right angle, of which his back was the base." (Thomas Love Peacock,* Nightmare Abbey and Crotchet Castle [New York, 1964], p. 158.) Powell's *most satiric sentences stay closer to this more lapidary manner of Peacock, with stronger evidence of "premeditated design" in satiric passages from the earlier prose.*

tence, or, as linguists like to say, right-branching. In most of the long sentences of *The Music of Time* this pattern predominates.

For the periodic sentence, linguists use the term left-branching: minor elements assembled to the left, before the main clause. A variation is the self-embedded construction, in which subject and predicate are separated by a subordinate syntactical element. If this minor element is long and involved enough, it can produce the suspended "periodic" effect, and when Powell wants to have fun at someone's expense in the early books, he will often resort to this construction (but seldom in the later).

> Bernard, who wore a collar made of a single band of starched linen that went rather more than once round his neck and was itself encircled by a silk tie passed through a ring, pressed the stub of his cigar into an ash-tray.   (W 68)

In this sentence from *What's Become of Waring* a satirical cut is once more made through an over-long prelude to an inconsequential action. My point in choosing it (there are two more constructions of the same type, beginning "Bernard," on that page) is to indicate complete reversal from the *Music of Time* example just quoted. There, the pipe got disposed, then the clothes described; here, there is a deliberate interruption to describe clothing, then a cigar gets stubbed out. The situations seem inherently satirical, the achievements each successful but in different stylistic ways.

The varieties of stylized sentences so far given are of course sporting with their material. Instead of the material having its way with the artist, the artist has his way with it. But if this grew to be too much the case, stylization would call in question the validity of the serious themes so far deemed paramount in Powell's work. " 'Stylization,' " says Susan Sontag, "is what is present in a work of art when an artist does propose the by-no-means inevitable distinction between matter and manner," when he predetermines his method of treatment, in other words. A predetermined method of treatment presupposes the author's superiority over his subject; "when the material of art is conceived of as 'subject matter,' " Miss Sontag concludes, "it is also experienced as capable of being exhausted."[1]

So, in the course of illustrating a satiric leaning in Powell which verges on the sententious, we come up against the issue of "treatment" or "mannerism"—the question of whether or not Powell tends to look on his subject as being capable of exhaustion. The question needs to be answered for the early books in particular, since we are leaving them. What of the claims made for their laconic but absorbing moodiness? Are these susceptible to dispute because of an arbitrary stylization that may have no real or deep concern for its material?

The answer I would give is that the kind of lapidary prose just illustrated is mostly encountered in circumstances that are digressive. The description of the master of ceremonies at the pageant is an effusion (it does provide half a moment of good fun) and the seduction-ploy from *Afternoon Men* represents an occasion when a maxim of Rochefoucauld might be in order. Powell has corroborated in interviews the combined Hemingway-Wyndham Lewis influence first observed by G. U. Ellis, and it seems to be the Lewis influence coming out here; in a review called "Satire in the Twenties" Powell gave a leading position to Lewis, whose style he described as "at once baroque and ascetic, utilitarian and outlandish. . . ."[2] That combination can be arrived at when a style is fashioned intellectually, as seems the case here. But just *because* the style of Wyndham Lewis is avowedly intellectual, it is a style that will not stop until the last nail is in the victim's coffin, and the last corrugation of a nailhead given its derisionary glint as the box goes under the sod.

A super-graphic style simply arrests pace, whether it is heavily punctuated or whether it is not.* And if this pattern proved to be the main staple of Powell's prose he might well be unreadable.

---

*A good example of a Lewis-like sentence trying to race along comes from What's Become of Waring. The sentence is as usual incidental, and in Lewis's manner catches the mechanical gyrations of its target, in this case Lipfield departing from a séance. "He jogged off towards Lothbury, clutching his umbrella and shrinking his shoulders as if to avoid a pursuing cohort of lamenting spirits summoned unwilling from the abyss" (W 102). The reader loses his wind following this along, stumbling on an average of a verbal every three words after the main clause.

However, it is not the staple pattern. Attention has had to be given to it because it does produce memorable satiric vignettes and it is recurrent. Yet my feeling is that the sharpness, even acidity, serves Powell mainly for surprise—enables him, as the notion takes him, to "cast a cold eye"—but that as a novelist he is more interested in getting things down without the aid of "distancing" factors like bathos or mannered archness. He seems actually most interested in capturing the almost unrecordable dead spots in life; in the early and late novels he does this in two different ways, and here is where the radically different styles do diverge.

In the last resort, his true originality as a stylist depends on realism, not exaggeration. In the early books his strategy is to resort to an unweighted, unpunctuated prose, while in *The Music of Time* everything is weighted, but weighted with the quality of *hesitancy*. For example, one always finds in the late style the *"not un-* formation" that George Orwell so deplored.[3] But once one realizes that key meanings in *The Music of Time* depend on the difference, say, between being "adventurous" and "not unadventurous," one sees that strictures on behalf of straightforward clarity will not apply. Constantine FitzGibbon translated a famous epigram of La Rochefoucauld the only way it could have been translated: "We always discover, in the misfortunes of our dearest friends, something not altogether displeasing."[4] To put the last phrase in positive form would have been the guarantee of falsification; the semi-pleasure phrased as it is is what is real.

To note facts like these is to begin to deal with the inexorable connection between style and meaning that causes a good writer to settle for only one way of saying what he needs to say. That is, he will almost always so settle; for the best writer will permit himself a sag or a flourish now and then. As Peter Quennell once said, "Whether in personal or in literary conduct, undue asceticism is always blighting; and as important as a capacity to resist temptation is an ability, displayed at the correct juncture, to succumb with grace and gusto; for, in every prose style that gives us genuine delight, an element of restraint and reserve is accompanied by occasional touches of exuberance. . . ."[5]

DIALOGUE

There is a way of suggesting why one kind of discursive prose supplanted another in Powell, and this can be done through some comments on dialogue. Though the proportion of non-dramatic prose increases drastically in *The Music of Time,* there is not a great deal of difference to be found in the way talk is recorded there. Certain trademark techniques reappear to settle dialogue in as a constant among variables. The one most nearly inimitable might be called the dialogue scroll; that is, a strip of conversation falling down a page as two speakers exchange questions, revelations, words of love or evasion, in compact patterns of a sort fairly staggering in resourcefulness—perhaps the kind of thing Powell delights most in discovering occasions for in his work, since it can be found from his first book to his last.

> "I'm called Lola."
> "No, really?"
> "Yes."
> "Who calls you Lola?"
> "I just call myself Lola."
> "Weren't you christened that?"
> "No."
> "One must have a name?"
> "What's your name?"
> "William," said Atwater. . . .   (AM 19)

That is from *Afternoon Men.* Atwater, the second speaker, is responsible for this scroll because he asks attenuating questions. He has already done the same thing often inside the first twenty pages of the first novel, and if one were to look at the conclusion of *The Kindly Ones,* one would find Powell ending the first sextet of *The Music of Time* with columns of dialogue too. Nick Jenkins in this case has found a man who might assist in getting his call-up into the army effectuated.

> "Could it be speeded up?"
> "What?"
> "Finding my name."

"Would you like that?"
"Yes."
"Don't see why not."
"You could?"
"M'm."
"Fairly soon?"
"How old are you?"   (KO 252)

The technique points to something inveterate in the author; the question-asking habit is persistent in his protagonists. Sometimes they just push the questions along in front of them as though to support themselves physically (Atwater's technique); urgency may get involved also, as happens at last with Nick. But it should not be thought that a question-and-answer pattern is primarily responsible for the dialogue scrolls. Some of the most moving moments in his writing, especially love scenes, are brought off through this compressed incremental technique. He can catch accents of conviction, stubbornness, or genuine idiosyncrasy as well as attenuation. Here, for example, is Nick's father, whom we only come to know in *The Kindly Ones,* arguing with Nick's mother. Mrs. Jenkins resents a servant's devotion to the father.

"He worships you," she would add.
"Oh, nonsense."
"He does."
"Of course not."
"I say he does."
"Don't be silly."   (KO 14)

The dialogue may appear effortless but is really molded to a very great degree. Two-, three-, and four-word sentences are fashioned with a shade of variation each time. As one speaker wards off the other, the odd thing that comes to underlie the passage is the presence of amity and compatibility. Just *how* one detects amity beneath words like these (a case could be made for the key phrase "I say": a repetition of "He does" would have produced nagging)—*how* a few words can do so much work may have to remain an imponderable. Just raising the question ought to show that such writing, economical almost beyond emulation, is no easy thing to achieve.

That Powell can continue to write as compactly as he chooses is one thing borne out by a method consistent across both styles. But where the patterns run similar and the speakers themselves do not, a very important reason may emerge for the laconic narrative of the early books and the "distinguished classical prose and rounded periods" of the later.[6] The fact that, in the last analysis, character dictates technique in Powell, becomes responsible not only for the things his people say but also for the way things are said by their creator when we are no longer listening to them.

The question involves wit, address, the capacity for rising to a challenge. Here, for instance, is an exchange between Nick and his friend Barnby, who wants to extract information from Nick as to the identity of a mistress he (Barnby) has acquired; it seems she would not divulge her name. Nick, having been shown a portrait Barnby had done of the girl, believes he has met her. " 'It would be only polite to reveal her identity by now,' Barnby said, returning the drawing to the portfolio and making a grimace" (AW 71). The point about what follows is that, halfway through, we realize Nick can name the girl. But to Barnby, so alert that he can begin to chime in with little additions to Nick's short divulgences, the girl becomes secondary to the push-pull of the dialogue itself. He is not so eager to get her name as he is relaxed and ironical toward the whole issue—and the irony shared between the two speakers amounts to a real exchange between them. Nick speaks first:

> "Dark eyes and reddish hair?"
> "The latter unbrushed."
> "Christian name, Anne?"
> "There was certainly an 'A' on her handkerchief. That was a clue I forgot to tell you."
> "Generally untidy?"
> "Decidedly. As to baths, I shouldn't think she overdid them."
> "I think I can place her."
> "Don't keep me in suspense."   (AW 72)

The fetching thing is how both characters spar along, matching wits. They *have* wit. And we get an inkling of depth from a little contest like this, just as we could from the exchange between Nick's father and mother. The clue is that the characters are really hearing each other.

On the other hand, the characters in the early books tend to exist in a state of "curious somnambulism," as Kingsley Amis once said—adding that they are likeable enough for all that.[7] Consider a not dissimilar patch of dialogue in *Afternoon Men*, involving Atwater and the two painters Pringle and Barlow. Pringle airs some complaints about country people and Atwater asks his usual questions. A certain girl is mentioned. Then we notice that Pringle stops listening and drifts off in one direction, tabulating his complaints, while Barlow in a sleepy way goes off in another.

> "They need waking up, these village people [said Pringle]. They don't understand modern methods."
> "Who is it now?"
> "The girl in the paper shop."
> "The one with iron spectacles?"
> "She said if I didn't like the papers being late why didn't I live elsewhere."
> "She's not a bad-looking girl," said Barlow. "Of a type."
> "Then there's the butcher," said Pringle. "But I woke them both up."
> Barlow said: "It's curious, that girl in the paper shop. If you took her glasses off she wouldn't be bad at all."
>
> (AM 169–170)

Pringle may have wakened the butcher and the shopgirl but he certainly did not do the same for Barlow. What passes for talk here is simply two people (each waiting his turn) thinking out loud. In *From a View to a Death* we meet a pair of women, Joanna Brandon's mother and her housekeeper, who become "great cronies" from this same obliging propensity. "Neither of them made any effort to listen to what the other was saying, so that often they would speak for hours together on two entirely dif-

ferent subjects" (FV 82). Amis had the right word in "somnambulism."

Now Powell has admitted that Barlow in *Afternoon Men* and
Barnby in *The Music of Time* were drawn from the same character,[8] but the whole matter of respect allotted Barnby is propor-
tional to his genuine countering-ability in a conversation like
the last given. It is a measure of the difference of Powell's whole
view, late as against early, that someone like Barnby becomes so
sympathetic while Barlow remains ungraspable, kept, as it were,
behind a glass partition. For a fiction writer to succeed he must
of course create real personalities (Barlow is by no means unreal).
But the amazing advance in the late fiction is the creation of
personalities through the medium of the characters' own manifest
abilities to comprehend the personalities of their friends. Barnby
once described to Nick how an old-fashioned novelist had tried
to catch up with the times—buying modern art and so forth:

> "So there he goes," said Barnby. "Head-first into the contem-
> porary world."
> He hunched his shoulders, and made a grimace, as if to ex-
> press the violence, even agony, that had accompanied St. John
> Clarke's aesthetic metamorphosis. By easy stages we moved off
> to dinner at Foppa's.   (AW 29)

We had noticed Barnby grimace before, but combined with awareness of his own or another's awkwardness, there is a leisure he
displays and it has something to do with the style of *The Music of
Time*. Its sometimes tortuous prose is invariably relieved by quiet
phraseology—the important phrase here being "By easy stages."
The phrase could apply to the modulation of dialogue when
speakers of Nick's own calibre are caught communicating. It defines in a large way the style which we shall try to epitomize in a
moment in *The Music of Time,* but it does not define the narrative style of the early fiction. This is a pure style that by no means
moves along in easy stages. Its effect on the reader may be that of
simplicity and effortlessness, but it seems to have cost pains unlike those expended in *The Music of Time*. They are the pains
of exclusion and the rigor of keeping color as much as possible
suppressed, of creating monochrome.

SPATIAL DEPLOYMENT: EARLY STYLE

The following paragraph from *Venusberg* is reproduced with the conjunctions italicized and it gives more of an idea of Powell's early style than any lapidary or ironic substitute could do:

> The wind had dropped a little *and* Count Scherbatcheff said *that* the worst was past *and* it would not be rough for the rest of the voyage. The passengers on board now formed a world of their own *and* it was difficult to imagine any time *when* acquaintance had not been limited to this half a dozen *and* all life proportioned to the boundaries set by the sea.   (V 28)

Sixty-eight words make up these two sentences and they are given no punctuation aside from a full stop. In the five novels from the thirties there are seventy paragraphs like this—paragraphs over sixty words long, sometimes twice that length, written in a pure syntax that requires only terminal punctuation. (I arbitrarily choose sixty words as a limit to produce a substantial paragraph, one that approaches say a quarter of a page. In the early books we have the high incidence of one such paragraph every fifteen pages, on the average. In the whole *Music of Time* there are only two such paragraphs [AW 158; LM 62–63].)

When I spoke of Powell's desire to record life's dead spots it was prose like this from *Venusberg* that I had in mind. The sentences in this example happen to work the same way and so their syntactical "purity" may stand out more pronouncedly. Though the constructions are compound-complex, each noun, verb, and modifier is placed so as naturally to preclude any pause or appropriated emphasis. (It is a syntax that Powell may have been helped to by Hemingway, but Hemingway would have avoided words like "acquaintance" and "proportioned.")

The first clause in each sentence gives a fact, and the second an idea rising from the fact, but the coordinate conjunctions keep the relationships neutral. (The progression is linear rather than logically causative.) Characters' opinions are now set up in subordinate constructions: "Count Scherbatcheff said *that*"; "it was difficult to imagine any time *when*." But as these opinions develop, the simple equating conjunction comes in again to prevent the grading of the information and it all falls into the same bin. The unique and matter-of-fact, to Powell, are one. Though the paragraph actually says that all life may be measured by a new governing situation—being confined at sea—the travelers settle into this displacement of the normal with no sense of drama at all.

The fact that the sentences are *long* and unpunctuated is interesting. Their "monochrome" quality (a term first used by Cyril Connolly[9]) arrives through a sense of the writer's hand being led into phrases and clauses that present themselves as objects would to a sweeping camera (rather than having to be blocked in by a Wyndham Lewis pen).* Continuity of mood allows for no shock. With a paragraph like the following, though it appears just after the disclosure of Major Fosdick's perversion, one may gather from the fifty-nine-word middle sentence how nerveless that mood is, how unstrung so far as moral tension is concerned:

> For a good many years now he had found it restful to do this [put on women's clothes] for an hour or two every day when he had the opportunity. He himself would have found it difficult to account for such an eccentricity to anyone whom he might have happened to encounter during one of these periods and it was for this reason that he was accustomed to gratify his whim only at times when there was a reasonable expectation that his privacy would be respected by his family. Publicly he himself would refer to these temporary retirements as his Forty Winks.
>
> (FV 17)

If Fosdick were to wink at himself forty times in his mirror there would then be irony enough in the last sentence to knock a reader flat. However, the whole drift of the passage, as of the vice, is placid: the indulgence is "restful," the slippage implied in "an hour or two" delivers the major up from manic punctiliousness, there is even a sense of his remaining fairly judicial through the repetition of "he himself" and in his "reasonable expectation" of privacy. And so that fifty-nine-word sentence trundles along with-

---

In Tarr *Lewis often used a strange punctuation mark, which looked like this, = , between sentences.*

out a pause—nothing like it can be found in the long *Music of Time* sentences—resulting not in irony but in an actual (and terrifying) disclosure of the Major's lulled condition.

The main thing to establish about Powell's early prose is that what *could* be read ironically has a limpness enabling it *at the same time* to be taken straight and savored for its pathos. The strength of the pathos will of course vary. Yet its potential presence in the monochrome style will bear out, I believe, the contentions made in the foregoing chapters: of Powell's offering a second look at comic figures, of his latent but "terrifyingly full-blooded" melancholy, and of his assertion that the impulse behind the early books was pure feeling. When pathos can hold its own against irony in a single context, one might say that a style has achieved a built-in defense of itself, neither the heart nor the head able to be challenged for want of its opposite. The Hemingway-Lewis contention is a fine recipe for balance.

One last word about these paragraphs modeled in an almost pure syntax—they tend to cluster in the emotionally important places in the early novels. Some examples quoted in part or in full in the last chapter bear this out: the scene in *Waring* when Hudson's love for the *femme fatale* is discovered, or the coda passage in *Afternoon Men,* for instance (see above, pages 69 and 54). In *Venusberg,* more than half of the long "monochromatic" paragraphs occur in the two key structural scenes between Lushington and the two counts: with Bobel in the hotel room and with Scherbatcheff in his grandmother's apartment. By looking at one of these passages describing the Scherbatcheffs we will be able to observe one last and decisive factor involved in Powell's early style.

> Now that his eyes had become accustomed to the half-light Lushington saw that a young man was lying at full length on the ground immediately under the window and in front of the man with the shaved head. This young man was writing in an exercise book by the light thrown by the oil-stove. He was writing lethargically with a stumpy pencil. The girl at the piano still played her five-finger exercises. Count Scherbatcheff said: . . . (V 96)

Scherbatcheff now continues a conversation that has no bearing on the details of this paragraph.

Meanwhile, the paragraph is striking in that it is really carried forward by a dozen prepositional phrases. Six of them in a row terminate the first sentence. The important thing is that all twelve are concrete and *locational*. Just as with the tendency to coordinate clauses rather than show causative relationships, so with this phrasal writing there is the sensation that space rather than time is being attended to by the writer. This is all part of the aura of non-retention that the early books create—the dialogue passing along without the cooperation of the speakers, recorded spatial events being followed by actions not deriving from them— for characters may notice their surroundings, but they can only get impetus from their preoccupations.*

This non-retention does not call into question the early characters' intelligence. It calls into question their responsiveness only. Frequently they themselves have the "all-observing" ability that Powell indicated was the young novelist's gift. Atwater and Lushington passively notate everything; Zouch actively notates everything.

> Zouch pressed forward and gained the morning room, which was lighter than the hall and hung with engravings. Someone was sitting reading a newspaper in the far corner of the room, but pretending that he did not see this person and quickening his pace, he reached the windows unaccosted and passed through and out into the thundery sunshine.   (FV 3)

There is plenty of perception here as Zouch arrives at Passenger Court: but there is pretension of the opposite, and so he goes

---

This method is not in the least related, by the way, to Joseph Frank's ideas about spatial form in his The Widening Gyre: Crisis and Mas ery in Modern Literature *(New Brunswick, 1963). Frank's notion of spatial construction takes rise from the modern fictional technique of superimposing many discrete moments of time to produce fully apprehended atemporal realities (as in Proust). Through what Frank calls "the principle of reflexive reference" (p. 14), novelists force readers to abandon temporal sequence in forming estimations, say, of character. But a technique emphasizing retention and value is involved here and these are the qualities evaded through Powell's styling.*

"forward" and "through" and "out," gaining as he goes. But gaining what? Immunity of a sort. His perceptions mean to him nothing worth pondering, but rather on-the-spot classification of what is in front of him, as it may or may not be useful to his plans. He deals with it directly, and directionally ("forward . . . through . . . out"). The fact that the early novels are told in the third person and confined to continuing-present action (like movies) helps give this sense of a milieu not much informed by time. Even the transition to first-person narration in *Waring* does not much moderate the non-retentive atmosphere. As the narrator says of the sudden revelation at the dance of Hudson's love for Roberta Payne, "The thought that Hudson had fallen for Roberta went out of my head as soon as it had come into it" (W 126).

Thus the style of the early novels continually suggests a spatial ambience, with repeated use of locational phrases, to underline the disconnection between characters and things. This is what G. U. Ellis meant when he said Powell's characters were "a law unto themselves, that is to say, their behaviour is not conditioned by the things that happen to them. . . ."[10] When Ellis concludes that "in telling us something of the experience he presents, he says virtually that experience tells us nothing,"[11] he has marked the difference between the early Powellian attitude toward time and the later.

Neutral, spatial descriptions become indicators of the deafness of people to the music of time, and this works as appropriately for Powell's drifters in the first two books as for the power seekers in the other three from the thirties. The drifters may be bumped together by minor spatial rearrangements, the power seekers may crash ahead in defiance of awkward facts in front of them, but in these we have just passive and active symptoms of the same non-retention. Here is that spurter-forward Maltravers, for example, in *Agents and Patients*, about to launch out on a diatribe against his wife:

> Maltravers took off his cap and threw it on the table. It fell with its peak in the butter. He said:
> "This afternoon I watched a man with a sword who was prodding another man. . . ."   (AP 15)

The peak of the cap going prepositionally into the butter makes no matter. It is simply there—indents the butter but not Maltravers' harangue—whereas something like this in *The Music of Time* would be consequential. (A drop of blood on Nick's father's riding breeches, for example, will put several people including his soldier-servant through such an ordeal that "the nervous strain he had been through caused Bracey to remain standing at attention, on and off, for several minutes together before he retired to the kitchen" [KO 27]. This may seem a small point but does show a sense of consequence foreign to the early manner.)

It may be remembered from the first chapter that when Nick Jenkins attended a cremation and afterwards found himself in bed with a girl in the dead man's house, he was overcome with a great sense of consequentialness. Notice on the other hand how Atwater is bumped into a love-joust with Harriet Twining strictly as the result of *spatial rearrangement handled prepositionally*. The two have just watched Pringle swim out of sight. (I have italicized the seventeen prepositions working phrasally or adverbially in the passage, the last four jammed ones being most important, just as they are least resonant emotionally, pointing as they do to strictly locomotive action.)

> Atwater got *up from* the grass. He looked *down at* the sea, but Pringle's head was no longer *in* sight. The mist *on* the horizon was thickening. There were a number *of* small boats *with* sails moving *along,* and farther away a black boat *with* a funnel and smoke. They turned away *from* the cliffs and going *through* the hedge made their way *across* some ploughlands. There were deep furrows, so that they had to step *from* the top *of* one furrow *to* the top *of* another and take either too long or too short steps. Harriet stumbled and took his arm. She said:
> "Are you in love with anybody, William?"   (AM 181)

The monotony of these prepositions—note even the phonal monotony at the end: "to step . . . to the top . . . too long . . . too short"—still performs that one other task, it seems to me, of suggesting melancholy. Is it because the aggregated prepositions prevent briskness, even though this couple have stopped gazing and begun to walk? Is it also because there are no true transitive verbs until that last phrase, "took his arm"? As always, exact qualities of style are difficult to pinpoint. One thing perhaps worth mentioning, however, is that the verb-preposition combinations like "got up," "looked down," "moving along," are able to do both locational and intransitive work, and seem able to create a terrible sort of detachment, a sense of people moving in front of a backdrop but having no contiguity to it.

At any rate, I should like to conclude with what is to me the most moving of all Powell's early paragraphs: the description of the death of Zouch that ends the penultimate chapter of *From a View to a Death*. In this paragraph of ten sentences there are forty prepositional constructions (only one sentence does not end with one of them). Leaving the prepositional phrases unstressed, I wish to call attention here to the idioms Powell resorts to that combine verb and preposition. Any of them could have been replaced by a verb alone—"coming down" by "falling" for instance. Far more than giving just an intransitive effect, these twelve leave a vague sense of arrest—of hovering and incompleteness—behind them. (Even the few transitive constructions here are kept in verbal rather than finite form: "losing his hat," "managed to hold his seat," "catching his hoofs.") I shall not analyze the paragraph further than singling out the idioms, preferring to leave it as representative of the best of that sort of prose that can find its way spatially when other connections need fumbling for.

Zouch began *to bump about* in the saddle. He managed to hold his seat and they *passed over* several inclines in the road without *coming down*. Along this part of the road there were a few cottages and a group of country people at the gate of one of these turned to watch him *gallop past*. It was soon after this that Creditor *came down*. He slid across a frozen puddle on a flat piece of the road by one of the cottages and *went over*. Zouch *came off*, landing on his head, losing his hat as he fell. He lay there *crumpled up* by the side of the hedge and his hat *rolled over and over* in the road until it dropped into the ditch. Creditor too, lay on the ground for a few seconds, kicking, and then somehow managed *to get up* and walked unevenly along the road, catching his hoofs in the reins, which *dragged along* below his head. He tried to trot but after a time he *gave this up.* Where Zouch had fallen there was some blood on the frost of the road.   (FV 201)

RETENTION AND VALUE: LATE STYLE

The mind naturally associates time and formulation, space and non-formulation. Just so, any writer's style might exchange loco-descriptive for temporal-evaluative phrases as he or his charac-ters began to take an interpretive turn. Zouch, for example, arriving at the Passengers' on his fatal last visit, is given a moment of reflection in which *The Music of Time* style is born, years be-fore its full arrival.

> As he went over the threshold, for an interminable second, one of those shapeless entities torn out of the abyss of time, it struck Zouch how different his feelings had been on an earlier visit to this house.   (FV 171)

Powell the spatial arranger has stopped work, as Zouch "for an interminable second" reviews how things had been "on an earlier visit." Of course the natural demands of the thought have made the prepositions work temporally. But they work in another way, too, for in Powell the change from space to time also involves a change from a linear record of things to a style that seeks parallels, and tries to set experience into categories.* Zouch's moment is thus described generically as "one of those shapeless entities torn out of the abyss of time": a similar moment in *The Kindly Ones* will materialize as "a savage incision across Time" (KO 164)— the effort is to give shape to the intangible: what spatial reference we now have is metaphoric. This does have something in common with Joseph Frank's "spatial form." When one tries to fathom

---

The final phrase of a much-hedged sentence from Casanova's Chinese Restaurant *shows Powell ready to use the very word: "The atmosphere of doom that hung over Maclintick's house, indeed over the whole quarter in which he lived—or so it seemed the night Moreland and I had called on him— proved categorical enough" (CR 216).*

one's experience, concepts will ultimately replace the dimensional tabula rasa of space.

Two more examples, dealing with sudden revelations to Nick Jenkins, serve to illustrate the retentiveness of the later style which forces its words and phrases to operate so differently from the earlier. I shall deal with them individually, but may say in advance it is no accident that Nick's phrases "I was conscious" and "I was aware" are the controlling elements in both instances.

> For a brief second, for an inexpressibly curtailed efflux of time, so short that its duration could be appreciated only in recollection, being immediately engulfed at the moment of birth, I was conscious of a sensation I had never before encountered: an awareness that Stringham was perhaps a trifle embarrassed.
>
> (QU 226)

R. P. Blackmur, writing once of T. S. Eliot's concentration of abstract emotions, spoke of these as developing out of "a totally different realm of experience [from the visual]—the realm in which the mind dramatises, at a given moment, its feelings towards a whole aspect of life."[12] That is the way to take Powell's passage. It would be tautological except that it is registering an almost unrecordable shock. (It goes without saying that the shock must be worth the candle—but Stringham's imperturbability had been so marked that a sign of embarrassment from him is a revelation.) Since the (now abstract) phrases show the sensation to be appreciable "only *in recollection*," the powerful spatializing words, "curtailed" and "engulfed," are reserved for transmitting the nature of the time-glimpse, and not for what is itself perceived. The perception is so fleeting that it can only be verified by proving what the moment was like. The following related passage shows how a whole paragraph can open out from one of these categorical moments; it deals with Nick's first hints of mutual attraction between himself and Jean Duport. Attention should be paid to the way the later sentences begin.

> I was aware of an unexpected drift towards intimacy; although this sudden sense of knowing her all at once much better was not simultaneously accompanied by any clear portrayal in my

> own mind of the kind of person she might really be. Perhaps
> intimacy of any sort, love or friendship, impedes all exactness of
> definition. For example, Mr. Deacon's character was plainer to
> me than Barnby's, although by then I knew Barnby better than
> I knew Mr. Deacon. In short, the persons we see most clearly are
> not necessarily those we know best. In any case, to attempt to
> describe a woman in the broad terms employable for a man is
> perhaps irrational.   (BM 193)

In terms of the narrow approach I have been taking in con-
trasting the two styles, the first thing to mark about this 113-word
paragraph is that of its seventeen prepositional phrases *not one*
is spatial. Even the "drift towards intimacy" (one could scarcely
find a more spatial word than "towards") is conceptual like most
of its neighbors. Once the lead sentence has raised its doubts about
knowing Jean well, the weight of the famous Powellian word
"perhaps" is felt—beginning the second sentence and ending the
whole passage (as had happened at the end of the sentence on
Stringham). More striking are the time-honored transitions which
start the next three sentences: "For example," "In short," "In any
case." They reveal a mind accustomed to trading on its continuity: keeping the foregoing ideas in mind as the present ones take
shape. The result is that the situation, while being generalized,
appears to have benefited from consideration of all possible ways
to protect its uniqueness.

In this way the painstaking value-words—phrases like "at the
same time" and "in the last resort" and a tremendous assortment
of easygoing dead metaphors that are now conjunctive adverbs—
become the standard and even redundant hallmark of a very
daring fictional style.

It is daring because while it may be droll it is not ironical and
does not move toward parody. Quite different from some of the
more astringent sorties Powell may make, these phrases, "in
short" and the others, are the most convincing indicators of Nick
Jenkins's real voice. "It was, in short, a complete give-away," he
says of a verbal slip he once made in front of Jean Duport's husband (KO 179).

The importance to *The Music of Time* of this formal, round-about, "*Times* leaderish" language[13] is that it establishes a mood of uninsistent authority. Uninsistent, because these expressions are so conventionally used that no one could charge their user with trying to be persuasive. So that Powell, in the end a writer whose emphases are steel-like, never appears to use any of the bulldozing methods so available to the modern professional, that generic novelist who moves heaven and earth with his plain Anglo-Saxon directness. This generic writer will not use phrases like "indeed" and "to be sure" because they have no force. The odd thing is that they were originally developed to transmit force —but are now expressive of a mind that is ready to use them for the opposite reason: to invest with cool and collected temper those passages in which they are prominent.

Powell's double negatives work the same way—toward non-insistence, high and ever-reasonable discriminatory powers. His use of the reflexive pronoun does the same. He will not say "Quiggin and me" but rather "the closed community of Quiggin and myself" (LM 112). Techniques like this have a way of standing the narrator off from himself. Instead of saying "When I arrived at Aldershot," Nick is likely to say, "Arrival at Aldershot brought an end to these reflections" (VB 114). Unsupported nouns like "Arrival," serving in place of actions, are encountered with very great regularity in late Powell. They enable him to get around "I" and "my" with consistency.

All these devices result in a created voice in whose accents a reader has confidence because it never appears to be trying wilfully to hammer things home. For example, Powell gives this early description of Widmerpool: "We left Widmerpool on the steps of the house: to all intents and purposes, a fish recently hauled from the water, making powerful though failing efforts at respiration" (QU 49). A hard-hitting novelist would have tightened this up into metaphor: "We left him on the steps of the house—a fish just hauled from the water," and so forth. But the key to Powell's sentence is "to all intents and purposes." The words have a "just about" or "almost" air about them that keeps Widmerpool from being manhandled.

Or, to reverse the process, let us conjecture how the following idea might have been put across. The wife of Nick's friend Moreland had a baby who died right after its birth. The couples are depressed, but then, "after some disagreeable weeks, two unexpected jobs turned up. Almost from one day to the next Moreland recovered his spirits. There was no reason why they should not have another child" (CR 129). Powell did not write that last sentence. Instead he wrote, "There was, *after all,* no reason why they should not *in due course* have another child." The first version would have passed in the work of any competent documentary novelist. We might even have been carried a notch closer to empathy with the couple there and then. ("After all" makes you go back into the past a bit, "in due course" makes you go into the future.) But the flavor of Powell's sentence, with its added mild concessions (that do not forget the complications of the begetting process), is the flavor of an original mind, wishing a friend well but not getting trapped into any hearty certitude by unconsidered enthusiasm.

I have concentrated on these fairly arbitrary transitions because, being originally colloquial and now formal in usage, they help explain one of the great resiliencies of Powell's later prose. They bridge the gap between his generalized, formal language and the surprising number of colloquialisms that nevertheless keep that language alive. And without this range—one discovers in Powell a no less than Joycean command of public idiom, as a matter of fact —his formal style could be fatally relegated to the ranks of those who find it impossible to speak plainly.*

For example, Henry James's style is replete with the kind of hesitancies just described in Powell; yet no one, I think, would compare the styles of the two men. Powell's greater affinity for the vernacular marks the difference, in my opinion. His first-person narrator will ease off investigation with rough-and-ready phrases—"With a woman it is impossible to say" (AW 86)— which would be foreign to James. As fine an instrument as James's was, it would be suicidal to write in a style like his after Joyce and Hemingway, Eliot and Yeats, and the revolution they produced that made writers votaries first of the spoken word, whatever else they might rely on to create their own voices.

Powell's formal predilection does not then tell the whole story though it tells a good deal more than half. In *The Music of Time* a man will be less likely to give a smile than to *dispense* one; we will not be told of another's intelligence but of the *mental equipment possessed by him;* people are not so likely to tell about their problems as to *ventilate* them. Similarly, ordinary ideas like "marriage" or "competition" will often be attenuated by reference to the "spheres" or "quarters," the "vehicles" or "machinery" that circumscribe the particular condition:

> Different couples approach with varied technique the matrimonial vehicle's infinitely complicated machinery.   (AW 59)

> In the conquest of Mrs. Wentworth, however, other spheres . . . had inevitably to be invaded by him [Barnby]. These hinterlands are frequently, even compulsively, crossed at one time or another by almost all who practise the arts. . . .   (BM 253)

In Powell's career, the first strong indications of this practice come from *John Aubrey and His Friends;* and also there, significantly, his technique of rescuing this style by colloquial cross-germination. The first of the following fragments shows an instance of the style going on unrelieved; but the second shows how the rescue can be made:

> It was, of course, all very well for Wood to recommend philosophy to Aubrey (whose natural equipment in that sphere was considerably superior to that possessed by Wood himself). . . .
> (JA 143)

> . . . although Aubrey was incapable of writing in a dull manner, he did not possess the ingenuity in literary mechanics necessary to galvanise into movement even so ramshackle a vehicle as the average play of his time.   (JA 289)

That word "ramshackle" marks a deliberate relapse in the middle not only of formal phraseology but also of formal syntax—a technique used so resourcefully that to characterize it as "relapse diction" would be to pin it down as Powell's most successful single idiosyncrasy. The following sentences about Moreland, in which I have also italicized the standard formalities, end with this relapsing technique and may show how an old situation can be freshly viewed:

> He was *not unattractive* to women. *At the same time,* his own romantic approach to emotional relationships had already caused him to *take some hard knocks* in *that very knockabout sphere.*   (KO 78)

The last two words meet across a formidable linguistic barrier; but they make quite a fine summary image (almost a visual rendition *à la* Marvell) of the war between the sexes.

As with this example, the ones that follow indicate the added turning force Powell can achieve by holding the relapse idioms for terminal positions. Perhaps they hardly need italics but there may be some clarity to be had through double emphasis:

[On doctrinaire criticism in the 1930s]

> In fact some such doctrinal method of attack was then becoming very much the mode; taking the place of the highly coloured critical flights of an earlier generation that still persisted in some quarters, or the severely technical criticism of the æsthetic puritans who had *ruled the roost* since the war.
>
>   (AW 117–118)

[On the eclectic General Conyers, an octogenarian]

> It was astonishing to me that he should have been reading about psychoanalysis, although his mental equipment was certainly in no way inferior to that of many persons who talked of such things *all day long.*   (LM 81)

[On Miss Weedon, the woman who is trying to cure Stringham of alcoholism]

> She merely continued to look at me with a kind of chilly amiability; as if, by making an immediate confession that I was a former friend of his, I had, so far as she was concerned, *just managed to save my bacon.*   (LM 163)

One can observe some asperity in these placings. Another way to work the relapse diction is to introduce it earlier, then double back and meliorate what has been roughened. Powell once described a group of lingerers at a party as a "residue" who were

> sinking to *a small band of those hard cases who can never tear themselves away* from what still remains, for an hour or so longer, if not of gaiety, then at least some sort of mellow companionship, and protection from the austerities of the outer world. (BM 139)

Here the relapse diction makes hard cases out of some partygoers halfway through a sentence, only to have them rescrutinized in formal cadences. Syntax completes the reversion: a trailing antithesis is filled out (*"if not* of gaiety, *then at least . . ."*), and then, unexpectedly, comes the final cause of the malingering: a craving for "protection." The hard cases are now seen to have their soft side. Again there is no irony, for their need to stay on is considered too completely for irony.

This alternation between orotund completeness of detail and sudden plain convincingness can be shown to operate in one last way, related to the others and especially observable in narrative rather than reflective sequences. In keeping with his formal practice, Powell has a relish for supplying summary synonyms that return earlier facets of an action to the reader's eyes. In the most celebrated episode of *A Buyer's Market,* Widmerpool's shower-bath of sugar at the hands of Barbara Goring, this synonym habit can be illustrated once and for all.

Having first described the sugar "pouring out on to Widmerpool's head in a dense and overwhelming *cascade,*" Powell gives a full paragraph to the results, ending with "He had writhed sideways to avoid the *downpour,* and a *cataract* of sugar had entered the space between neck and collar; yet another *jet* streaming between eyes and spectacles" (BM 70-71). If this seems to be attempting to outdo Robert Louis Stevenson in the dredging up of substitutes, it is not nearly all. As the incident began Powell had described the contents of the sideboard, then located the sugar castor among "this residue." In the next sentence the sugar will be called "this sugar" and the castor "this receptacle." Barbara now proceeds to hold the inverted castor over Widmerpool's head like the sword of Damocles—but it does not behave like "that normally inactive weapon." When the sugar consequently pours out, we learn that "Widmerpool's rather sparse hair had been liberally greased with a dressing—*the sweetish smell of which* I remembered as somewhat disagreeable when applied in France—*this lubricant* retaining the grains of sugar. . . ." These grains become, in turn, "the glittering incrustations that enveloped his head and shoulders."

Now no reader of *The Music of Time* can have failed to notice a demonstrative mania (as an unfriendly voice might put it) that is found in only slightly exaggerated form in the Widmerpool sugar episode. It almost seems the same kind of *tic* that caused the eighteenth-century poets to elaborate every normal object or event by way of their compulsive poetic diction. But the greatest of them, like Pope, always knew what they were doing, as does Powell, and the proof can be offered once again by the demonstration of their effortless recourse to the opposite policy when that may have suited them (Pope's vernacular epistles, for example).[14]

The simplest way to avoid the "demonstrative-plus-summary-noun" technique would be to make use of the demonstrative alone, which would produce simple, vague reference, and this in fact turns out to be a method Powell makes astonishingly thorough use of. "I am going to marry, I have decided that," says the character Moreland in *Casanova's Chinese Restaurant;* a little later the pattern has been taken up in Nick's prose, as he mentions Moreland's occasional successes with female music fanatics. "Moreland did not care for that. He liked wider horizons" (CR 6, 8).

As with the "relapse diction," the best quick way to illustrate emotional directness would be to discover some terminal uses to which this related verbal resource is put. It happens that Powell often does reserve these pared-down demonstratives for the ends of paragraphs—all sense of leisure evaporating as the short, finality-ridden sentences are placed down. Here are two paragraphs, separated by a couple of pages in *Casanova's Chinese Restaurant* but both pertaining to the most powerful moment in that novel, when Charles Stringham's snake-charming of the virago Audrey Maclintick is brought to an end by Stringham's guardian Miss Weedon.

> "We have been talking about marriage," said Mrs Maclintick aggressively. . . .
> "It sounds a very interesting discussion," said Miss Weedon.
> She spoke in a tone damaging to Mrs Maclintick's self-esteem.
> Miss Weedon was undoubtedly prepared to take anybody on; Mrs Maclintick; anybody. I admired her for that.   (CR 181)

And when this determined woman has secured Stringham, she makes this announcement:

> "We could give this lady a lift home too, if she liked," said Miss Weedon.
> She glanced at Mrs Maclintick as if prepared to accept the conveyance of her body at whatever the cost. It was a handsome offer on Miss Weedon's part, a very handsome offer. No just person could have denied that.   (CR 184)

The pattern of each of these three-sentence paragraphs of narration will repay close notice. The first sentence in each is unpunctuated and trenchant; the last in each ends on the unadorned "that"-demonstrative. Meanwhile in the middle ones come the most crucial attacks that can be mounted by this style. In the Widmerpool sequence everything had depended on the search for synonyms and variation, but here there is no such leisure and we get the reverse—hard repetition: "take anybody on . . . anybody"; "a handsome offer . . . a very handsome offer." There is no time to think up summary labels. The capture of Stringham and the degradation of Widmerpool are two equally dramatic events, but only one has the sense of emergency written into it.

In cases of admiration, decision, sudden disclosures that reverse Nick's judgments, this kind of writing will customarily result. Most common perhaps are variations on a theme often struck in *The Music of Time,* when Nick records some reversal affecting his own complacency or self-esteem. Without evasion he will record straight out that this or that fact "had to be admitted." In *The Kindly Ones,* when he is over his affair with Jean Duport, he meets her ex-husband and learns some devastating facts about side-lovers Jean had had while estranged from Duport (and presumably in love with Nick himself). Just before Duport begins to elaborate, Nick ends a paragraph on the assured note that "present recital could in no way affect the past. That was history" (KO 176). However, as unforeseen news breaks, Nick is hit with some pretty gritty information, and the three paragraphs that terminate his reflections end accordingly:

> If her lovers were horrifying, I too had been of their order. That had to be admitted.   (KO 180)

> I suddenly found what I had regarded as immutable—the not entirely unsublime past—roughly reshaped by the rude hands of Duport. That was justice, I thought, if you like.   (KO 181)

> [Having given Duport *The Arab Art of Love*, a kind of wry gesture of amends]

> It would be better not to draw attention to the chapter on the Deceits and Treacheries of Women. He could find that for himself.   (KO 182)

These long and admissive paragraphs, ending this way, show that when Nick is brought up against incontrovertible facts Powell's language is unqualified and direct. This quality in his style is more to be encountered in the second and third trilogies of *The Music of Time* than in the first. It happens that most of my examples of the more tentative and exploring style have been taken from the first trilogy, and most of the "relapsing" illustrations from the second. This is simply convenient, because it is proportionately more or less faithful to the book—though the style does not radically change in favor of one mode or the other, and remains one integrally formal style throughout. The reasons for the proportion changes are related to Nick's being drawn in and getting involved in things: through the first trilogy he has been marked down as a slow starter.

Starkness, then, of all things, becomes the quality that seems to me to involve the most risk and attest the greatest linguistic genius in *The Music of Time*—starkness even exceeding the inviolate scrupulosity of the thirties' prose, because it is reflected through a patient and uninsistent mind. At times there does emerge a quality of insistence. When this happens, often enough in later entries, some passages resemble the simpler prose of the first phase, in that afterthoughts disappear. However, the sense of a toughened mind is there, so that regardless of simplified diction or syntax there will rarely if ever be a return to the limpid quality of the earliest style. This makes a considerable difference, as I shall show by citing, in conclusion, three short passages from the books that end the *Music of Time* trilogies, but citing them in reverse order. All represent starkness, but the flow is different in each. One is unpunctuated; one measuredly punctuated; the third heavily punctuated in the most usual *Music of Time* fashion.

The passage from *The Military Philosophers* includes a thirty-two word sentence that has no pause. It would therefore appear to resemble the early style with its pristine syntax. But Nick is resolved in this instance to put up with no ingratiating nonsense from Odo Stevens, the man who split the Lovells up and indirectly caused their deaths:

> I was determined to endure for as short a time as possible only what was absolutely unavoidable in the exhibition of self-confessed remorse Stevens was obviously proposing to mount for my benefit. . . . That was the long and the short of it.
>
> (MP 125)

So the uninterrupted burst here has nothing in common with the spatially arranged syntax from the thirties' books, but rather develops out of a mental determination neither to mince words nor to waste time over false emotion about to be displayed. The early characters of Powell were never able to set themselves against that sort of speciousness, as it unrolled in front of them.

As for not mincing words, in turning to the example from *The Kindly Ones,* it seems to me that the hardest-boiled modern mannerist would hardly dare to write a sentence like this one, annotating some facts about young Nick Jenkins's friends with respect to World War I:

> The Fenwicks' father was killed; Mary Barber's father was killed; Richard Vaughan's father was killed; the Westmacott twins' father was killed.   (KO 74)

Something so unaccommodated as this is more typical of the later trilogies. It is at the end of the first, with its *Acceptance World* title of transition, that Nick tends to move toward a general position permitting, in the appropriate circumstances, such an utterly uncompromising laying down of facts. What helps him toward this position in the last pages of *The Acceptance World* is a banal French postcard sent him by Jean Duport. It produces this paragraph of reflection, a quartet of sentences themselves quite banal. Yet, on reconsidering, one might decide that the moment has been carried by Powell in a style and mood that have fused.

> Yet, after all, even the crude image of the postcard depicted with at least a degree of truth one side of love's outward appearance. That had to be admitted. Some of love was like the picture. I had enacted such scenes with Jean: Templer with Mona: now Mona was enacting them with Quiggin: Barnby and Umfraville with Anne Stepney: Stringham with her sister Peggy: Peggy now in the arms of her cousin: Uncle Giles, very probably, with Mrs. Erdleigh: Mrs. Erdleigh with Jimmy Stripling: Jimmy Stripling, if it came to that, with Jean: and Duport, too.
> (AW 212–213)

Several volumes after this, Nick will be recording the judgment that "All love affairs are different cases, yet, at the same time, each is the same case" (VB 190). Here he is finding that out. On inspection, it will be seen in the final sentence that between each set of colons there is some additive or variation that does not let one member of the series actually repeat the other in form. There is no driving rhetorical impact to the series. But at last the afterthoughts come round to producing the names of those who made a mockery of Nick's special love for Jean—her husband and one extra clandestine lover. The phrase that brings them in is quite an equalizer: "if it came to that."

THE MUSIC OF TIME:
First Movement

THE STRUCTURE OF "THE MUSIC OF TIME"

There is a point in *A Passage to India* when Forster writes of Aziz and Godbole that "the comparatively simple mind of the Mohammedan was encountering Ancient Night."[1] Godbole is the possessor of knowledge about India and things older than time, older than the Marabar caves. Everything he says and does carries arcane significance in *A Passage to India,* though he is an apparently innocuous character. I mention him here because with such a figure it is a good principle to ponder sayings however casually delivered, and because Anthony Powell has put a version of Godbole into *The Music of Time*. Powell was hardly thinking of Forster's character. But his Mrs. Myra Erdleigh, a fortune teller, among other things, to Nick Jenkins's Uncle Giles, is the marker of trilogies in *The Music of Time,* and, just as Godbole had done for Forster, she retires only to return as the presiding genius of Powell's novel.

By the time she appears in the ninth volume, one has learned to respect her. Since she is involved in predictions as well as character-readings, she even affords chances for guessing what may be on the way—though it had best be a gingerly undertaking. In *The*

Military Philosophers, Mrs. Erdleigh defines the deadliness of
Pamela Flitton (the most lethal woman Powell has presented in
his whole saga), her own serene power outmanaging the bitter
composure of this beauty who storms off into a blacked-out night
and an air raid. Pamela obeys a nature which "loves disaster and
death" (MP 131), and projects that same wretched fascination onto
the men she captures. Now the remote culprit behind the down-
fall of many a figure in *The Music of Time* is Widmerpool, a
"hydrous" character as Robert Morris calls him (Pamela Flitton
is also "under a watery sign" [MP 133]).[2] Since Mrs. Erdleigh has
predicted a wildly jealous husband in Pamela's future, the girl's
eventual marriage to Widmerpool alerts us to possibilities of
retribution that seem fated for him in the final trilogy. About
time, some readers may say under their breaths—but these same
readers know it is useless to frame in advance any assurances
about Widmerpool. What Mrs. Erdleigh imports for Nick remains
even less clear and cannot be talked about at this stage.

The point is, she does appear in volumes three, six, and nine,
and the structure of the first half of *The Music of Time,* being
complete, can be seen to have arranged itself along lines which
she had, one might say, anticipated. Before *The Military Philosophers,* she had been last seen slipping away from Uncle Giles's
cremation in *The Kindly Ones,* having served as one of the
"votaries of the Furies" that gave that book its title, and she had
appeared in *The Acceptance World* as well.

Compared to her, Godbole is non-committal. When Aziz encountered the Hindu, he discovered "He was handling a human
toy that refused to work"[3]—he could get nothing from Godbole
about those disquieting caves. But Mrs. Erdleigh, also a kind of
toy or vehicle (her gliding movements make Nick think of her as
"like an automaton on castors" [AW 81]), told Nick on first
meeting him that because he lived "between two worlds" he had
to come to equilibrium by trying "to understand life" (AW 14,
15). These are not platitudes but serious issues in *The Music of
Time.* Because they sound like platitudes, Nick can conveniently
make light of some of her "trivial comment, mixed with a few
home truths of a personal nature . . . the commonplaces of for-

tune-telling" (AW 16). While Powell will not admit that Nick is encountering Ancient Night, he does say that her ritual with the cards had about it "something infinitely ancient, as if Mrs. Erdleigh had existed long before the gods we knew, even those belonging to the most distant past" (AW 12).

Nick is impressed enough by Mrs. Erdleigh to wonder—and this sentence is thematic—whether "Perhaps I was irrevocably transfixed, just as she described, half-way between dissipation and diffidence" (AW 15). Now the pull of either of these two "worlds"—of dissipation or of diffidence—is a pull away from the world of action. In Powell's logic, sensuality (or dissipation) is just as much an impediment to action as is reticence (or diffidence). But the indulgence of either leads to understanding: the diffident person is forever watchful, learning by others' experience (as Nick tends to do), and the one who yields to dissipation can gain painful self-knowledge. He may also earn the kind of "vision of reality" that Yeats maintained art provided.[4]

Powell at least continues to associate sensuality with the arts, and warns against carrying the gains of the sensual life over into the world of action. Zouch paid with his life when he tried to convert sensuality to power in *From a View to a Death*. Of course he was an inferior artist. In *A Buyer's Market,* Nick thinks over the painter Barnby's situation (winning a woman away from an industrialist) and reflects that "the arts themselves . . . by their ultimately sensual essence, are, in the long run, inimical to those who pursue power for its own sake. Conversely, the artist who traffics in power does so, if not necessarily disastrously, at least at considerable risk" (BM 253).

The point of these quotations for the moment is to tie together sensuality and artistic vision in Nick's mind, rather than to emphasize yet any dangerous beckonings of the byways of power. Nick, an only son imbued with a sense of dignity from a very "correct" upbringing, runs different risks from Barnby, who is not diffident. Nick's problem is that both diffidence and dissipation can educate him, but only when the two are in conjunction, not opposition. (The restraints implicit in diffidence prevent the relaxation necessary to dissipation, and *vice versa*.)

There are larger connotations to these two words, connotations that finally are responsible for the restriction of their sway to the first movement of *The Music of Time*. Granting they open two avenues of knoweldge, they remain highly personal words. One can protect *oneself* through diffidence, indulge *oneself* in dissipation, and in the first trilogy Nick lives on this selective basis. In the second trilogy, conversely, having absorbed a good deal of knowledge, Nick becomes involved in actions and relationships willy-nilly. The designs of the trilogies are then traced according to this shift from personal preoccupations to wider involvements. Thus in the second trilogy another pair of key words—these having more public connotations—replace the original pair. There is a tendency, germinating from the second book of each trilogy, for the uncommitted artist Barnby to be Nick's mentor, and then for the musician Moreland, who is marriage-befuddled, to take Barnby's place. The best sign of keyword-displacement is a Moreland comment on the abdication of King Edward VIII, which event forms a background for *Casanova's Chinese Restaurant*. The public reverberations of the King's act make it the best of many symbols to emphasize the wide applicability of private decisions.

> I met Moreland in the street just after the story had broken in the newspapers.
> "Isn't this just my luck?" he said. "Now nobody is going to listen to music, look at a picture, or read a book, for months on end. We can all settle down happily to discussions every evening about Love and Duty."
> "Fascinating subjects."   (CR 136–137)

Nick, now married and working away at a literary career, is serious about these "Fascinating subjects." The second trilogy abounds with gossip about such things, to the exasperation of such admirers as V. S. Pritchett.[5] The cause is not that Nick's and his friends' lives have slowed down into vicarious routines, but that they feel others' lives as extensions of their own. That point is made and a major difference marked between the two trilogies when, in the middle of the second, Powell cuts back to some gossip overheard around the period of *A Buyer's Market*. That was when Nick, down from the university, had first met the artist-bohemian group among whom he would make many long-standing acquaintanceships. (Moreland significantly had been met then but never was mentioned in the first trilogy.) "I listened to what was being said," Nick records, "without feeling—as I came to feel later—that I was, in one sense, part and parcel of the same community; that when people gossiped about matters like Carolo and his girl, one was listening to a morsel, if only an infinitesimal morsel, of one's own life" (CR 25).

Love and Duty, seen in this extended way, though still principles at odds, become the morally attuned twins of dissipation and diffidence.

By taking up such pairs of terms, I have begun to discuss the movements of *The Music of Time* as though they were constructed on metaphysical rather than social principles. This seems to be the case. Social and historical documentation continue to arrest readers, naturally. But the struggle not only to record but to understand the recent past leads to the effort to mythologize it. Whole years are left out of the first sextet of *The Music of Time*, whereas half an installment may be reserved for the adventures of a single night (*A Buyer's Market*). No character suffers any social depletion because of treatment based on working out a myth. Even Mrs. Erdleigh, the "genius" of the novel, is a character socially solid enough to inherit Uncle Giles's £7,300 estate. Mrs. Erdleigh marks off the trilogies in a metaphysical way, however. She once passes a remark that may contain the richest clue of all to the structures, even perhaps to the titles of *The Music of Time* volumes. This moment, in the middle of *The Acceptance World*, is carefully hedged in by Powell because one of Mrs. Erdleigh's disciples goes too far in endorsing that woman's Program of Life and is brought up short by the grating voice of a Marxist sceptic. That is the way Powell handles occult proselytizing of any sort, but here it is the disciple who is proselytizing, Mrs. Erdleigh permitting herself only a soft insinuation:

"You must understand the thread that runs through life,"
said Stripling, now speaking rather wildly, and looking stranger
than ever. "It does not matter that there may be impurities and
errors in one man's method of seeking the Way. What matters is
that he *is* seeking it—and knows there is a Way to be found."

"Commencement—Opposition—Equilibrium," said Mrs. Erdleigh in her softest voice, as if to offer Stripling some well-
earned moral support. "You can't get away from it—Thesis—
Antithesis—Synthesis."

"That's just what I mean," said Stripling, as if her words
brought him instant relief. "Brahma—Vishnu—Siva."

"It all sounded quite Hegelian until you brought in the In-
dian gods," said Quiggin angrily.   (AW 90)

The first thing that can be said, making due allowance for
humor, is that Mrs. Erdleigh's belief in "Commencement—Opposition—Equilibrium" summarizes the pattern of each of the
first two trilogies. There is even the chance—this may be an accident—that putting the component volumes side by side begins to
reveal this.

A Question of Upbringing   *At Lady Molly's*

A Buyer's Market   *Casanova's Chinese Restaurant*

The Acceptance World   *The Kindly Ones*

The words "Market" and "Restaurant," in the titles accorded
second position, fit immediately the "Opposition" premise of Mrs.
Erdleigh's triad. Observe that Nick makes one commencement,
through public school and university, completing his upbringing;
that he later makes a second commencement, entering aristocratic
precincts—the milieu of Lady Molly Jeavons and the Tolland
family. The results of these indoctrinations lead to the opening
of two marts. The first is generalized, the second more specialized.
The buyer's market tempts in a general way because Nick is invited to wander into different social levels and to take for the
asking—to make his way with people (parties are the places of
offering), if he can but rise to the occasion. But Casanova's Chi-

nese Restaurant, the mismatched name itself suggesting "a whole new state of mind or way of life" (CR 29), has marriage on the bill of fare—temptation with a foretaste of obligation, oppression —and perhaps some inevitable indigestion.

Why these middle books work themselves out as phases of "Opposition" may be gathered from James Hall's comment on the first of them. "The conscious choices begin in *A Buyer's Market*," says Hall. "The supposed goods of the world fail to inspire a sustained enthusiasm in Nick. All is for sale, the buyer waits."[6] In other words a tremendous mixture of possibilities baffles the young man who has "commenced." Should he plunge or hold off, that is the buyer's problem: will a mixed lot of duties make a great hash of love, that is the diner's.

The first volume of each trilogy, and this is fitting, ended wryly but reassuringly. At the end of *A Question of Upbringing*, one of Nick's friends, Charles Stringham, had stood him up in London. Nick then relied on something known, family protocol, and so on the last page made his way to Uncle Giles's standby restaurant and spent his evening with his uncle (who was found reading *Some Things That Matter*), discussing the family Trust. At the end of *At Lady Molly's*, the man who dogs Nick's heels through the whole series, Widmerpool, has survived a disastrous engagement and emerged his old self. He tells Nick, who is engaged now himself, how wise it is to preconsider "such a thing as marrage. . . . I have thought about the subject a good deal, and you are always welcome to my views" (LM 239).

Both second volumes, again fittingly, ended on spine-chilling notes. Their concluding images, from the pastimes of Russian billiards and ghost railway rides, leave unsettling impressions that a dreadful die has been cast. It is less important now to supply the contexts of these endings than to suggest that "Opposition" has taken its toll and paved the way (it might be better to say "mined the way") into the third volumes, both promising "Equilibrium." That promise they deliver, though not in the same way.

It is in the world of a sensual postcard sent from France "that I seemed now to find myself" says Nick in the last line of *The Ac-*

ceptance World. Jean Duport had sent him the card, confirming an assignation. The acceptance of sensuality has meant the relegation of diffidence and discretion to a subordinate position: in fact these now *serve* the sensual union and that is how a synthesis has been achieved as the trilogy ends. "You must be discreet," Jean had said at the onset of the affair.

> "All right."
> "But really discreet."
> "I promise."
> "You will?"
> "Yes."   (AW 105)

At the end of *The Kindly Ones,* in sentences as short as these—we have already looked at them in the style chapter—another sort of equilibrium is reached. At Molly Jeavons's house Nick has run into that captain who can move names up on Reservist rolls; the war has begun and "You'll probably come my way in due course," says the captain; Nick is then told that, yes, the process can be speeded up:

> "What arm is your choice?"
> "Infantry." . . .
> "And you'd like to get cracking?"
> "Yes."   (KO 253)

Duty has clearly risen to the top here: love (Nick's love for his wife) has not been extinguished but never takes center stage in the second trilogy. So the first two movements of *The Music of Time* end antithetically, love in *The Kindly Ones* relegated to a position in support of duty, because of what "the kindly ones," the pursuing furies, have burned into Nick's and some of his friends' consciousness about the entanglements of romantic love. In particular, Nick learns at the end of *The Kindly Ones* that he had not understood Jean Duport at all. That is why she is the most Proustian character in the whole series. He had missed the fact, while in love with Jean, that her abandon with him was mostly whim. It remained for her husband to reveal accidentally to Nick that there had been yet another lover of Jean during Nick's own "tenure." Nick's romantic notions of love end forever at this disclosure. The army and duty await him, and a marriage to remain faithful to, although it is placed second.

With no concluding fourth trilogy available, it is less valuable to try to shape up the third movement as painstakingly just now. The Thesis-Antithesis-Synthesis progression is under way there, as the last chapter will show. This much may be said now: in the third trilogy, the key structural opposition turns out to pit a respect for the Rules of War against a penchant for intrigue. Nick's "mentor" here is not an artist-type but a philosopher, though an unprofessional one, David Pennistone. The outcome is similar to that of the second trilogy in that respect for the aboveboard wins out: protocol, consideration for the other party, faithfulness to regulation are embodied in various heroes or semiheroes in this new trilogy. Going by the book must not amount to a fetish, however, as we gather when treated to the spectacle of some wonderful red-tape obstructionists—the worst a civilian called Blackhead, roosting at the top of the War Office in a file-filled room where all logistical requests are blocked. In other words, one more balance must be reached by subordinating the less legitimate of the antithetical attractions (as diffidence was subordinated to dissipation, Love to Duty). Thus Nick's major contribution to the war effort, the evacuation of some restive Belgian Resistance troops in danger of being shot by the Allies, goes almost by the liaison officer's book, but not quite. He makes one crucial bypass of his immediate superior, Colonel Finn, in telling the Belgian military attaché how to contact a member of the British Cabinet to get this evacuation expedited. Respect for probity in one's military job has become endemic to the last volume, and paramount to Powell's theme, but there was still that vital tincture of covert dealing in this final wartime action performed by Nick. His reflection is characteristic: "Thinking over the incident after, it was easy to see how a taste for intrigue, as Finn called it, could develop in people" (MP 195).

Realizing that private intrigue is subordinated to public probity in this third trilogy, one might project that the whole structure of the now open-ended *Music of Time* might well run, trilogy by trilogy, according to this patern of commitments: private-public-public-[private]. Such a design would seem likely, at least, if the fourth trilogy begins to pose opposites that must be balanced by a man returning to family and civilian life (Nick is now a father) but also to the life of a practicing artist. It is too dangerous to assume that Powell, always reticent about the intimate artistic processes, will turn toward the shaping of Nick's life as a writer. The conclusion of Proust's great work tended this way, but Powell has not been working along the design of converting the transmutable past to art. So it would be hazardous to make guesses, even though the post-war years were the years when Powell tackled *The Music of Time.*

There are one or two clues, however, that a final return to something like what was offered in the first trilogy, secret commitment to the self, lies in prospect. If this is a true forecast, and it may not be, there would be no disfigurement to the subordinative bent noted in Powell. In his intricate structuring, there will always be meaningful subordination of something. The self is never romantically unleashed. The leading clue comes from Mrs. Erdleigh and points to silent, guarded maturation as a last line to follow for Nick. She says, "Let the palimpsest of your mind absorb the words of Eliphas Lévi—to know, to will, to dare, to be silent." "The last most of all?" Nick asks her, and she replies, "Some think so" (MP 138). One may be reminded of the Joycean dicta of silence, cunning, and exile prescribed for the artist. Exile by no means applies for Nick Jenkins. If silence and cunning apply, reversals will occur in the fourth trilogy. The superior categories of Duty and the Rules of Life in War which govern the second and third will be subverted to inferior positions of influence and Powell's great book will at last have come to balance.

THE SUN NEVER SETS

In 1949, about the time he was starting work on *The Music of Time,* Powell commented in a review on Beardsley on the passing of the ivory-tower artist: "for as someone was saying only the other day—now that so much of the Empire has gone, one simply cannot get the ivory."[7] Now while Nick Jenkins never does aspire to an ivory tower, *A Question of Upbringing,* set in Powell's Eton-Oxford years (about 1921 to 1926), offers no sign to Nick that the Empire is indeed in decline. And in his 1934 memoir of Eton, Powell had recorded the general assumption, "or so it seemed to me, that every boy would at one time or another be in some such position as viceroy of India and must be brought up with this end in view."[8]

No sign of decline—perhaps this is saying too much. There are a few. They are overshadowed by the orthodoxy of the four sections of *A Question of Upbringing,* following Nick at public school, then to the homes of his two best friends, Charles Stringham and Peter Templer, next to France for seasoning with "*Une vraie famille de soldats,*" the Leroys (QU 113), finally to the university. Charles Stringham joins Nick late at the university because of his own trip to Kenya. That African sojourn had enabled Charles to look over prospects for his own future, but there Imperial opportunism halted, and Stringham's return hails the beginning of a terrible downslide.

Since Stringham had been the most gifted and wealthiest of Nick's friends at school, his decline, beginning so early in *The Music of Time* (and not checked till the end of the sextet), might have pointed to something "imperially" wrong, except that Nick understands Charles's family predicament: the fact that his mother's divorce and remarriage have set the father drinking in Kenya, and Stringham himself into a Hamlet-like position at home with mother and stepfather. Something also troubles the backgrounds of Nick's other friends at school, more gauche than Stringham—Templer and Widmerpool. Thus we get the rationale behind the novel's title. "But what we do know," as James Ward Lee has said, "is that there is no 'question' to [Nick's] upbringing as there is to Widmerpool's, Templer's, or Stringham's."[9] It is therefore natural that Nick should fail to detect problems in the beginning that might relate to a broader social upheaval, and that he should sense a difference between his own regular advancement and the more striking behavior of his acquaintances as they leave adolescence—and be able implicitly to lay this down (as Nick Carraway did on the first page of *The Great Gatsby*) to "a sense of the fundamental decencies" that happens to be "parcelled out unequally at birth."[10]

At Peter Templer's seaside house—Nick's impression of it as "an enormously swollen villa" (QU 73) doing its owners moral damage in the reader's eyes—Nick encounters Sunny Farebrother, who is paying court to the elder Templer, a stock market expert now retired from the City. The name itself conjures up a kind of defender of the Empire, and it is soon revealed that Sunny Farebrother has won the D. S. O.

Farebrother seems to have two roles in the first sextet. The more obvious is the role that keeps Nick's vision occluded—that of fraternal, frank, athletic servant-of-the-realm. (But if he is these things, Nick wonders why he is so willing to genuflect before the Templers, and even worse, why he has to carry his cricket bat with him wherever he goes so as to make the right impression.) The problem is that the Empire *has* changed, and that D. S. O. Farebrothers not only must but are ready to compromise to make their financial way. In the third trilogy, Farebrother is identified as an intriguer who has won an O. B. E. "sitting in a chair," by his own account; by that time Nick can say of him, "he was well able to look after himself and his business in that unwarlike position, however assured he might also be in combat" (SA 196). In *A Question of Upbringing,* however, when Nick cannot measure him, Farebrother seems placed in a wider thematic role when one of the Templer family fails to carry out a practical joke against him. It is one of the first signs of chance operating against plan: an attempt is made to put a chamber pot in Farebrother's hatbox, but Farebrother happens to walk in on the operation and all the mortification is transferred to the culprit (Jimmy Stripling, son-in-law of old Templer). The important thing is that Farebrother wins in this little contest because he exhibits a specious dignity; he does not really understand what is going on with the chamber pot. This in little is a kind of symbol of what marks Nick in the first novel—his reliance on dignity, and forfeiture of understanding. This is part of the pattern of "Commencement." Admiration for men of Farebrother's stripe is natural but must be outgrown.

In Touraine province, at a *maison* called La Grenadière, the novel's third section brings Nick's education a step further under the direction of Madame Leroy. But free choices seem precluded here. She appears to be "a kind of sorceress," and living at her house suggests "a stage in some clandestine order's ritual of initiation" (QU 162).

At La Grenadière the most unusual of Nick's schoolmates, Kenneth Widmerpool, has turned up, and he has not the slightest feeling of being at sea under the flag of a sorceress. The humorous thing is that the Widmerpools, mother and son, should pitch onto a French "finishing-up" course as proper for Kenneth. (Widmerpool's father had been a supplier of liquid manure to a noble family.) This Widmerpool development is radically different from, say, Stringham's going to Kenya. If all Etonians might be thought of as potential viceroys, the irony is that the ones who see nothing surprising in this are the plebian Widmerpools, who are quite eager to try out their diplomatic spurs on such early proving grounds as La Grenadière.

Not only does Widmerpool show his diplomacy in patching up a quarrel, arising from a tennis incident, between a Swede and a Norwegian also staying at the Leroys', but he has some lessons for Nick as well. "Jenkins, do you mind home truths?" he asks (QU 154). And he lets Nick in on the information that he is too critical, too ready to dismiss as beneath contempt any sort of choleric behavior, because of the loss of dignity entailed (as the Swede and the Norwegian had lost theirs).

There are two girls at the Leroys'—they were the secret cause of the Scandinavians' quarrel—and one of the things Nick collaterally suffered from was not knowing that to declare oneself sooner or later is a direct necessity with women. In one of the most marvelous moments of the novel, on Nick's last day in France, he does go up to one of these girls and, seizing her hand in a summer-house (her head is averted), begins a set speech, only to find he is talking to someone else—a married woman of the Leroy entourage, in fact.

> . . . Having made the mistake, there was nothing for it but to behave as if it were indeed Madame Dubuisson who had made my visit to La Grenadière seem so romantic. Taking her other hand, I quickly used up the remaining phrases that I had rehearsed so often for Suzette.
> The only redeeming feature of the whole business was that Madame Dubuisson herself gave not the smallest sign of being in the least surprised . . . and the curious thing was that its effect had been to provide some genuine form of emotional release. It was almost as if Madame Dubuisson had, indeed, been the focus of my interest while I had been at La Grenadière.
> (QU 165)

This is a marvelous insight, considering that modern fiction is so prone to overrate intense emotions and equate them with their objects. The commuting of emotions, once these are allowed to escape from their origins in thought, is another home truth, and it squares oddly enough with the charge Widmerpool had entered against Nick: that he guarded a sense of his own specialness, which led him to disparage the impulsive Scandinavians. The passage that makes this self-respect clearest of all, so that it becomes the major theme of the first trilogy, develops from yet another exchange with Widmerpool at this time. Widmerpool hints knowledge of Stringham's problems—the mother's divorce. Nick refuses to listen.

> I should have liked to hear more of this last matter; but, Stringham being a friend of mine, I felt that it would be beneath my dignity to discuss his family affairs with someone who, like Widmerpool, knew of them only through hearsay. Later in life, I learnt that many things one may require have to be weighed against one's dignity, which can be an insuperable bar-

rier against advancement in almost any direction. However, in those days, choice between dignity and unsatisfied curiosity was less clear to me as a cruel decision that had to be made.

(QU 130)

Nick's typical casting forward to what he will learn helps lend force here; the really strong touch comes with the phrase "things one may *require*." There is no sidestepping the seriousness toward which the passage has been tilted.

Since the Widmerpools had decided that Kenneth ought to go right into business and "cut out Oxford or Cambridge" (QU 133), Nick moves on to Oxford unencumbered by this harbinger of change. Sillery, the don at Oxford who takes up many promising young men, makes things appear as stable as ever they were in the Kingdom: lending books to hard-reading boys, for example, or being able to exhibit a protégé who, like Sunny Farebrother, combines those qualities of looks, charm, and deference that used to lead to great careers. This protégé, Bill Truscott, has begun his career as secretary to the magnate Sir Magnus Donners. (In the matter of a book's time he will be evicted from the Donners-Brebner Corporation by Widmerpool.)

Only two things smack of the unexpected in the reassuring university atmosphere. The first is that both Sillery and Truscott are favorably taken by an aggressive North Country scholarship boy called Quiggin. The other is that Sillery convinces Charles Stringham's mother that Charles ought to go down from the university in his first term to accept a job alongside Truscott as a Donners aide.

"What about a degree?" Nick asks Charles. Stringham replies: "Bill Truscott reports Sir Magnus as demanding who the hell wants a degree these days; and saying all he needs is men who know the world, and can act and think quickly" (QU 206).

Well and good. Yet, it occurs to Nick, "Sillery's part in this matter was certainly of interest. He might have been expected . . . to encourage as many undergraduates as possible to remain . . ." (QU 206). Even more bewildering is that Sillery does en-

courage Quiggin, finding him much more interesting than Stringham. Here is an amazing reversal of standards as far as "questions
of upbringing" are concerned. Nick actually watches Sillery rub
his hands together, "entranced" over Quiggin's coarse remarks
about the decline of Oxford:

> "Very good, Quiggin, very good," said Sillery. "You find we
> all fall woefully short of your own exacting standards—formed,
> no doubt, in a more austere tradition."   (QU 181)

With Sillery fawning on an heiress like Stringham's mother,
yet infatuated with the penniless Quiggin, Powell's attack on the
Left in *The Music of Time* begins. "All the same, if [Sillery]
was known to incline, on the whole, to the Right socially, politi-
cally he veered increasingly to the Left" (QU 170). If we encounter Sillery at a swank party in *A Buyer's Market,* toadying up
to a Balkan prince, in *The Acceptance World* he will be found
at a demonstration of hunger-marchers in Hyde Park. Powell will
continue to expose this same syndrome, Sillery being merely the
first of a line that includes St. John Clarke (famous novelist),
Milly Andriadis (famous hostess), Alf Tolland (famous "Road to
Wigan peer"[11]). All permit themselves to be badgered by false
left-wing Alastors (different from the real furies who breathe in
the second trilogy). Powell indicates why in describing Mrs. Andriadis' toleration of a young Trotskyite—whose pyjamas she is
wearing in the scene in which we meet him. (He would have been
a pure "messenger" figure in a pre-war Powell novel.) "His uncompromising behaviour no doubt expressed to perfection the
role to which he was assigned in her mind: the scourge of frivo-
lous persons of the sort she knew so well" (AW 168–169). *Herself
included*—that is the point. Powell is uncovering sheer guilt-de-
rived masochism. Had the Trotskyite's pyjama sleeves not been
too long, perhaps Nick would have seen this woman rub her hands
together while bent like a flagellant under the diatribes of a man
who is meanwhile making free of her house and chattels. So, out
of the same masochistic compensation, does Sillery relish the gruff
attacks Quiggin makes while eating Sillery's own buns. The don

is compensating for his own trickery, for his hobnobbing, perhaps even for his dereliction of duty. (Conniving to get Stringham out of his college hardly speaks well of a professional educator.) By the end of *A Question of Upbringing,* Nick has begun to see that roles on which the Empire has long counted are being discharged with something less than integrity.

A LONG LONDON NIGHT

Dereliction of duty figures more openly as *A Buyer's Market* starts out on the first of its own four movements (Nick now about twenty-two, working for a publisher of art books). It is an aspersion cast against Sir Gavin Walpole-Wilson, Nick's host on the evening of a debutante ball in Belgrave Square. Sir Gavin had been forced into early retirement because of an ambassadorial blunder in South America. He is a likeable melancholic, whose type is being replaced, and well he knows it, by entrepreneurs like Sir Magnus Donners; indeed, the novel's third section ends after a weird day at Donners's country castle, with weary Sir Gavin fully eclipsed by Sir Magnus.

Nick's first love is the niece often chaperoned by the Walpole-Wilsons, Barbara Goring. By the end of the night of the Belgravia dance, a night carried through the second section to the book's halfway point by the Mayfair party of Mrs. Andriadis, Nick has shed himself of the infatuation with this girl and is in fact well on his way to the acceptance world. It is therefore in the Walpole-Wilson environment that release from the question of upbringing finally becomes imminent.

Two symbols connect this unfruitful love affair with Nick's vestigial faith in Empire. The first, more overt, is that his love was awakened by a chance meeting with Barbara near the Albert Memorial: "where, beside the kneeling elephant, the Bedouin forever rests on his haunches in hopeless contemplation of Kensington Gardens' trees and thickets, the blackened sockets of his eyes ranging endlessly over the rich foliage of these oases of the mirage" (BM 18).

Words like "mirage" and "hopeless" cut into this coming-together of Nick and Barbara, and likewise there is something spurious about the painting called *Boyhood of Cyrus* which Nick associates with Barbara. This painting hangs at the Walpole-Wilsons' where he often sees her. Its executant was old Mr. Deacon, more dated as an artist than Sir Gavin as a diplomat; nevertheless, as Arthur Mizener has said, "In *A Buyer's Market* Mr. Deacon's carefully described painting, *The Boyhood of Cyrus,* is the key psychological particular of Jenkins' passion for Barbara Goring. . . ."[12]

The main association may be an unstated one. The boyhood of the Persian emperor seems to conjure up that sense of specialness —of having been singled out—that has been remarked in Nick thus far. The painting, to give an instance of extreme contrast, is a far cry from the statue this same Mr. Deacon collects for his antique shop, a copy of *Truth Unveiled by Time*. This is referred to in the counterpart volume *Casanova's Chinese Restaurant*. It is something like an answer to *Boyhood of Cyrus*. It proves projections wrong, projections about love and maybe with them assumptions about a stable empire. The painting had suited Nick's puppy love, meanwhile. It could promise a lot, even though fulfillment were a good distance off. Nick as prospective lover shares something with Cyrus as prospective emperor. The "assured" future is consoling. Powell even has Nick reflect about this sort of love, "where the sensual element has been reduced to a minimum," as shading over into the area of power. As he says, "If we both ate at the Walpole-Wilsons', she was at least under my eye" (BM 24).

The debutante dance in the first section of *A Buyer's Market* features Barbara's pouring sugar onto Widmerpool's head—for Widmerpool is a would-be suitor too!—though before Nick learns this he plays with a mind's-eye picture, *Boyhood of Widmerpool* (BM 30). *After* he learns it, and realizes this man covered with sugar had been a rival, he makes a gain in *A Buyer's Market,* though a gain effectuated through his dignity: "I had made an egregious mistake in falling in love with Barbara" (BW 73).

That gain is the only sure thing stamped in his memory by the end of the second section, in which he has had his first brush with the real world of energy. Milly Andriadis had once been mistress to royalty: she is now mistress to Charles Stringham, who meets Nick at a midnight coffee-stall and drags him and some others to Milly's party. If the tune played here is the same as Nick has heard but an hour ago, there is this difference: at Milly's party "a hunchback wearing a velvet smoking-jacket was playing [it on] an accordian, writhing backwards and forwards as he attacked his instrument with demiurgic frenzy" (BM 105). It is at this party that Magnus Donners first comes onstage. And Stringham slips away from it, outraging Milly, but giving also an early sign that he cannot cope physically with that which would draw on his energy. It is frightening to realize that though Stringham had compelled Nick to come to the party, he could not bear its brunt himself. "At least I can rely on you, Nick, as an old friend," he says in his last sentences on Milly's premises, "to accompany me to a haunt of vice. Somewhere where the stains on the table-cloth make the flesh creep . . ." (BM 145). Since his mistress is there in the fullest eagerness to keep him by her, we are learning, for the first time, that Stringham is affected not only with restless-ness but with the urge to vicarious life. *Others* have put those stains on the table cloths. It is meanwhile at this same party that Widmerpool, in reaction to the sugar humiliation, makes off with a trollop named Gypsy Jones (for whose abortion he will later feel himself obliged to pay).

If these revelations about Stringham and Widmerpool are stun-ning in the abruptness with which they strike, we might suspect that a crisis of sorts is at hand. So true does this prove to be that in retrospect Nick says he became aware "that such latitudes are entered by a door through which there is, in a sense, no return" (BM 160). (And he will reiterate this statement in *Casanova's Chinese Restaurant.*) Stringham, on the run, and Widmerpool, compromised into involvement, continue to mark extremes; but the pointer has finally shown itself ready to swing toward involve-ment as a prerequisite to pleasure.

For this reason, here approaching the middle of the first trilogy, Powell makes a last resounding emphasis on the force of upbringing; Nick, from the mid-point on, will begin to slip its shackles. As far as imagery goes, just after Nick and Widmerpool leave the debutante ball and are about to encounter Stringham at the coffee-stall, Powell chooses a spot where the Empire fittingly can seem to totter.

> By this time we had come to Grosvenor Place, in sight of the triumphal arch, across the summit of which, like a vast paper-weight or capital ornament of an Empire clock, the Quadriga's horses, against a sky of indigo and silver, careered desperately towards the abyss.   (BM 82)

(That verb "career" will appear again in the last sentence of the novel, and on the last page also Westminster cathedral will impart "a sense of vertigo, a dizziness almost alarming in its intensity. . . .") But Powell accomplishes something richer still, to make the abyss more exotic and intimidating—the abyss, that is, opening now between strict Belgravia and daring Mayfair (and places yet lower down the scale). He casts the whole scene of Mrs. Andriadis' party as though it were seen through the disapproving eyes of Uncle Giles. This provides a kind of vizor, a last bit of Jenkins armor, Giles's way being to spot "latent imperfections" in any situation conducive to enthrallment.

But appraising the guests at Milly's party this standoffish way, watching the beauties surround Prince Theodoric or Sir Magnus Donners, learning that this Hill Street house itself belongs to Peter Templer's sister Jean and her husband Bob Duport ("while I myself, at the same time, lived a comparative hand-to-mouth existence in rooms" [BM 141])—these observations finally lead to mortification. Making his way to those rooms in the Shepherd Market, Nick is forced to conclude that "From the point of view of either sentiment or snobbery, giving both terms their widest connotation, the night had been an empty one" (BM 153). Sentiment—he had not made off with a girl "to take the place of Barbara"; snobbery—he had done nothing to consolidate his position with anyone important at that party. Right down to the alliteration, the words anticipate that suspended state between dissipation and diffidence soon to be acknowledged and finally equilibrized in *The Acceptance World.* Now who should loom up against the backdrop of dawn at the Shepherd Market but Uncle Giles, almost like a genie or a ghost, as much as to say, well, how did you like the look that I lent you?

Nick is astonished to find his uncle prowling the streets at this hour, but Giles only registers mild surprise that his nephew lives in these precincts. This queer fact— that to an individual himself there is scarcely anything strange about where he happens to arrive (having been in his own skin all the time it took to get there) —drives itself home with great force to Nick. In fact, Giles's presence drives out thoughts Nick had had, on his way to his room, of recording the fatuity of the party in the icy manner of Montaigne. (How fatuous this would itself have been: he would only have been licking his wounds.) Instead, he allows mystery to take hold of him, not Montaigne. The Andriadis guests he thought he could etch, and here is a man known so long whom he can't begin to account for. More than a chastening thought, this encounter with Giles defines Nick's quest for the rest of *The Music of Time.*

> While I undressed I reflected on the difficulty of believing in the existence of certain human beings, my uncle among them, even in the face of unquestionable evidence . . . that each had dreams and desires like other men. Was it possible to take Uncle Giles seriously? And yet he was, no doubt, serious enough to himself. If a clue to that problem could be found, other mysteries of life might be revealed. I was still pondering Uncle Giles and his ways when I dropped into an uneasy sleep.
>
> (BM 158)

DOWNSLOPE TO ADVENTURE

Nowhere else in *The Music of Time* are the events of a single night permitted to consume half a novel. So it makes good sense when, in *Casanova's Chinese Restaurant, Powell* reverts to this night's formative influence. A die was cast then which would lead Nick into Bohemian life.

The phrase Nick uses, borrowed from Mr. Deacon, about "the pilgrimage from the sawdust floor to the Aubusson carpet and back again" (CR 16), applies only partly to himself. He went after all from Belgravia's waxed parquet to Mayfair's magic carpet, and in *A Buyer's Market* passes through one other social declension before reaching sawdust floors. This is a world of patronizing wealth, a shade less exclusive than Milly Andriadis', represented by Sir Magnus Donners's moated castle Stourwater. When Nick met Jean Templer at her father's house, though that businessman was not quite in the class of Donners, the place had seemed "a sea-palace . . . where any adventure might be expected" (QU 73). In a magnified way, Stourwater presents this aura too, and there at a luncheon party Nick meets Jean again. It is she who distinguishes the niceties that make the Stourwater gathering more the kind that would have business at the back of it—where bargains are struck, even emotional ones—rather than the sheer emotional sorting out seen to prevail at Milly's.

Nick does not quite catch the implication that a wider, less exacting market might be played by a girl like Jean. When he does, in the aptly titled *Acceptance World,* she will remind him of his obtuseness; as it is, she nearly bowls him over by discussing the depiction of Lust in a medieval tapestry of the Seven Deadly Sins—over lunch no less.

> "You were so deep in the tapestry," she said.
> "I was wondering about the couple in the little house on the hill."
> "They have a special devil—or is he a satyr?—to themselves."
> "He seems to be collaborating, doesn't he?"
> "Just lending a hand, I think."
> "A guest, I suppose—or member of the staff?"
> "Oh, a friend of the family," she said. "All newly-married couples have someone of that sort about. Sometimes several. Didn't you know? I see you can't be married."
> "But how do you know they are newly married?"
> "They've got such a smart little house," she said. "They must be newly married. And rather well off, too, I should say."
>
> (BM 192)

Jean's innuendo here is too disquieting for Nick. The facts are that *she* has a smart little house, that *he* has been a "friend of the family." Powell's own irony goes well beyond this, since there are scalding moments ahead in *The Music of Time* that will owe themselves to that phrase about young wives having an extra partner about, "Sometimes several." Nick is stopped in his tracks by this conversation, however. When, at the end of this visit and section three of *A Buyer's Market,* he half advances, then retreats from Jean, a sub-motif for *The Music of Time* has made itself felt. This is because of Nick's real inkling of the nature of love. What may be called the love-hate motif is aired when Nick wants to say some parting word to Jean: "yet so far was this feeling remote from a simple desire to see more of her that, in a way, I almost equally hoped that I might fail to find her again before we left Stourwater, at a time that a simultaneous anxiety to search for her also tormented me" (BM 214). The love-hate tension is felt here through mere overtures toward intimacy. At any rate, Nick buys time. Jean's slyness is frightening because to follow her beckoning would mean giving oneself up, one's security, *the knowledge too of not having yet been humiliated,* one's sense of no one else having anything *on* one. Such are some of the sources of hate in that compromise so often designated "love-hate" in *The Music of Time*—and elsewhere of course: *"Odi et amo,"* as the poet says.

Most disturbingly, a paradigm of all this seems hinted in another activity that afternoon at Stourwater. Stringham (now Donners's secretary) and Widmerpool (soon to be his henchman) both figure in this. Donners has taken a party of guests down to his dungeons, and when one of the girls is shackled to a wall in some horseplay, Sir Magnus throbs with excitement. But Nick does not witness this incident, and when he arrives seconds later to be told of it by Stringham, something horrific results. "The Chief was in ecstasies," confides Stringham. Nick is put aback by this, "because nothing could have been more matter-of-fact" than Donners's voice and demeanor an instant after the girl had been unchained (BM 211). To the untrained eye, the Chief's ecstasy was unobservable, the horror being that Stringham's delectation is more exquisite than Donners's. For Donners's may be secret, but Stringham's comes in perceiving that secret and having his own clandestine fun with the perception.*

This is a paradigm of Nick's own situation in that Stringham's involution seems to derive from that selfsame pull always half-operating on Nick, to withdraw and watch, finally, perhaps, to take pleasure from the non-exposure. Pondering Jean as a Rubens subject (which he does on saying goodbye to her), seeing Mrs. Andriadis' party through Giles's eyes, are symptoms of the same holding-at-arm's-length. To relate the underground episode to moments at Stourwater with Jean might yet seem farfetched, were it not for the cause of Nick's own belated arrival at the dungeon. On the way along with the troop of guests, his shoelace had come untied and, from an adjacent outer passage, Widmerpool had called his name. Nick has a momentary fantasy that the man has been imprisoned, wondering with "almost unbearable anxiety . . . what crime, or dereliction of duty, he must have committed to suffer such treatment at the hands of his tyrant" (BM 205). Though nothing so awful of course has happened, yet it is through a barred aperture that Widmerpool informs Nick of that abortion he has paid for. Graphic enough in its own right, does not the information bear on the other side of Nick's dilemma? Here is an acquaintance who has taken a mad plunge (as for love-hate, no one is hated more in *The Music of Time* than Gypsy Jones by Widmerpool), and here is the indignity framed by bars, no less. Widmerpool caged: a fine subterranean symbol of what it may mean to take a rash step.

---

*When Donners had made a leering remark at the start of the dungeon tour, "I could see from Stringham's face," said Nick, "that he was suppressing a tremendous burst of laughter. It struck me, at this moment, that such occasions, the enjoyment of secret laughter, remained for him the peak of pleasure, for he looked suddenly happier; more buoyant . . ." (BM 202). Stringham—this was even true with his impersonations when Nick knew him at school—always expert at spotting people's weak or secret sides, has by now contrived a way of obtaining amusement at their expense without exposing himself. What is so desperate is that self-protection has made him similar to, even more perverse than, the voyeur Donners—who is his active counterpart, in a way necessary to his existence.

Still, whether Widmerpool seems exposed in the Stourwater section, or Stringham protected, the importance of energy is re-clarified there. Just as I used a phrase of Mr. Deacon's a moment ago as showing direction in this book, so did Robert Morris pick up a Deacon aphorism—"Gothic manners don't mix with Greek morals" (BM 113)—and apply it to conflicts in *A Buyer's Market.* Stourwater is Gothic and so are occupants like Donners and Widmerpool; Stringham would be the sly Greek here; and Morris's well-taken point is that "thrusting as Gothic manners are, they clearly dominate the freedom and looseness of Greek morals: the one involving willful participation, the other imaginative passivity."[13] While Nick is caught in the middle, still hesitating to commit himself, the thrust of the novel's action after the halfway point clearly points toward Gothic involvement; and as we know, the book's final section will lead to the metaphor of Russian billiards and the conclusion that life has "begun in earnest at last. . . ." (BM 274).

A fourth party is now in store for Nick, this one in Mr. Deacon's rooms, and as the divisions have taken him down four social rungs he has gotten closer to adventure. Mr. Deacon, specifically referred to as an adventurer (BM 227), takes a fall on the night of his party that later proves fatal. This causes Powell to blend the party scene into one describing Deacon's funeral.

As Widmerpool had rebounded from his sugar incident into the arms of Gypsy Jones, so is Nick propelled toward Gypsy. She makes game of Widmerpool to Nick as they chat on Deacon's sofa, and the attraction-repulsion mood arrives again. "There was something odious about her that made her, at the same time—I had to face this—an object of desire" (BM 249).

The party scene shows Powell at the top of his form, for, where one might expect its fifteen pages (BM 235–250) to produce a kind of *Breakfast at Tiffany's* decor, the whole middle is scooped out of it and for eleven pages (BM 237–247) we are delivered over to Mark Members and J. G. Quiggin. During this time, as they stand paying each other guarded compliments, Nick's uneasy, almost grudging respect for their literary talents comes forward. A great deal is thus accomplished by Powell. As he keeps the Bohemian gathering "in hover" he passes along the notion that. these men too are in a buyer's market, only theirs is a literary one. Able meanwhile to express the tedium of the party by not referring to it, Powell leads up finally to the high adventure, for Nick, of sexual intercourse. As Nick owns, "that night at Mr. Deacon's seemed to crystallise certain matters. Perhaps this crystallisation had something to do with the presence there of Members and Quiggin . . ." (BM 242).

Nick has been a slow starter also in the field of letters, and is made conscious by Members and Quiggin of having dragged his feet. Connect to this the fact that Gypsy has a weakness for people who talk books, and a couple of strands emerge that will help bring Nick to bed with her. It is incumbent on Powell, in other words, to take Nick over the border of sensuality, and part of the impetus is the restlessness making itself felt *on many sides:* that is the point of the Quiggin-Members interlude.

His friend Barnby's summons by telephone to an assignation, the fact that Nick has learned, with irrational regret, that Jean Duport is "expecting"—even perhaps the recent news of Charles Stringham's marriage—all these things added to Gypsy Jones's easygoing sexuality help bring her and Nick together in her alcove at Mr. Deacon's place the day of that man's funeral. One needs to insist on such intricate causation because Powell does, more repeatedly in this one scene than perhaps anywhere else in *The Music of Time.* "Nothing in life," he has Nick say, "can ever be entirely divorced from myriad other incidents; and it is remarkable, though no doubt logical, that action, built up from innumerable causes . . . is almost always provided with an apparently ideal moment for its final expression" (BM 254).

There are two results: the copulation, as Nick goes through with it, seems formalized; and there is no trauma—since the really pervasive sense Nick had was of "a general subordination to an intricate design of cause and effect . . ." (BM 257). One is entitled to regard lightly enough these words and this incident; it nevertheless remains true that "subordination" is a Powellian keyword for catching the tune of the music of time (whereas Widmerpool, rushing into collusion with Gypsy, suffers severe trauma). There is no sense, on the other hand, of equilibrium having been reached in this passing episode, which does not so much contain its own significance as point to a future where more emotion may be tapped. What is then reserved for the last page of *A Buyer's Market* is a heavy underscoring of the feeling that life had "begun in earnest at last, and we ourselves, scarcely aware that any change has taken place, are careering uncontrollably down the slippery avenues of eternity" (BM 274).

WORLD WITHIN WORLD

The bottom, not yet in sight in that last description, is reached in the Slump years, 1931–1932, which are the setting of *The Acceptance World*. The title derives from Widmerpool's new job as a bill-broker, working for credit houses which "accept" debts owed to businesses by, for example, overseas clients. The acceptance houses contract to pay these debts in advance of the actual delivery of goods. The suggestion in part three of *A Buyer's Market*, that emotional as well as financial bargains might be struck, tended to pave the way for Powell's new title, the unidealistic business phrase becoming germane especially at the end of the third novel's action.

Where "the buyer waits" is the theme of the second novel, now the buyer makes his move. What he "accepts" is another person, his collateral being himself. From the opening pages Nick is guided toward this "plunge" by Mrs. Erdleigh. And from these pages on—because of their setting at Uncle Giles's slack-grey hotel in Bayswater—a brooding note is prolonged and seems to say that his deep dive is the antidote to tension, economic as well as personal, in the times. For example, *The Acceptance World* is the only novel in the sextet which brings Nick into social contact as the result of his making his living. He goes to the Ritz in the second section to meet Mark Members, with whom he wishes to discuss the preface for a book Nick's firm is doing on *The Art of Horace Isbister*. He meets Peter Templer and his wife Mona at the Ritz instead—along with Peter's sister Jean—and, on the way back to Peter's house with them, his love affair with Jean begins.

It is appropriate that they should kiss, in the rear of Peter's car, just at a point where an "electrically illuminated young lady in a bathing dress dives eternally through the petrol-tainted air; night and day, winter and summer, never reaching the water of the pool to which she endlessly glides" (AW 64). Appropriate because this sign is a giant advertisement, adjunct to business and repeater of a cycle of frustration.

By no means will Nick's affair with Jean be drab—that is not the point. Rather, their behavior as lovers is circumstanced by practical problems, various pressing timetables, which serve as reminders of the provisional, almost escapist quality of their love. It ought to be seen as the one pulsing signal in a gray world *and* as something reactive and therefore unable to supply its own fuel. It is conditional, this affair. Bob Duport's business decline seems as much a cause of his estrangement from his wife as "other women" do—and Bob's business recovery will reunite the couple at the end. All this emphasizes what might be called the "conductivity" of the Slump, as Powell senses this, in contrast to the insularity of Jean and Nick within it. Two sentences of his, in fact, capture this idea of escapism just as the Templers arrive at their house with their impromptu guest, and Jean whispers to Nick what bedroom he will be able to find her in. The sentences are made possible because Peter Templer happens to own an Isbister, which Nick sees on entering. "Isbister's huge portrait of Mr. Templer still hung in the hall, a reminder of everyday life and unsolved business problems. Such things seemed far removed from this mysterious, snowy world of unreality, where all miracles could occur" (AW 66).

Some very nearly miraculous things happen in the third and fourth sections of *The Acceptance World*. A kind of remote cause of them is the ailing writer St. John Clarke, who has bolted to the left and replaced the valuable Members as his secretary by Quiggin, a move duly noted by Nick as "a landmark in the general disintegration of society in its traditional form" (AW 121). In the fifth section, a social landmark of wider implication will be reached unsocialistically after an Old Boys' Dinner, producing the climax of the whole first trilogy when Charles Stringham is bested in a physical struggle with Widmerpool.

The day after Nick falls in love with Jean at the Templers', Quiggin is invited there to appease Mona Templer's interest in social action, and the spirit of Karl Marx comes through on Planchette. The outrage this induces in Quiggin is quickly converted to alarm as Planchette's handwriting changes in size and begins indicating the ill health of St. John Clarke, whom the new secretary has just left. Back Quiggin rushes from Maidenhead to London, his skepticism toward the Other World transformed in an instant.

It is only consonant with Powell's (or Nick's) rationalism to leave room for the possibility of actual spiritual information being passed along. Mrs. Erdleigh, who happens to be on the scene, naturally accepts the results of the board's manipulations. Nick neither accepts nor rejects—his characteristic response is "Search me" (AW 96)—and having made it clear no sleight of hand has been involved, he leaves the question open as the only rational view to take of the supernatural and/or the psychic. (A definition of rationalism, as opposed to positivism, surely needs to be grounded on the expectation of some irrational or unaccountable activity forever potential in life: the reverse, positivism, is sheer superstition by the very *unempirical* way it insists on empiricism.) Thus it is left up to Peter Templer (earlier called a "spoiled intellectual"), and not up to Nick, to say, "It was extraordinary all that stuff about Marx coming up. I suppose it was swilling about in old Quiggin's head and somehow got released" (AW 102).

A key fact is revealed about Jean (and by extension, it may be, about Planchette) during this session. It was she who introduced the game to the assembled company. It will not work while she is one of the three on the board. The two most obviously excited people, Mona Templer and Jimmy Stripling (now Mrs. Erdleigh's disciple), have sat down to the game with Jean. The sentences that precede Planchette's activity are these:

> Jean and Mona had been trying their luck with Stripling as third partner. Jean now rose from the table, and, dropping one of those glances at once affectionate and enquiring that raised such a storm within me, she said: "You have a go." (AW 93)

And Planchette does begin to work, crackles of emotion having come into play within each participant. While such heightened emotion seems indispensable, so does the fact that Nick has replaced Jean at the table. The inference is—it must not go unnoticed, having relevance to their union from start to finish—that Jean is *not* crackling with emotion. Planchette is merely diversionary, and so is the love, so are all the loves, she dabbles in, regardless of the intensity and allure and control she brings to love. Later, as this weekend ends and Nick tries to fix an assignation with her, he says, "She seemed to have no sense of the urgency of making some arrangement quickly—so that we should not lose touch with each other. . . . In spite of apparent coldness of manner her eyes were full of tears" (AW 104–105).

Seen so often by Nick in a detached attitude (as Susan Nunnery was in Powell's first book), Jean is enigmatic beyond definition, though not altogether different than Nick, intelligent like him and quiet. Perhaps that is it, that they are alike; although she is not a product of the upbringing that so intransigently is working him along a course of gradual loyalty. Like her brother Peter, there is something tragic about her—moreso in her nature than residing in her affair with Nick *per se*. Though associated with many pictures in Nick's mind, it is his initial image of her, from *A Question of Upbringing*, that persists and that will recur in *The Kindly Ones* when the sextet ends. The image derives from the measuredness in the way Jean stops and looks toward her brother and Nick, while in the act of sliding a garage door closed. She has a carved quality about her,

> such as might be found in an Old Master drawing, Flemish or German perhaps, depicting some young and virginal saint; the racquet, held awkwardly at an angle to her body, suggesting at the same time an obscure implement associated with martyrdom.   (QU 74)

The sense is rightly the shivering one of her having been formed forever: "martyrdom" suiting an inalterability conveyed this early though not defined. Yet once more will this "fixed" sensation occur, via the same image. It is in *The Military Philosophers*, which ends with the admission that Nick and Jean have become different persons. But different with respect to each other, for the presence of the image itself would seem to belie essential inner change.

St. John Clarke's illness, curiously enough, not only disbands the Planchette circle but will reach out to touch Nick's love affair next. Quiggin may have rushed out of the Templers' house distraught, but he would soon be taking up with Mona Templer. And Nick, crossing Hyde Park to fulfill an assignation with Jean, is to encounter a Marxist procession and behold Clarke being pushed in a wheelchair by Quiggin and Mona. Their loverlike stride is so incriminating as to knock him completely off his.

This event indicates that while "polite surprise" may be Nick's ordinary reaction, major transitions in *The Music of Time* are accompanied by Nick's being stunned right out of his senses—rarely as that may happen. Nick cannot help telling Jean what he has just seen in the park; it is her sister-in-law's infidelity, after all. What follows calls up one of Powell's main thematic statements: "nothing in life is planned—or everything is—because in the dance every step is ultimately the corollary of the step before; the consequence of being the kind of person one chances to be" (AW 63).

As their conversation curves around Mona and Peter, and Nick reverts to the day of Planchette and makes disparaging remarks about Jimmy Stripling, Jean suddenly and destructively announces that she has had an affair with this man, in Nick's view a revolting boor. It seems that a chance *event* has caused Jean to make this revelation (stimulated to jealousy or whatever, because of Mona's move). Yet the essential thing is that one day or another, and very likely sooner than later, Jean would have told Nick of Stripling. The chance event only plays into the hands of the kind of character "one chances to be." Thus before this scene Powell places an important reflection by Nick, on the matter of his "being out of key" with Jean during early moments of time spent with her: suggesting "a whole principle of behaviour: a deliberate act of the will by which she exercised power. At times it was almost as if she intended me to feel that unexpected accident, rather than a carefully arranged plan, had brought us together on some given occasion . . ." (AW 136–137). These words show Jean to be actuated by a plan that reveals itself in the guise of contriving accidents. The correlation between apparently haphazard event and its cause in character could not be more pointedly made. The power Jean intended to exert, through the revelation of a disgusting fact, was toward a paradoxically "increased intimacy" between herself and Nick. This is borne out as the two walk away from her flat (AW 144), and confirmed in the last words of the fourth section: "in some way the day had righted itself, and once more the two of us seemed close together" (AW 169).

Though I intend at the end of the next chapter to encounter the problem of will in all these novels, it should be apparent by the drift of these extracts that Jean has wilfully—through will-oriented instinct, it might be more accurate to say—caused that mystifying piece of news to be dropped to wound and ensnare Nick, and that character and timing rather than event ultimately accounted for these modifications. In the next and last section of *The Acceptance World,* when Widmerpool commandeers a taxi (something Nick could not do), Powell doubles on the idea:

> Widmerpool acted quickly. He strolled to the kerb. A cab seemed to rise out of the earth at that moment. Perhaps all action, even summoning a taxi when none is there, is basically a matter of the will. Certainly there had been no sign of a conveyance a second before. Widmerpool made a curious, pumping movement, using the whole of his arm, as if dragging down the taxi by a rope.   (AW 204)

This taxi is needed to get the drunken Stringham home from the Old Boys' Dinner. That ceremony itself had ended because of the collapse of the guest of honor, the old housemaster Le Bas. He had collapsed in the middle of Widmerpool's amazing speech on statistics, a *coup de table* that confounds all the Old Boys. The structure of the first trilogy is to be completed now as Nick, conscious of "a whole social upheaval: a positively cosmic change in life's system" (AW 209), witnesses Widmerpool's forcible consignment of Stringham to the latter's bed. Widmerpool is also the agent for separating Nick and Jean, since it is through his offices that Bob Duport gets back on his feet in the business world. (Jean's will, as we shall see, was working overtime in this regard.) It is of Bob's return that Jean and Nick talk on the novel's last page, providing the poignant sense of compromise with which it ends; "the acceptance world," Nick now knows, will always balance whatever ecstasies it provides with bitterness. And though the poignance has a settled quality about it that is right for the end volume of the trilogy, still it was only moments before that the "cosmic change" had come, with the man of grace and wit impounded by the man of action.

A picture of Widmerpool and Stringham in grotesque struggle in the last section of the trilogy takes the reader back to the end of the opening section of *A Question of Upbringing*. At that point Stringham had tricked Le Bas and then browbeat Widmerpool. ("We left Widmerpool on the steps of the house: to all intents and purposes, a fish recently hauled from the water, making powerful though failing efforts at respiration" [QU 49].) But that schoolboy afternoon had ended with Nick's image of the other two at chapel, where it became clear that Stringham *retained* the stain of things thought and done where Widmerpool had the recuperability of obtuseness.

> Stringham was opposite, standing with his arms folded, not singing. . . . He looked grave, lost in thought, almost seraphic: like a carved figure symbolising some virtue like Resignation or Self-sacrifice. . . . On the other side, away to the left, Widmerpool was holding a book in front of him, singing hard: his mouth opening and shutting sharply, more than ever like some uncommon specimen of marine life. He turned his eyes from time to time towards the rafters and high spaces of the roof.
>
> (QU 50–51)

And now years later it would be Stringham who was left, as it were, making "powerful though failing efforts at respiration." His dignity stood him in no stead at the end, when Widmerpool was pinning him on his bed. He might yell out in his lovable way, "So these are the famous Widmerpool good manners, are they?" (AW 208). He might try the bewitchment of the perfect phrase: "But

ingress and egress of one's own bed is unassailable" (AW 207).
Widmerpool will simply reply, "Much better stay where you are."

   One final thing that "the acceptance world" means is that regard
for form or dread of the ungainly simply will not carry one through
life, and that the dance to the music of time does require movements, gyrations, that must put one off one's dignity. Widmerpool's victory is by no means the only indication of this truism
(in fact it would be perverse to go any further and allow Widmerpool to become a hero in the novel). Even as far back as *Afternoon
Men* Powell was indeed making the point through Verelst. Thus
his choice of ending the trilogy with an Old Boys' Dinner is very
potent. At the end of the first section of *A Question of Upbringing*,
when the boys who would be Old Boys tempered their impetuous-
ness by behaving circumspectly in chapel, Powell had written,
"Youth and Time here had made, as it were, some compromise"
(QU 50). At the dinner, these Old Boys were roughly doing the
same thing until Widmerpool elbowed into the limelight and
virtually caused Le Bas's stroke, the problem being that dignity
forbade that Le Bas should interfere with the hideous drivel
Widmerpool was delivering. An image used to describe poor Le
Bas, as the Old Boys form a line to shake his hand, goes to the
heart of the milieu of Powell's first trilogy in the terms now under
consideration. "After the final handshake," records Nick, "he
took up one of those painful, almost tortured positions habitually
affected by him, this particular one seeming to indicate that he
had just landed on his heels in the sand after making the long
jump" (AW 180–181). It is a fine fleshing-forth of the man always
encountered in would-be dignified situations, but unable to square
his own posture with the apparent requirements. If it is a sort of
symbol, through this one man's regimented routine, of any man's
uneasiness—with the relief of physical activity kept far beyond
the possibilities of the setting (a receiving line at the Ritz)—one
senses a poignant corollary nonetheless in that physical activity
seems the only recipe that might cure the awkwardness. This was
the kind of thing brought home to Nick as he shed his dignity
over the course of the three books. Perhaps not wholly justifiably,
one is led back to the couple on the French postcard poised in the

preliminaries of physical activity—the amorous postcard sent in the last pages by Jean to Nick. That couple command attention after the final, quietly shrugging dialogue of the novel. "Did Peter mention that Bob is back in England?" Jean has asked Nick.

> "Yes."
> "That may make difficulties."
> "I know."
> "Don't let's talk of them."
> "No."
> "Darling Nick."

Outside, a clock struck the hour. Though ominous, things still had their enchantment. . . . Perhaps, in spite of everything, the couple of the postcard could not be dismissed so easily. It was in their world that I seemed now to find myself.

(AW 214)

5

THE MUSIC OF TIME:
Second Movement

Since in the second trilogy of his novel Powell will demonstrate, over the span from 1934 to 1939, the gradual ripening of circumstances that will bring the Furies down on the English, it needs to be said that for this second movement he creates a background of almost flameproof solidity which will enable his principals to weather the firestorm. Now clearly the world of Templers and Duports, impinging on Nick at the end of *The Acceptance World,* is one that *will* kindle under the Furies' blast. These people have too many restless imperatives: for example,

> to possess no social ambitions whatever, though at the same time to be disfigured by no grave social defects. The women had to be good-looking, the men tolerably proficient at golf and bridge, without making a fetish of those pastimes. Both sexes . . . were expected to drink fairly heavily; although, here again, intoxication must not be carried to excess.   (AW 39)

Such imperatives are the kind well known to bring on ulcers, not to mention greater torments. In the two end volumes of the trilogy, *At Lady Molly's* and *The Kindly Ones,* Peter Templer is encoun-

138

tered, by chance as always, pursuing his rounds on these terms. Mona having left him, he is spotted in the first book at a night-club, to which he has taken the wife of another businessman. "She is called Betty. I can never remember her married name. Taylor, is it? Porter? Something like that. We met at a dreadful bridge party the other day" (LM 187). It does not much matter what her sur-name is because it is soon to be changed to Templer. And when Nick runs into Peter at Stourwater, this girl is mad; a great cli-macteric in *The Kindly Ones* is on tap; and the time-range of the second trilogy is rapidly filled in before that terrible scene:

> That outward appearance was the old Templer, just as he had looked at Dicky Umfraville's nightclub four or five years before. Now, as he strode up the path with the same swagger, I saw there was a change in him. . . . He looked hard, even rather sav-age, as if he had made up his mind to endure life rather than, as formerly, to enjoy it.   (KO 101)

Torment is in the air in *The Kindly Ones,* but it was also in *Casanova's Chinese Restaurant,* in which stillbirth and suicide occur, and even in *At Lady Molly's.* But to backtrack once again, that original description of Peter Templer's regimen had ended with this addendum of his: "You know, I really rather hate the well-born" (AW 39). In this lay a secret, not to stand to the detri-ment of Peter's character,* but to account for the predisposition to breakdown of inhabitants of the acceptance world.

If any charge of snobbism were ever to be levelled at Powell, in other words, it would have to come up against feelings that begin to be registered in *At Lady Molly's,* the very strongest feelings, not simply arguments. This includes the feeling that old consanguin-eous families are indoctrinated in hard realism in such an unbro-ken fashion as to render them less than vulnerable to shocks of the times.

As Nick says in The Kindly Ones, *"He was always kind, I noticed, when he spoke to Betty, would probably have done anything in his power—short of altering his own way of life, which perhaps no one can truly do—to allevi-ate this painful situation" (KO 122).*

It is important to emphasize this wide-based resistance attributed by Powell to the many-branched, established old lines. Robert Morris, for example, does not miss the stabilizing effect on Nick of the aristocrat Molly Jeavons, from whom this new book gets its name. But Morris, like other Powell critics, is inclined to overestimate disintegration in upper-class English society, not finding it as tough in the end as Powell does. I therefore disagree with such general statements of his as, "Powell views the aristocracy as bordering on . . . a private *Götterdämmerung*. . . ."[1] Lady Molly is not a "sport," but rather one of many resilient representatives of the old consanguineous families.

So we need to observe that the milieu into which Nick is introduced, that of Molly Jeavons and the Tollands—and less immediately of the great houses Dogdene and Thrubworth—is first of all *untormented.* The key to the meaning of the whole second trilogy lies in this fact, and structurally it explains why its first and last subsections are centered at Lady Molly's somewhat tumbledown house in South Kensington. Lady Molly was once Marchioness of Sleaford and chatelaine of Dogdene, but rather than be bothered repining about her displacement, she keeps much vitality percolating in the dark red brick house. There are overtones of affliction here: there is a borrowed butler who will dampen any visitor's spirits at the street door; and, on the top floors, always someone whom Molly has taken in, perhaps in mortal sickness, or else, as in the case of Stringham, put out of action by alcoholism. Though Molly is a ragger and tease, she is quite the opposite of a Fury. Indeed, the last Fury we meet in this trilogy is Mrs. Erdleigh, bent in her suave and quiet way on administering a hypodermic to a man who has asked for a visitation from Furies. This next-to-last scene will be supplanted by one at Lady Molly's, where one more poor fellow will be ransomed from the streets for a time, and where Nick's chance for a speedy call-up into the Reserves will materialize.

After the death of Lord Sleaford, Molly married Ted Jeavons, a man badly wounded in World War I, whom she fairly well dominates. The strain of talking to this by turns absent-minded, by turns animated man (not of aristocratic stock) again seems to imply borderlines of torment. But this assessment is misleading and Jeavons, one of the great heroes of *The Music of Time* by virtue of heights of realism that he reaches, is one who, with some title to be hounded by past and present, remains unhounded all the same.

This second trilogy, leading to war, takes the measure of many Englishmen but will not be able to get on the other side of the Jeavonses. Not that they are idealized. They are not necessarily happy; and Nick detects a strand of ruthlessness in Molly's way of life. He himself could not have been absorbed into the Jeavons circle had he not had credentials going beyond his connection at a film studio with Chips Lovell, Molly's nephew. All the same, the almost cruel directness in vogue at Lady Molly's, if compared with the style of entertainment of Milly Andriadis, say, has the nap of something infinitely more interesting, human, and non-competitive about it.

Widmerpool proves this because he enters the household *as* a competitor.

Widmerpool's arrival closes out section one. He is squiring an old friend of Molly's, Mrs. Haycock, to whom he is engaged—she is the daughter of a peer. However, Widmerpool comes to realize that Mrs. Haycock requires a trial trip in bed before marriage, and he fails with her during a weekend at Dogdene, bringing the engagement to an end.

Plans are his undoing, and as a planner Widmerpool doesn't fit in among the old campaigners in Molly's circle. These include General Conyers, who married Mrs. Haycock's elder sister apparently on whim when "on the brink of fifty" (LM 5), and who got into a great cavalry charge in the Boer War also more or less on whim, as he tells Nick in their strange and intimate conversation at the novel's end. If there was some difficulty in getting him "mounted" for that charge, it happens he has just been the one to tell Nick of the difficulties there had been at Dogdene in getting *Widmerpool* mounted! That may sound facetious, yet the General himself had led the topic in this direction by comparing marriage to war. "What was it Foch said? War not an exact science, but a terrible and passionate drama? Something like that. Fact is, marriage is rather like that too" (LM 234). Conjunctions of this sort help give the whole trilogy form: *Casanova's Chinese Restaurant* is a marriage book; *The Kindly Ones,* a war-fomenting one.

Powell separates Widmerpool from the Jeavons circle because these others belong to the war generation, and also because the competitive man wants to have and hang on to: Widmerpool wants to "have" Mrs. Haycock and hang onto her title. His wants are directly related to his inability to "perform" at Dogdene. A fundamental contrast then comes up when it is revealed that Jeavons had a wartime affair of a week's duration with this same Mildred Haycock. She was then the Honourable Mildred Blaides, ambulance driver. With great matter-of-factness, Jeavons explains how surprised he was to see Mildred again when she and Widmerpool arrived at his house. Nick wants to know what Mildred said and gets the answer,

> "Not a word. Didn't recognise me. After all, I suppose I've got to take my place in what must be a pretty long list by now."
> "You didn't say anything yourself?"
> "Didn't want to seem to presume on a war-time commission, so I kept mum."   (LM 177)

These words pass between Jeavons and Nick at a nightclub they have wandered to by chance and where Jeavons out of the blue not only tells his tale to Nick but also astonishes him by breaking into a song of war vintage, displaying a rich voice, too. A naughty thirties' song that someone sings draws subdued anger from him a moment later. There is no doubt that a moral inference may be drawn from this combination—reinforced by the fact that on the very last page of the sextet, as Nick's slate is wiped clean to be turned now to the record of service in uniform, Ted Jeavons (who has happened to come into the room) suddenly begins to sing:

> "There's a long, long trail a-winding
> Into the land of . . . my dreams . . ."

There is not a shade of sentimentality here, because Jeavons is singing only for the sake of the noise in his throat, giving just a moment of release to "that full, deep, unexpectedly attractive voice . . ." (KO 254).

Jeavons's self-effacement, his never presuming on his wartime commission or his marriage to a noblewoman—and his somewhat misfit nature, including an attraction to gadgetry—all make him into a subdued sort of Gatsby; a Gatsby hurt more by the war (physically) and therefore somewhat less of a haunted dreamer, but touched with this quality all the same. He is not altogether an adventurer, but to use one of Hugh Moreland's distinctions, he is *not unadventurous*. This phrase is a key to the kind of heroism most likely to survive the realities of life and the life of the will, which are seen so clearly in *The Music of Time* and which must be the subject of fuller remarks in a moment.

One might almost call Jeavons a classical Gatsby (if such an idea is possible to entertain), in that he has some of the other's chivalry but is not competitive. Differences admitted, and even noting that Powell's figure seems apparently conceived as a minor character, I still feel forced to an equation of this sort because of the extraordinary emotional pull Jeavons seems to exert. He has richness and candor—both more often muted than not, for he is, more often than not, sleepy or just shambling along. Certainly that critic needs to be refuted who credits Powell with a "perfect detachment" from Jeavons, and wonders whether this "may have at last too rigidly limiting an effect on these books as works of art?"[2]

Widmerpool once annoyed Nick by sniggering in the middle of the subject of his proposed affair with Mrs. Haycock. ("The problem could be treated, as it were, clinically, or humorously; a combination of the two approaches was distasteful" [LM 61].) By contrast, Powell's respect for Jeavons's emotional realness comes across in Jeavons's retrospective account of the real thing. (Of how many secondhand recountings of an affair in fiction could it be said that the whole effect is bracing?) Jeavons may make Nick laugh by referring to the young Mildred as "the Honourable":

> However, he himself remained totally serious in his demeanour. He sat there looking straight at me, as if the profound moral beauty of his own story delighted him rather than any purely anecdotal quality, romantic or banal, according to how you took it. (LM 176)

The interesting thing is that Nick, as usual, is able to shape categories for how such information might be transmitted. Widmerpool offends by splitting the categories ("clinical" and "humorous"). But Jeavons does not fall into either of the categories ("romantic or banal, according to how you took it"), and—here more than ever like Gatsby—astonishes by his fidelity to his own norm. Nick once said of Uncle Giles that he had the "determination to be—without adequate moral or intellectual equipment—absolutely different from everybody else" (AW 2). But Jeavons *has* adequate moral equipment. Consider that when Molly met him convalescing, in Chips Lovell's phrase, "The extraordinary thing was they didn't start a love affair or anything" (LM 17). Consider that he felt he had no claim at all on Mildred Blaides, at the time of his week with her *or* twenty years later. As Jeavons looks Nick in the eye and uncreates his categories for him, he conveys the fact that the war *was* a murderous thing, and that the ambulance driver who became his partner for an assuaging week *was* "the Honourable" after all.

To round off Powell's view of Jeavons one must turn to the end of *The Kindly Ones,* where the fact that he married above his social station is revealed as something he has calibrated perfectly. He has no airs and no hesitancies. He can even deliver round aristocratic maxims on the value of retaining, say, one's home-farm.

> To have prefaced this recommendation with the avowal that he himself came from a walk of life where people did not own home-farms would have seemed to Jeavons otiose, wearisome, egotistical. Everything about him, he knew, proclaiming that fact, he would have regarded such personal emphasis as in the worst of taste, as well as being without interest. . . . The notion that he might be trying to pass himself off as a fellow-owner of a home-farm would have seemed to Jeavons laughable.
>
> (KO 234)

The whole exposure to Ted and Molly Jeavons may amount to, in short, a new "upbringing" for Nick, and particularly in this trilogy a character like Jeavons tends to replace Uncle Giles (from whose raffish shadow Nick seems to need to emerge). Where Giles would tend to excuse his own irresponsibilities through a sour grapes attitude that always saw Fate's deck stacked against him, Jeavons in his unegotistical way becomes a kind of pointer to the responsibility-in-escrow, as it might be called, that has always lain in store for Nick. Giles was a kind of beckoner-away from duty; and Giles caused Nick to become far less priggish than he might have been (necessary to the theme of the first trilogy); but Jeavons has the positive effect on him of a man who does not consider his own every move as the first and last thing of interest in his day.

COMMENCEMENT

At Lady Molly's has five sections, and the first and fifth end with the announcement and dissolution of Widmerpool's engagement. The fourth is devoted mainly to Ted Jeavons, but at its end Nick alludes to his own engagement to Isobel Tolland. Powell handles the courtship in a revolutionary way by having Nick report next to nothing about it.

It is not all a question of reticence. Powell simply indicates how in that large family of Tollands (the stepmother being Lady Molly's sister), other events overshadow the engagement of a younger daughter anyhow. The chief one of these concerns two other competitors in this novel: the new young head of the Tolland clan, Lord Warminster (called Erridge by his family, but known to some intimates as Alf); and the old standby Quiggin. Though they put their heads together over left-wing causes, these men compete over Peter Templer's ex–wife Mona.* Erridge's spiriting her off to China becomes the great staple of Tolland coversation; but more than providing for a screen to keep Nick's affairs overshadowed,

---

A thumbnail summary of Erridge in The Kindly Ones *supports indirectly the point made earlier about the lack of torment in the old large families: "Erridge, a rebel whose life had been exasperatingly lacking in persecution, had enjoyed independence of parental control, plenty of money, assured social position, early in life" (KO 205). So he must needs become half a tramp, investigate slums in the north, promise to finance a socialist magazine—all really in the service of his own ego.*

Powell makes the Erridge-Quiggin connection important to Nick by making it responsible for his meeting Isobel.

He meets her in the middle section of the novel in what is, from the point of view of style at least, the most astonishing scene sequence in *The Music of Time*. The second section, leading up to it, had been framed by meetings with Widmerpool and Quiggin. Momentary touches of "the red-hot pincers" nothwithstanding (LM 68), Nick has been able to live unoppressed by the memory of Jean. All the same, a pretty unbuoyant twenty-nine, he owns up to himself on his way from luncheon with Widmerpool: "I tried to persuade myself that the gloom that had descended upon me was induced by Widmerpool's prolonged political dissertations [he thinks Hitler's Germany can be bargained with], but in my heart I knew that its true cause was all this talk of marriage" (LM 65). The end of part two finds him "kicking [his] heels" with a girl in a movie queue, "as if life's co-educational school . . . had come to a sudden standstill . . ." (LM 97). Out from that movie, however, comes J. G. Quiggin. Nick, we recall, works for a filmscript studio. Quiggin invites him to his cottage in the country, having at the back of his mind the chance of Nick's movie contacts leading to some employment for Mona as a bit actress. At least it will divert Mona to talk over such things.

Quiggin makes a mystery, as part three begins, about who owns the cottage (it is Erridge in fact). The result of his evasiveness, and of Erridge's too when he walks in later, is to arouse a certain stubbornness in Nick altogether more overt than his manner had previously allowed. It is a dramatic crux, for instance, that Nick can deliver such sentences as the following, about a publisher crony of Quiggin's: "Poor Craggs, indeed. That just about describes him. He has the most loathsomely oily voice in the whole of Bloomsbury" (LM 110).

Only preliminary, this is still stunningly aggressive, coming from Nick. Absolute magic is going to result from it. The whole theme of *The Music of Time*—that character determines event; that unplanned action forever overturns what is planned; that the will nevertheless must be energized before life can be caught; and that tiny increments from the past (like Nick's state of kicking his heels) lead to the moods that create crises—this entire theme will be driven out in the open by Nick's scorching atypical remark on Craggs, though not only by that of course.

By what else? By the fact that when Erridge enters the cottage, bearded, grubby, and the picture of timidity, Nick notices "that under this burden of shyness he did not care in the least whether he butted in on Quiggin, or on anyone else. What he wanted was his own way" (LM 114-115). Nick's reaction is, "I saw no reason, for my own part, why he should be let off anything. If he lent Quiggin the cottage, he must put up with Quiggin's guests . . ." (LM 118). Therefore Nick obstinately turns the conversation, irritating both Erridge and Quiggin by declaring he has met some of Erridge's family through Lady Molly. Erridge now halts out an invitation to dinner that the secretive Quiggin cannot head Nick off from accepting. The stakes in these exchanges have been trivial —simply the covert will of Quiggin and Erridge opposed to Nick's understandable reluctance to be bypassed as though he were not alive and actually sitting there on a kitchen chair in that cottage of Erridge's. He has no ulterior motive, in other words—but he has broken out of his usual diffidence. And the absolute magic I spoke of is that Nick has now earned his wife and mate and so she appears.

The next night, at Thrubworth, Isobel appears, with her sister Susan, who is herself just engaged. They take their brother Erridge's dinner party by surprise, and cause great resentment in Mona in fact, who had begun her annexation of Erridge at dinner. No one else resents the Tolland girls—except perhaps the curt butler Smith, forced to bring champagne in honor of Susan's engagement. The announcement of this, "planned with great dash," as Nick says, "had not been entirely carried off with the required air of indifference," for first Susan and then Isobel "blush violently . . ." (LM 139). "Violently" has become the adverb of the day, from the moment the girls burst into the room and make its atmosphere change "suddenly, violently. One became all at once aware of the delicious, sparkling proximity of young feminine beings. The room was transformed" (LM 135). Consider the kind of words to be met with now on successive pages: "poetic enchantment" (LM 137), "haphazard," "incalculable," "startling oddness" (LM 138), "suddenly overwhelmed," "violently" (LM 139), "astonished," "daring manoeuvre" (LM 140), "dangerously exciting," "utterly unforeseen" (LM 141), and, on the heels of the "unprecedented" request for champagne, these sentences: "Even so, the shock was terrific. Smith started so violently that the coffee cups rattled on the tray" (LM 142).

There is simply nothing to match this fierce and glowing language anywhere else in Powell, all of it following a paragraph which had begun,

> Would it be too explicit, too exaggerated, to say that when I set eyes on Isobel Tolland, I knew at once that I should marry her?

and which had ended,

> But what—it may reasonably be asked—what about the fact that only a short time before I had been desperately in love with Jean Duport; was still, indeed, not sure that I had been wholly cured? Were the delights and agonies of all that to be tied up with ribbon, so to speak, and thrown into a drawer to be forgotten? What about the girls with whom I seemed to stand nightly in cinema queues? What, indeed?   (LM 136)

In this great scene, even the crotchety Quiggin is transformed. He becomes in his own way a contributor to the surcharged atmosphere—parrying Susan Tolland's quotation from Coleridge with one from, of all poems, *Kubla Khan,* demanding the wine itself that so confounded the dipsomaniac butler Smith. And when Smith at last opens and pours this, it courses out in "a stream of the palest of pale gold, like wine in a fairy story . . ." (LM 146)—the last bottle of champagne in Thrubworth Park.

Quiggin is to have a misadventure himself stemming from this evening; the signs are already in the air, Mona having been reduced to haggardness by the attention paid to these girls. This leads directly to her bolt to China with Erridge. Thus Quiggin and Widmerpool take severe falls in this novel. But the point to make—especially in view of Quiggin's infectious high spirits at the "engagement" party—is the one James Hall makes. "The interesting thing about Quiggin and Widmerpool," says Hall, "is not their failures, though, so much as their honesty and even humanity."[3] As for Nick, all his reticence about his marriage in pages to come in *The Music of Time* is compensated by this one scene that sets the imagination so to work. A famous view of Yeats's is hereby corroborated:

> Even the wisest man grows tense
> With some sort of violence
> Before he can accomplish fate,
> Know his work or choose his mate.[4]

OPPOSITION—FROM A QUITE SEPARATE
ENTITY

If Powell can charge an atmosphere he can certainly uncharge one too, and *drain* is the force underrunning *Casanova's Chinese Restaurant*. When we next see Isobel, for instance, she is allowed two sentences: "How were they all?"—"I shan't be sorry to come home" (CR 97). Here in the second part of the new book, with allusions having been made to the Spanish war and the impending marriage of Edward VIII, we are brought to 1936, and Isobel, now married two years to Nick, has had a miscarriage.

Meeting Moreland at the hospital, where Moreland's wife is in labor, causes Nick to acquiesce in paying a call on the music critic Maclintick in Pimlico—an errand of mercy, in a sense, because this man's wife is *not* in the hospital. The Maclinticks live in a dwelling "threatened by a row of mean shops advancing from one end of the street and a fearful slum crowding up from the other" (CR 107); the seeming aggressiveness of those participles anticipates the mood of Audrey Maclintick, forever accusing even the elements themselves for the marriage situation that is festering her life away.

Thus to come from Thrubworth in the middle of *At Lady Molly's* to Pimlico in the middle of this novel is to come from "wine in a fairy story" to the beverage Maclintick uses to check his wife's tongue—"the slight 'pop' of [the cork's] emergence appearing to embody the material of a reply to his wife, at least all the reply he intended to give" (CR 110). And that is only the beginning.

Though critics have often said *Casanova's Chinese Restaurant* has one great scene—the one where Stringham "snake-charms" Mrs. Maclintick at a party[5]—I believe the deliberate draining effect of the novel makes them feel this way and that the other scenes are as excellent in their way; that the one in question now might be as original as any of Powell's and probably as hard to write as any. "Opposition" having been set up, in this trilogy, in the uncanny institution of marriage, Powell has depressed the register of his language here as he had elevated it accordingly in the violent "commencement" scene.

At the Maclinticks' house, all actions seem to derive from a continuous dull smoulder, something encountered there no matter what time the house is entered. So Moreland, entering, and avoiding an eye-to-eye meeting with Audrey, "spoke a few desultory words about the weather, then made for the bookcase"; and Maclintick, coming downstairs, greets Nick and Moreland and "Without saying more, he made straight for a cupboard from which he took bottles and glasses" (CR 109, 110). Audrey, in her turn a little later, "now made for the basement, telling us she would shout in due course an invitation to descend" (CR 114). The headlong quality of that repeated verb phrase tells a good deal about nerves in this place, and by the end of dinner everyone is on his feet and Audrey has accused her husband of a final contemptibleness—incompetence as a critic: ". . . sitting upstairs messing about with a lot of stuff that is really out of your reach—that you are not quite up to"—that is her style (CR 121-122). Present during this scene is the uncouth musician, Carolo, with whom Audrey will run off at the novel's end; he scribbles music in a corner while the others dine. But "dine" is not Powell's word, for note again how, by modulation of diction, he achieves sordidness without recourse to heavy-handedness. "He often meals with us," says Mrs. Maclintick (CR 113); whereas Maclintick has a standing objection "to their lodger working while he and his wife were making a meal . . ." (CR 115).

Powell makes a vicious transparent texture through this treatment, though not only in this section. When Mrs. Maclintick says "The place gives me the pip" (CR 117), she echoes a chance phrase from much earlier, used by Barnby to describe Moreland's bad luck with an actress. "The girl had a headache that night—curse, too, I expect," says Barnby (CR 7). Realism, yes—the aim here being to invite attention to the residuals inseparable from womanhood (similarly a physician's pompous equation of "abortion" and "miscarriage" causes these words to be repeated and repeated). The opening paragraph of the novel, which drew an incisive comment from Arthur Mizener, works in the same direction. It describes a door left standing in the cavity made by a direct bomb hit on a pub called the Mortimer (from which description Powell will cut back to early days at the Mortimer):

> Walls on both sides were shrunk away, but along its lintel, in niggling copybook handwriting, could still be distinguished the word *Ladies*. Beyond, on the far side of the twin pillars and crossbar, nothing whatever remained of that promised retreat, the threshold falling steeply to an abyss of rubble. . . .
>
> (CR 1)

Says Mizener, "If such a world ever possessed 'ladies,' its promise of a retreat for them was surely false, and the vulgar elegance of the promise has, without losing its absurdity, become somehow pathetic since brutal violence has so ludicrously exposed its coy refinement."[6]

"Brutal violence" points toward the force that, looming on the horizon, will bring the second trilogy to equilibrium in *The Kindly Ones;* and Powell's opening juxtaposition of war and *"Ladies"* extends a theme already alluded to through General Conyers, that the handling of women (or being mishandled by them) is a microcosm of war. As for the exposé of "coy refinement," the second trilogy, like the first, had started with the magnetizing of Nick toward correctness and the *retenu* associated with noble families.

The problem is not that Nick needs safeguarding from snobbery; that battle has already been won. It is rather that the more people try to filter and refine their way of taking the world, the more they will be forced to take it in straight, unsavory doses. The toughness of the Tolland clan, for example, has been attested; yet Nick's mother-in-law, who writes biographies of forceful women, has a manner about her which almost necessitates that women's rest rooms be summoned into unhallowed view. In Lady Warminster's drawing room, says Nick, anything might be said,

> though nothing indecorous discussed openly. Layer upon layer of wrapping, box after box revealing in the Chinese manner yet another box, must conceal all doubtful secrets; only the discipline of infinite obliquity made it lawful to examine the seamy side of life. If these mysteries were observed everything might be contemplated: however unsavoury: however unspeakable.   (LM 211)

Charles Stringham's mother is another such woman. She is especially an arch manipulator of husbands. In *Casanova's Chinese Restaurant* she will meet her taskmaster in the hermaphroditic little dancer Norman Chandler. The point of mentioning Stringham's mother is that the most significant artifact in the novel, a reproduction of *Truth Unveiled by Time,* was discovered by Chandler and comes to rest almost accusingly in Mrs. Foxe's drawing room (where the great scene actuated by her son Stringham will take place).

Of this Bernini reproduction Mr. Deacon once remarked that "in the original marble Bernini has made the wench look as unpalatable as the heartless quality she represents" (CR 13). The observation ties in with other "unveilings" that characterize the texture of this novel. Two last ones may be mentioned—the first to show that Powell can treat grossly a respectable work of art, when the occasion demands. He describes, in Bronzino's *Venus, Cupid, Folly, and Time,* how "Time in the background, whiskered like the Emperor Franz-Josef, looms behind a blue curtain as if evasively vacating the bathroom" (CR 16). It may seem, in these early pages, that the reminders of temporal "necessities" are getting positively Swiftian. But when Powell does expose a toilet, although the color of what enters it will be right, the liquid itself will be one euphemistic grade away: in this case an undrinkable tawny port that Moreland is flushing (it is his first appearance in *The Music of Time*). What Moreland is saying counts heavily meanwhile:

> "If you were legally allowed three wives," asked Moreland, as we watched the cascade of amber foam gush noisily away, "whom would you choose?"   (CR 6)

It is one of Powell's greatest juxtapositions.

The first section of *Casanova's Chinese Restaurant* contains a flashback to the time of *A Buyer's Market,* when Nick first met Mr. Deacon and through him Barnby and Moreland. In the 1936 setting of the later sections, the action commences with the hospital meeting of the two young husbands. Widmerpool having opted out of the marriage market, and Stringham's union having collapsed from inanition, it is Moreland and the other new character Maclintick whose trials reflect the indigestibleness of matrimony symbolized by the title. The first section, moving forward from 1929 to 1933, introduces Matilda Wilson, an actress and once a Magnus Donners girl, whom Moreland marries. The section ends with Nick's announcement of his own wedding a year later (1934—the same year as Powell's own).

For Nick, marriage represents opposition more through its mysterious restrictions than anything else—the restriction on seeing friends for instance. In the later sections Nick and Moreland drift apart, even though their wives get along very well together, simply because of marriage's tendency to drive itself between friends by appropriating most, if not all, intimacies.

Matilda, like Moreland, is a winning character and has a temperament similar to his—a gift for the arts, intellectual penetration, real consideration for others. She seems such a fine match for Moreland because of her everyday efficiency, and even the loss of their child, who does not live a day, is not as destructive as another novelist might have made it. What undoes them is their lack of affinity for the marriage state itself.

It is Moreland, not Matilda, who is badly hurt when their partnership finally breaks (in *The Kindly Ones*). In *Casanova's Chinese Restaurant* it nears collapse but is righted temporarily

by Moreland, because of the tremendous emotional shock de
livered to him by Maclintick's suicide. Yet well before·this, something virtually constitutional in each partner warns that they
cannot stay together. At the beginning of a long and revealing
conversation Nick has with Matilda, in part three, she asks,

> "Is it fun to be married to anyone?"
>
> "That is rather a big question. If you admit that fun exists
> at all—perhaps you don't—you cannot lay it down categorically
> that no married people get any fun from the state of being
> married."
>
> "But I mean *married* to someone," said Matilda, speaking
> quite passionately. "Not to sleep with them, or talk to them, or
> go about with them. To be *married* to them. I have been mar-
> ried a couple of times and I sometimes begin to doubt it."
>
> (CR 157)

For his part Moreland squirms over the same nebulous draining quality attached to the word itself. Of his wife's pregnancy
he says,

> "Matilda has not been at all easy to deal with since it started.
> Of course, I know that is in the best possible tradition. All the
> same, it makes one wonder, with Maclintick, how long one will
> be able to remain married. No, I don't mean that exactly. It is
> not that I am any less fond of Matilda, so much as that mar-
> riage—this quite separate entity—somehow comes between us.
> However, I expect things will be all right as soon as the baby
> arrives. Forgive these morbid reflections. I should really write
> them for the Sunday papers, get paid a huge fortune for it and
> receive an enormous fan-mail. The fact is, I am going through
> one of those awful periods when I cannot work. You know what
> hell that is."   (CR 123)

The way Moreland turns his words against himself, as with
this "Sunday papers" flourish, is one of the endearing things about
him. He would eschew melodrama any time. Yet that is precisely
part of his fix. For he is greatly sensitive to the daily non-profes-
sional thing he may run into: is prone to react to small things with
deep disturbance. He is immensely winning in the way he can dis-

pose of *some* annoyances, but these are in his professional sphere
—as when, at the nursing home with Nick, he will not scruple to
break decorum when their doctor pens them in with fatuous
musical pronouncements. "Moreland disengaged us brutally from
him" (CR 104). (Nick would have waited that doctor out.)

But Moreland is more likely to tread water when a challenge or
an upset does not offend him professionally. What is wanting, despite the characters' belittling in the novel of Don Juan and even
of that better man Casanova himself—what is wanting on Moreland's part is the ability to exercise power in his marriage.

Since power is such a dangerous thing, generally, in *The Music
of Time*, it is difficult to reconcile the distrust of it felt behind the
fabric of the novel with the clear need for it to function in marriage. Yet that need *is* clear. In *At Lady Molly's* Nick says roundly
that "Marriage . . . is a form of action, of violence almost: an assertion of the will" (LM 203). "Hardly a *sine qua non* of action,"
says Moreland as though in answer two books later. (Though the
exchange is set in *The Kindly Ones*, it comes early in his and
Nick's friendship.) "But a testing experience, surely," says Nick,
refusing to be moved (KO 77).

In his bones Moreland seems to recognize the truth of Nick's
words, as when before his wedding he and Nick go to see Matilda
in *The Duchess of Malfi*. "He shuddered slightly when she replied
to Bosola's lines: 'Know you me, I am a blunt soldier,' with: 'The
better; sure there wants fire where there are no lively sparks of
roughness' " (CR 45). At dinner after this performance one of
Moreland's own great moments arrives; unfortunately its sparks
of roughness are struck at the expense of music critics rather than
lovers. *Tamburlaine the Great* being mentioned, Moreland roars
out in a startling way, " 'Holla, ye pampered jades of Asia. What,
can ye draw but twenty miles a day?' " He goes on to postulate
himself hauled in triumph to concerts: "I should like to be
dragged along by all the music critics, arranged in order of height,
tallest in front, midgets at the back. That will give you some clue
to what the procession would look like. I have always been interested in Tamerlaine." (Yet just at this point cold water is
thrown by Moreland's wife-to-be, Matilda—a dangerous fore-

shadowing: "You may be interested in Tamerlaine, darling," she says, "but you are not in the least interested in my career" [CR 55].)

Maclintick's almost dog-like fidelity to Moreland seems to ask for this kind of outburst; at the same time, Moreland will make this up to Maclintick with a great example of humanity later. But the sad thing is that this real access of power can be stimulated in Moreland only by art, where his roots penetrate. At least sometimes, Powell insinuates, this kind of divine whip-cracking is needed in marriage.

Maclintick remains the most convincing defaulter from power, unable to bring any sort to bear anywhere. He can't decide what restaurant to go to, so goes with the others to Casanova's though he dislikes it; he protests hatred of fine clothes and fine parties, yet goes to the one Mrs. Foxe gives for Moreland, in ill-got-up evening clothes, capable only of being obnoxious. This sort of impotence (not sexual), magnified through daily susceptibility to it, will cause his suicide.

I suppose the only resolution of the question lies in the comment made earlier with respect to the thirties' novels—that Powell, still distrusting power when it is "programmed," continues to sense times when the instinct to power must be yielded to, and molds those occasions that offer themselves to be molded. Either a man accepts the invitation to power then, or else he suffers the consequences of reneging.

Insofar as this is an exterior kind of power that needs demonstrating—especially over women—no scene in the novel bears out the contention better than its most celebrated one. Charles Stringham arrives drunk at a party his mother gives in honor of a symphony by Hugh Moreland. One of the first things Stringham does is captivate Mrs. Maclintick. He calls her "Little Bo-Peep" because of the idiotic frock in which she is dressed, and from this point on he has her under his thumb—absolutely transformed from virago to coquette. As Nick says, "I saw at once that this must be the right way to treat her; that a deficiency of horseplay on the part of her husband and his friends was probably the cause of her endemic sulkiness" (CR 167) .

It is hard to say what is achieved through this power. Its spontaneousness is of course essential.* Capturing Audrey Maclintick, Stringham then goes on to capture Moreland too, through his eloquent discourse on marriage. But when in this discourse Stringham indicates that what he objects to is not "the active bad behaviour" in marriage, the idea of exterior power displayed by one partner over the other must be seen as only a partial answer to the problem of marriage. Such power could control active behavior, certainly, but as Stringham says, "What broke me was the passive resistance. That was what got me down" (CR 176). And it is with words like these that his monologue takes greatest effect, approaching the consolation of art, in fact, so far as his listeners are concerned: for Moreland and the others "seemed to be finding some release from themselves, and their individual lives, in what was being said" (CR 179).

When Evelyn Waugh reviewed this novel, he paid due tribute to this scene but asked a searching question about the "quite separate entity" of marriage:

> How do they [Powell's characters] distinguish the relationship from other forms of concubinage? That they do make a distinction is apparent from the gravity with which they discuss it, but Mr. Powell gives no hint of its origin and character. Is it purely superstitious and atavistic?[7]

Certainly the irrationality, in Powell, connected with the planning and entering of marriage, makes those last adjectives of Waugh's appropriate. I would say, without pretending to get around them—but with Stringham's relief-bringing information on the subject fresh in mind—that a temptation to jeopardize oneself is involved, and that if this is atavism it is a moral type of it. In other words, besides the sporadic exterior power that Nick has alluded to, there also comes up, due to the nature of the marriage state, an interior power struggle undergone by each

---

*Hall's comment is a telling one: "Stringham charms Mrs. Maclintick by a simple offhand assumption of power to do so." (The Tragic Comedians, p. 148.)

partner singly. Since in the emancipated 1930s the husband is not in charge and each partner becomes his or her own moral taskmaster, the jeopardy is that of allowing one's own worst self to come to the fore. In *A Buyer's Market* "opposition" came up through sexual diffidence in view of the prospect of humiliation and entanglement—as though one's best self were jeopardized. With the legal holds offered through marriage, the danger is more now that of the liberation of selfish instincts. "Love-hate" remains but there is a shift of perspective. Thus part of the power struggle is not related to the other partner but reserved within oneself. The occasions any marriage offers for taking righteous revenge are alone enough to indicate this. A broken Moreland, at the end of *The Kindly Ones,* says that "One of the worst things about life is not how nasty the nasty people are. You know that already. It is how nasty the nice people can be" (KO 246). In saying this about Matilda he not only makes us think of his own lack of power in marriage, but also of such an utterance as Matilda's passionate "I mean *married* to someone": her dread of her own worst self lying under her perplexity.

The scene with Stringham at his mother's house offers views of both kinds of power at once. It indicates the significance of exterior power because Stringham does temporarily dominate the situation. But whatever consolation Stringham could pass on to those listening to him was based on his own interior failure, by dint of which he could attest so eloquently to the passive drains of marriage. Not only has his own marriage been ruined; the rub is that even now he is interrupted short of spiriting Mrs. Maclintick off to one of his haunts. He is prevented by his mother's ex-secretary, Miss Weedon, who has become virtually his keeper in the upstairs rooms at Lady Molly's. His relatives have all but incarcerated him there for alcoholism. And the assuagement Stringham has offered Mrs. Maclintick doesn't carry past the event. "Stringham had made no great impression on her," says Powell in a remorseless sentence at the party's conclusion (CR 186).

Before Stringham's arrival in this long third section at Mrs. Foxe's, Nick had a talk with Matilda and learned of serious trouble in her and Moreland's marriage. His feelings became engaged on behalf of Moreland—and for Stringham in his turn—in a new way. In the corresponding early book, *A Buyer's Market,* the Andriadis party had seemed to demand some response from Nick on his own behalf.*

What has happened is that Moreland has become involved with Nick's sister-in-law Priscilla Tolland. Nick had looked the other way at the first implicating sign (when he learned—on the page where the "Love-Duty" theme phrase came up—that Moreland had given Priscilla a ticket to his symphony). Why Nick had connived, thrown up a "smoke-screen" before Isobel for example, poses one question for us to explore, and how he reacts when Matilda forces him to face the fact poses another.

"But why should a smoke-screen be required?" (CR 138). The answer is: because of his genuine liking for all the parties concerned, and his not *wishing* to see happen what apparently will happen to this fine adjunct couple, the Morelands. Furthermore, the Love-Duty tension is an unresolved one because of something underlying the whole ethos of English society as caught and rendered by Powell: in this society one sanction operates distinctly: *no one shall be condemned for pursuing Love:* and meanwhile, at its heart but never so openly acknowledged, the sense of Duty remains forever nailed. Hence the smoke-screen. "In the end I convinced myself," says Nick (CR 183), that nothing was afoot, but he is to have no such luck at staying clear of the situation.

As Matilda begins allusively to broach this issue and Nick suddenly feels "as if ice-cold water were dripping . . . down my spine" (CR 155), it is not only that he goes through discomfort for More-

---

Incidentally, Mrs. Foxe asks his aid in getting Stringham off her premises, just as Mrs. Andriadis asked him to keep Stringham on hers, a point noted by Nick with a pang and·helping to link these middle books. When they end with the ominous references to Russian billiards and the ghost railway ride, the emphasis in the second instance is on the two *friends, Moreland and Nick, riding down the roller coaster "together," and moving "with dreadful, ever increasing momentum toward a shape that lay across the line" (CR 229).*

land's and Priscilla's sake. The problem of dignity arises here as well. Where earlier that problem rose up as an impediment to personal advance ("in those days, [it was a] choice between dignity and unsatisfied curiosity" [QU 130]), here the factor of dignity counts for more, because this business of marriage has such legitimacy in its claims. Offenses within it do not affect the self-esteem of just one person (as was the case all through the first trilogy). So as Matilda continues to tell Nick things, it is on her behalf in turn that he checks himself, where to have done the same in the first trilogy would have been a sign of regression. Their conversation provides one of the most telling announcements of the scales tipping in favor of Duty in *The Music of Time*. The substance of it is that Matilda has made some references to her past as Magnus Donners's "girl"; then swung round to her double concern of the moment, her husband and her husband's music. "I longed to hear more about Sir Magnus Donners," says Nick.

> However, the moment to acquire such information, the moment for such frivolities, if it had ever existed, was now past. The tone had become too serious. I could not imagine what the next revelation would be; certainly nothing so light-hearted as a first-hand account of a millionaire's sexual fantasies.
>
> (CR 159–160)

And now Nick has to hear what he has been avoiding. He typically admits he deserved this—but given his observant nature, it comes across all the more as the measure of his friendship when he shows how he has hooded his eyes.

> "And now [says Matilda] he has gone and fallen in love with your sister-in-law, Priscilla."
> "But——"
> Matilda laughed at the way in which I failed to find any answer. There was really nothing for me to say. If it was true, it was true. From one point of view, I felt it unjust that I should be visited in this manner with Matilda's mortification; from another, well deserved, in that I had not already acquainted myself with what was going on round me.   (CR 160)

Nick's embarrassment is acute and undergone of course on behalf of his friend Moreland. Moreland deserves to be felt for in this way, for though he cannot preserve a marriage where Nick evidently can, Moreland has something further to teach Nick about friendship.

In the last section of the novel, the abandonment of Maclintick by his wife leads Moreland to take Nick back into "a pocket in time," a visit to the suicidal Maclintick. Maclintick holds himself together and their talk throws back to "the days of the Mortimer and Casanova's Chinese Restaurant" (CR 216), framing the novel, in fact. There are even some moments of laughter (but berserk laughter—Maclintick is unreclaimable). It may be his professional stymie rather than his marital one that has been most hampering. Powell (through Moreland) has made it clear that Maclintick has a real affinity for good music, is devoted to it, can *recognize* it: yet as a critic is unable in the world to make good on these gifts. (Maclintick has been sacked by his paper, and cannot finish his book.) The corrosion that results could be inferred as the great cause for the man's inability to indulge in what was seen to be so important before—horseplay. Nothing that Moreland can do can allay this grinding down process.

But during this last section two final insights are given into Moreland's character. "He was a person," says Nick,

> not well equipped to deal with human troubles. . . . He also lacked that subjective, ruthless love of presiding over other people's affairs which often makes basically heartless people adept at offering effective consolation. . . . In short, nothing but true compassion for Maclintick's circumstances could have brought Moreland to the house that night. It was an act of friendship of some magnitude.   (CR 206)

Indecisive, unable to be ruthless, Moreland has no mission he can complete at Maclintick's, but does have one when his friend takes his life three days later: no less than releasing Priscilla Tolland from a deathy world. Two hundred pages earlier Nick had referred to "that professionally musical world which, towards the

end of his life, so completely engulfed him" (CR 9), and now at
Moreland's unmistakable hint that he will break off with Priscilla,
Nick reverts to similar phrasing.

> "But what are you explaining to me?"
> "That any rumours you hear in future can be given an un-
> qualified denial."
> "I see."
> "Forgive my bluntness."
> "It suits you."
> "I hope I have made myself clear." . . .
> "And [Priscilla] thinks the same?"
> "Yes."
> I too could see what he meant. At least I thought I could.
> Moreland meant that Maclintick, in doing away with himself,
> had drawn attention, indeed heavily underlined, the conditions
> of life to which Moreland himself was inexorably committed;
> a world to which Priscilla did not yet belong, even if she were
> on her way to belonging there.   (CR 220)

It is a grand and profound gesture, especially as we are to learn
(in *The Kindly Ones*) that Moreland was "crazy about her," and
that he and Priscilla had never slept together.

"Forgive my bluntness." There is something heroic here. It is
of course the bluntness of negative determination—an instance,
one notes, of interior rather than exterior force. Powell's favorite
American writer, Scott Fitzgerald, was almost in the same year (in
his case, 1935) in a circumstance similar to Moreland's. A few
words in a letter Fitzgerald wrote to break off an incipient affair—
while Zelda was in a sanatorium—contain the explanation of
Moreland's action after the suicide, and, oddly enough, the seeds
also of Nick's own first feelings, his smoke-screen, trying to hold
knowledge off. To the young woman Fitzgerald wrote, "There are
emotions just as important as ours running concurrently with
them—and there is literally no standard in life other than a sense
of duty. When people get mixed up they try to throw out a sort of
obscuring mist, and then the sharp shock of a *fàct*—a collision
seems to be the only thing to make them sober-minded again."[8]
It was Maclintick's death which provided the sobering collision

for Moreland. He had to be a man of some magnitude, all the same, to give a person he loved a release from an orbit he could have kept her in.

MEN OF ENGLAND, TRIPLE-TEAMED

Anthony Powell's novels never become overwhelmingly symbolical or allegorical, and perhaps because his women seem linked in symbolical roles in *The Kindly Ones,* he provides in this novel a few pointers toward the pure materialism that may lie behind many of their actions. If the first two sections reach their high moments because deranged women bring events to a standstill, the last two sections conclude with non-deranged women homing in on profits: Myra Erdleigh is discovered, at Uncle Giles's cremation, to be his only beneficiary; Matilda Moreland has returned to Sir Magnus Donners, with expectations of becoming Lady Donners. As if in confirmation of materialistic motives, Powell offers us Isobel Jenkins's word—for instance when she tells Nick, "Matty rather likes talking of her [early] days with Sir Magnus if one is *tête-à-tête.* They represent, I think, the most restful moment of her life" (KO 89).

All of which may merely prove that there are more ways than one to be a Fury.

In *The Kindly Ones,* women become Furies—avengers, Eumenides—in three ways really. Or, since a Powell critic once held that "The women exist more for the men than in their own right,"[9] we might say that men are exposed to assault on three fronts. Metaphysically, as well as publicly and privately, Powell suggests the operation of forces, combined and unstoppable, that wreak vengeance on faults in civilized life and in so doing define the first-half boundaries of *The Music of Time.* The 1914 War is spawned as part one of *The Kindly Ones* ends; the 1939 War as part four ends.

Nick Jenkins is living at Stonehurst near the military base of Aldershot in part one. He is eight years old; we meet his parents now and discover that the combination in Nick of rational skepticism and open-mindedness derive in part from his father and mother (the former basically a logical positivist, the latter intuitive and ready to credit many happenings to mystic causes). In two jumps of fifteen and ten years, the second section develops Nick's friendship with Moreland and leads to a scene at Sir Magnus Donners's, set sometime after the Munich crisis of 1938. The last two quarters of the novel cover the year or so remaining of peacetime. Pressures of augmenting disaster are felt in every section, but more lingeringly in the later ones since part one deals all at once with the 1914 situation and the bringing of Nick's childhood "suddenly, even rather brutally, to a close" (KO 74).

Besides the efficiency of opening the sextet's last volume with a setting antedating all other material so far, there is also another good reason for the rapid and then slow approaches to the two framing wars. As Nick says, 1938 was "a decidedly eerie period in which to be living. Unlike the Stonehurst epoch, when . . . war had come for most people utterly without warning . . . war was now materialising in slow motion. Like one of the Stonehurst 'ghosts,' war towered by the bed when you awoke in the morning . . . a looming, menacing shape of ever greater height, ever thickening density" (KO 86–87).

Those "ghosts" mentioned have bearing on the general psychic disturbance in 1914 and take us back to the tripartite origin of the Furies, as Powell seems to be adumbrating this. The parlormaid at Stonehurst, Billson, is most susceptible to its notorious ghosts, and they seem partly the cause of her breakdown, taking startling dramatic form on the day that the Archduke Franz-Ferdinand is assassinated in Bosnia.

Lest it be thought these ghosts are just gratuitous, it ought to be said that near Stonehurst dwells an all-too-material man who is metaphysically unsound—a tamperer with diet, a magician, a leader of an infatuated cult supported mainly by females. Billson once donated a cake to this Dr. Trelawney's cause, an event that brought on some disgruntlement in the kitchen at Stonehurst. This in turn led to her seeing a ghost. Actually, in introducing us to the Jenkinses' haunted house, Powell brings in three important new male characters, Trelawney's presence felt from outside. Inside are the soldier-servant, Bracey, devoted to Nick's father, but otherwise daunted by the treacheries of soldiers; and the cook, Albert, devoted to Nick's mother, but daunted otherwise by the aggressions of women.*

I believe these men seed the air for the Furies in three different ways, though Powell does not deal with them in any such cut-and-dried fashion as my remarks may suggest. Bracey sulks in a kind of public and Albert in a kind of private depression, and their paranoia maddens Billson at last, since she and they form a triangle. (She wants Albert, Bracey wants her.) This triangle could well have been as allegorical as Sartre's in *No Exit*, which it resembles, yet comes across in a realistic way. Structurally speaking, it is as though Powell, by having Trelawney in the wings, has created the sense of there being something wrong in the very air in 1914. The keyword used throughout is "uneasy," especially when Nick dreams about Trelawney. In the meantime, Powell can lead up to national and domestic crises in more prosaic, step-by-step fashion, through the record of the Billson-Albert-Bracey affair. As Melvin Maddocks has said of this book, "It is a superb stroke by Mr. Powell that he probes the first cracks in the trembling structure—and the first portents of world madness—in the settings of kitchen and stable."[10]

Realism predominates because kitchen and stable contain so much intense life to eight-year-old Nick, who is always on hand with his trip-hammer questions. He learns that Albert puts up shutters in the stables out of fear of suffragettes. At the Aldershot parade ground, he is shown a self-mutilated soldier by Bracey. Such fear-inflicted behavior "by no means entirely repelled me," he says; "on the contrary, [it] provided an additional touch of uneasy excitement." At which point, near the parade ground, "A bugle, shrill, yet desperately sad, sounded far away down the lines" (KO 26).

Trelawney seems contemptuous of the mundane world and its drives for security, yet is once seen registering a parcel for mailing—an early and funny sign of his own dependency which is doubled on much later when he needs hypodermic boosts. As he falls to his foe, the world, so does Bracey, who is killed in action, and so does Albert, who is caught and managed by a wife.

With such a forlorn call to attention coming on the heels of
Nick's attraction to self-protective devices, we have a little
paradigm of the first movement of *The Music of Time:* the uneasy slide from duty to dissipation. Playing at war on the fringes
of the Stonehurst grounds, Nick has yet another anticipation of
striking out in pure individualism—a necessary thing, and yet the
great problem of so many in the series who remain self-committed.
The sentence that results is one of the most moving in all of *The
Music of Time:*

> Here, among these woods and clearings, sand and fern, silence
> and the smell of pine brought a kind of release to the heart,
> together with a deep-down wish for something, something more
> than battles, perhaps not battles at all; something realised,
> even then, as nebulous, blissful, all but unattainable: a feeling
> of uneasiness, profound and oppressive, yet oddly pleasurable at
> times, at other times so painful as to be almost impossible to
> bear.   (KO 9)

The shifts after the predicate of this sentence ("brought a kind
of release to the heart") do not permit that release to last any time
at all; they combine incompatibles just as all through his work
Powell combines them, but especially when private, boyhood-of-
Cyrus feelings are allowed to lead the way: producing love and
hate, anxiety in the midst of delight.

For this reason—that loyalty to something beyond the self is the
only way of quelling that uneasy mixture of feelings—the figure
who must pass on in *The Kindly Ones* is the one who has been
Nick's older surrogate all along, Uncle Giles. It is he who arrives
at Nick's house the day of Billson's disaster, to announce the news
of the archduke's assassination. To start the third part of the
novel, where Nick's own circumstances are concerned (as opposed
to the general settling-in of the Furies in the second part), the
watershed event will be Giles's death.

Billson for her part had done nothing less than enter the
Jenkinses' drawing-room naked, to hand in her notice. She had
learned that day that Albert had been trapped into marriage; she
had seen the ghost that morning. It is an astonishing scene, told in
retrospect because Nick was not there to see it. Nick's mother

thought the end of the world had come, and could not act; his father was stunned like Mr. Passenger of old, in this instant "that summarised, in the unclothed figure of Billson, human lack of co-ordination and abandonment of self-control in the face of emotional misery" (KO 59). Their guest General Conyers did act to save the day, putting a shawl from the piano round Billson and leading her out. "The point, I repeat," says Nick, "was that action had been taken, will-power brought into play. The spell cast by Billson's nakedness was broken. Life was normal again" (KO 61).

Conyers a few pages later can parallel this by driving Dr. Trelawney good-naturedly off the grounds. (Trelawney had attempted some proselytizing, but the General—who amazingly knows the key Trelawney slogans—tells him he has a premonition that he should not commit himself to Oneness just at this time.) "Off you go now—at the double," says the General (KO 68). And Giles's arrival bears out the General's premonition. But Giles's information about the archduke immediately widens the scale of diabolism and madness, and is not the sort that can be acted on in an instant. Conyers can do no more than recognize the fact of a World War that is to be.

Dr. Trelawney is not allowed to be forgotten as the second section of *The Kindly Ones* begins, because we are informed, from some of Moreland's conversation, that he too had had "a precocious awareness" of the magician in childhood (KO 82). In one of his remarks a coupling is made that will bear on the end of section two: "There was talk of nameless rites, drugs, disagreeable forms of discipline—the sort of thing that might rather appeal to Sir Magnus Donners" (KO 84).

This part of the novel soon moving forward to 1938, Nick visits the Morelands at a cottage provided them by Donners. In *At Lady Molly's* a cottage had been lent to Quiggin and Mona, and Mona had run off with the donor, Erridge. Thus portents arise and cause the reader some anguish. Though the nearby Stourwater is not so authentic as Thrubworth ("Nobody warned me it was made of cardboard," says Isobel Jenkins [KO 106]), one fears that property-power may prevail again—and one more cataclysmic scene is now laid there. In it Betty Templer, Peter's afflicted wife, becomes the Fury replacing Billson. She moans like a dog when Peter, one of seven guests of Donners, mimes the sin of Lust in front of the great tapestry, before which Donners has photographed his whole party pantomiming the Deadly Sins. (The Morelands and Jenkinses are in this party, the seventh "sinner" being Donners's current girl, Anne Umfraville.)

There are similarities between the Stonehurst and Stourwater crises, but the differences are more important.* For all their un-preparedness, one has a sense of the greater recuperability of the people at Stonehurst: there the Furies strike because of emotions long pent-up, whereas at Stourwater they descend through the fouler air of used-up passions. Another way of saying this is that, with Donners replacing Trelawney as a somewhat less concen-trated spirit behind events, the one who arrives on the scene to divert everyone from Betty's collapse—and wearing a uniform no less—is Widmerpool, grotesque stand-in for General Conyers. Widmerpool has been up to now a pacifist and Hitler-truster. Even now—after Munich—he is most concerned with business exigencies, assisting Donners in a project of cornering the chro-mite market. (The uniform is rather factitious—he has just been to a Territorials' meeting.) Moved to compare the two episodes on the spot, Nick says that

> This was all the same kind of thing. Betty wanted Templer's love, just as Billson wanted Albert's; Albert's marriage had pre-cipitated a breakdown in just the same way as Templer's extrav-agances with Anne Umfraville. Here, unfortunately, was no General Conyers to take charge of the situation. . . .
>
> (KO 133)

So far as the scene's relevance to the second war is concerned, part of the slow-motion horror of that war's arrival is caught in the fact that no one is able to meet situations, since certain greeds

---

*The Stone *and* water *in the names may not be accidental, any more than are the solid and fluid connotations of* Moreland *and* Widmerpool. *"Nar-cissus-like," says W. D. Quesenbery, "the men of Will are associated with water." ("Anthony Powell: The Anatomy of Decay," Critique, VII [Spring 1964], 13.) Powell doesn't make a program out of this sort of thing but there certainly are some sporadic examples.*

have been operating for so long and halving English society. Thus this symbolic breakdown, touched off by Peter Templer's compulsive philandering, is not attended to as the previous one had been. Betty Templer is neglected (having got to her room under her own power), and a ridiculous shift occurs as Widmerpool, almost feminine he is so spruce, engrosses Donners in business talk. Though the two shake hands as Conyers and Trelawney had, there is this difference: at Stonehurst Conyers (the *soldier*) had been inside and had taken charge, whereas at Stourwater it is Donners (the *magician*) who is running things, and not failing "to extract a passing thrill of pleasure from Betty Templer's *crise*"—Widmerpool or no Widmerpool (KO 133).

Immune from shock here himself, Widmerpool will meet his own persecutor at the novel's end, when war has come. This is Gypsy Jones, the communist scamp who had brought him into disgrace in *A Buyer's Market*. He is almost goose-stepping along in self-importance when he and Nick encounter her, broadcasting from a soapbox, and the recognition overpowers Widmerpool—so much so that Nick is forced to admit, "I had myself shown lack of feeling in treating so lightly his former love for Gypsy Jones" (KO 229). It is another instance of the past taking a savage swipe, and Nick has by now had his share of that in this novel.

Why Nick is with Captain Widmerpool at the end is interesting. With war declared, Nick has been chafing to get into active service and goes to see Conyers, now immensely aged, to find whether the General can expedite his call-up. The General says to try a junior officer. An extravagant shock awaits Nick: he now hears that the widowed General has decided to remarry. "I had just enough control not to laugh aloud" (KO 212). It would have been worse for him if he had. The spinster chosen turns out to be Miss Weedon, Stringham's old guardian and one of the most formidable women in *The Music of Time*. But, says Nick of the General, "If he could handle Billson naked, he could probably handle Miss Weedon clothed—or naked, too, if it came to that. I felt admiration for his energy, his determination to cling to life. There was nothing defeatist about him" (KO 217). With these sentences the action of *The Kindly Ones* has come full circle. The nuclear Billson event has now been mentioned near the end of every subsequent section: to conclude the Betty Templer episode; to conclude section three as Nick dreams that Trelawney has made Billson pregnant (KO 199); and now at Nick's visit to Conyers's flat.

But there is a crucial difference here. It may be observed that every woman with a sizable role in *The Kindly Ones* is a Fury (except Nick's wife and his mother), until we reach this dangerous person Miss Weedon. And she had been a Fury in *Casanova's Chinese Restaurant.* (Not only that, but it looks as though she will resume a retributive role with the new husband she acquires after Conyers's death in *The Military Philosophers* [MP 151].) But Conyers deserves no "kindly one." He was a rake in youth but an exemplary husband after marrying the first Mrs. Conyers. And even if, as Nick often thinks, Conyers would as soon break or kill a man as look at him, it would all be done in the spirit of what was needed by the situation, not what General Conyers personally required. So a woman who has actually been fearsome is dismissed from the Furies' roster by Powell. It is quite a marvelous touch, achieved by Nick's remembering an allusion Moreland had employed when Miss Weedon had commandeered Stringham in the earlier book. The allusion is inappropriate at Conyers's flat. For "Miss Weedon had suddenly become . . . a very different sort of person, almost girlish in her manner, far from the Medusa she had once been designated by Moreland" (KO 214).

Such odd resolutions coming here and there in this book provide the light by which we can see that Powell is not recording full-scale collapse. If the 1914 people were more recuperative than the next generation, Jeavons's late arousal and Conyers's non-defeatism are strong signs of some wider ability to cope with things—signs that can be trusted. The revelation of this bethothal makes Nick get a move on. He does so through a quick recursion to the same thematic idea earlier connected with Jeavons:

> Certainly General Conyers was not unadventurous. Was he an adventurer? I thought over his advice about the army. Then the answer came to me. I must get in touch with Widmerpool.

I wondered why I had not thought of that earlier. I telephoned
to his office. They put me through to a secretary.   (KO 218)

Of course, since plans miscarry in *The Music of Time,* it is not
Widmerpool who will get Nick's reserve commission activated.
But Widmerpool on this evening has something he wants Nick's
help in at Lady Molly's, so he takes Nick there with him, where
the man Nick must meet happens to be stopping—it is Jeavons's
brother, "Staff-Captain at the War House" (KO 232), and Nick's
fate is settled.

Though Nick's mother and wife are not Furies, we must realize
he has not escaped tormentresses himself. Just before her collapse,
Betty Templer had reduced Nick to a stammering state in which
he could not say what line of work he was in. This had happened
when they were seated before the Luxuria panel in Donners's din-
ing room—where Nick had sat next to Jean ten years before. There
is something morally inescapable about this, as though the consequences of a heightened way of living in the chase of pleasure
(even the pursuit of the arts) can bring real harm—harm to others.
(While Peter Templer and Anne Umfraville were enacting their
version of Lust, Nick could only judge the spectacle aesthetically
and Betty's anguish left him utterly unprepared.)

The novel's third section—containing the climax of the whole
first sextet, operating in tandem with the climax of *The Acceptance World* —subjects Nick to a Fury-by-proxy, Jean herself.
She does not appear. Her husband Bob Duport is the agent, met
by Nick during his disagreeable trip to supervise Uncle Giles's
cremation. Giles died at a seaside hotel run by the old Jenkins
servant Albert. Duport is staying there temporarily—so, by the
way, is Trelawney.

Giles may be conceived as incorporating the metaphysical, public, and private aspects of disorder that were distributed among
Trelawney, Bracey, and Albert in section one. At least that may
help explain the three symbolic inspections Nick makes in going
over Giles's effects. He turns up a horoscope (metaphysical), an
army commission (public), and a love manual (private). Each
has bearing on Nick himself. Giles's horoscope points to the

handicaps and the final unreliability of the man who serves him-self. Next, there is Queen Victoria's army commission to Giles. The document is really very funny and Nick cannot resist being tendentious—

> His Conduct, in the army or out of it, could not possibly be described as Good. In devotion to duty, for example, he could not be compared with Bracey, a man no less pursued, so far as that went, by Furies. [Note the hint of Giles subsuming differ-ent roles—the presence of Trelawney and Albert makes for fur-ther corroboration.] There remained Uncle Giles's Courage. . . . Certainly it could be urged that he had the Courage of his own opinions; the Queen had to be satisfied with that. In short, the only one of her admonitions Uncle Giles had ever shown the least sign of taking to heart was the charge to command his subordinates to obey him.   (KO 158)

But Nick checks himself from taking "facile irony . . . too far." Instead he had best consider "what sort of a figure I should my-self cut as a soldier" (KO 159). At which point he makes the third discovery in his uncle's Gladstone bag: the Sheik Nefzaoui's private treatise on *The Arab Art of Love*. This is the volume Nick gives Bob Duport, who has caused him to learn of Jean's worst treachery of all, not with Jimmy Stripling but with Jimmy Brent. And if Nick can in the end understand Widmerpool's an-guish at meeting Gypsy Jones, it is because he has faced himself and his own degradation in section three. "If [Jean's] lovers were horrifying, I too had been of their order. That had to be ad-mitted" (KO 180).

I said in an earlier chapter that the narrator's secrecy in *What's Become of Waring* would be expiated in *The Music of Time*. This happens when Duport, who never learns the secret of Nick's love for Jean, is hence able to deliver the agonizing surprise of Jean's betrayal at a time when Nick thinks history cannot touch him. (Agony finally makes its inroads as the loyalty theme of the first sextet accomplishes itself.) Passing *The Arab Art of Love* to Duport, Nick feels he is making "secret amends for having had a love affair with his wife . . ." (KO 182). But the transference also marks Nick's deliverance from ever again making a priority of love, "that treacherous concept" (KO 181). So this is an expiation in two ways. It pays a man back for a concrete wrong visited on him; at the same time it acknowledges the mistake of having gone too far in personal indulgence, miscalled the service of love—which service when untempered by claims of duty is a synonym for the service of the self. In this second, broader sense, we can see why it is so fitting that Nick should have this revelation, and perform the expiation, just at the time when Giles, as an influence, has slid out of his life. Giles has always represented self-exculpation, the opposite of duty. It is no accident that the death of Giles coincides with the conception of a child by Isobel, a child that will be born in the first war volume, *The Valley of Bones*.

Critics of Powell who stress his comedy would say this is all coming down intolerably hard on Nick. But if this private peripety is hard to face, and if it will lead to Nick's hard and clear public decision to get into harness for war, there remains the metaphysical climax of the whole series. And that is *not* a painful event. Because of the peculiar timing that is involved in it, this event turns out to validate all the instincts Nick has had to let his character form as it has chanced to form.

The moment occurs when Dr. Trelawney is locked in the bathroom of Albert's hotel. This moment is climactic because it permits Nick to exercise accidental power that has come his way through the sheer repetitiveness of his way of life. Although he has observed others achieve power in their own native ways, he has never been tempted into the cultivation of a mental power-program such as Trelawney's. But Nick has remembered from childhood—because that is the way he is—the old charmed slogan of Trelawney and what the acolyte's answer is supposed to be. Now he and Duport have just returned to the hotel (the news about Jean is not an hour old) to discover that Trelawney is having an asthmatic attack in the bathroom and cannot work the key.

> "What," said Duport, "the good Dr. Trelawney, the bearded
> one? We'll have him out in a trice. Lead us to him."
> This sudden crisis cheered Duport enormously. Action was

what he needed. I thought of Moreland's remarks about men of
action, wondering whether Duport would qualify.   (KO 130)

The presence of Duport, Widmerpool's business confrere, is
important; and so is Nick's question, because though Duport is a
man of action, it is Nick who will qualify. First Duport endeavors
to break the door down, and this failing, he tries an "authorita-
tive" instruction about re-inserting the key. This brings a pause
to Trelawney's horrible panting from within.

> . . . Then the ritual sentence sounded through the door:
> "The Essence of the All is the Godhead of the True."
> Duport turned to me and shook his head.
> "We often get that," he said.
> This seemed the moment, now or never, when the spell must
> prove its worth. I leant towards his keyhole and spoke the con-
> cordant rejoinder:
> "The Vision of Visions heals the Blindness of Sight."
> Duport laughed.
> "What on earth are you talking about?" he said.
> "That's the right answer."
> "How on earth did you know?"   (KO 185–186)

But Nick does not need to answer. Fumblings and clickings are
heard from within, and then Trelawney unlocks the door. Nothing could be sillier, perhaps, than this scene, but Nick's *now or
never* (and many phrases about that asthma attack) have lent
seriousness to the event. An even greater consideration is that
structurally the elements of the scene reverse those in which
Widmerpool put Stringham to bed in *The Acceptance World*.
That was an event accomplished in space; this owes its resolution to timing. That was an occasion on which "the moving spirit
had been Widmerpool," suggesting to the onlooker Nick "a
positively cosmic change in life's system" (AW 209) ; yet Nick
despite such an acknowledgment never took an unnatural step
toward emulation of the spatially-oriented Widmerpools. Now
in an arcane manner all has come to new balance. Here is a reversal of that reversal. (And here an old dodderer has been re-

leased, whereas there the young dodderer Stringham had been restrained.)

In space, the man who acts achieves power *over* another (for better or worse); through timing, the man who acts dispenses power *to* another, or assuages. Meanwhile the power of the word has conferred on Nick the unsought status of man of action. And here is some fitness because it is in a writer's nature to trust to the word, to the axiom "Knowledge is Power"—although of course this does not connote the spatial concept of the imposition of power by direct physical will. An enlistment into the army, where action and loyalty will become matters of course, is so much the next logical step that Powell does not begin to require dramatic motivation for it—determined though Nick is when the final pages come.

Section three is over now, except for one raging, eclipsed, Ulysses-in-Nighttown scene. In it Trelawney mouths giant power slogans, but all are undercut because he is in the hands of his timeless nurse, Mrs. Erdleigh. Nick last sees in Mrs. Erdleigh's hands a hypodermic for Trelawney, and hears his last rising shriek invoking "votaries of the Furies who use branches of cedar, alder, hawthorn, saffron . . ." (KO 198). Irony of ironies, Duport has left that testament of austere sexual authority, *The Arab Art of Love*, in the room where Mrs. Erdleigh now begins whatever ministrations she will use to transport Trelawney to the Astral Plane. It is the day of one more anomaly of the will—the day the ministers of Hitler and Stalin signed their infamous non-aggression pact.

SPACE AND TIME

"I can only do ladylike things such as playing the piano," says a gloomy Moreland on the eve of war. "I suppose I shall go on doing that if there's a show-down" (KO 98). Behind his downright statement seems to lie Moreland's conviction that "Being an artist . . . partakes of certain feminine characteristics . . ." (KO 248). There is some correspondence when Mrs. Erdleigh meets Nick and judges him to be inclined in one of only two directions:

"You are musical?"

"No."

"Then you write—I think you have written a book?"

(AW 14)

The correspondence lies in the fact that music is the most temporal of the arts, and that Nick, time-oriented as a writer, shows the same passive-intuitive tendencies as Moreland.

It is not unusual for the element of time to be associated with the female, and that of space with the male principle. In *Time and Western Man,* for instance, Wyndham Lewis deplores "the ascendancy of Time (which also happens to be the feminine principle in this partnership) over Space,"[11] and we may note that one of Powell's space-oriented characters, the ballet dancer Norman Chandler, was a reader of Lewis's book (CR 48).* Powell generally does associate the passive and feminine with the temporal arts (music and writing), and the masculine-active with space (painting and sculpture, the stage). He is much less prone than Lewis in assigning moral preference to one over the other mode; when he does seem to choose, in this late work, it is in the direction opposite to Lewis's.

Since the relation between Time and Space was "a favourite subject of Moreland's" (CR 34), the occasion on which those capitalized nouns come up for a hearing is at Casanova's Restaurant on the day Nick meets Moreland. The subject is the furtherance of love affairs. Moreland has said that it is not the bedroom where energy gets used up, but "making efforts to get there. Problems of Time and Space as usual" (CR 34). But Barnby in his turn is inclined to dismiss all the theorizing—"I don't wonder seduction seems a problem, if you get Time and Space confused"—and this is a scene in which Barnby makes an assignation with a waitress with incredible ease while the others avert their heads. Powell's respect for Barnby amounts to a respect for clock-time, too: he appreciates the actual successiveness of Time in a way that is quite un-Proustian.

---

*Lewis speaks of ballet as being "essentially 'chaste and masculine'. . . ." (Time and Western Man, p. 32.)

There is a tendency in *The Music of Time* to relegate to a temporal existence self-conscious people like Moreland, and to relegate to a spatial existence such an unselfconscious person as Barnby. It is the former type who take those reflective, ruminative approaches to marriage. But in the case of Barnby, spatial proximity is all he needs to get something started with the waitress. He simply arranges haphazardly an appointment for her to come to his studio—significantly, the day itself, or how many days away it may be, doesn't matter.

Time matters to Moreland because, being self-conscious, he tends to be conscious of the selves of other people. Now this is a more or less original concept in Powell, I think. That is, the prevailing notion about self-conscious people would seem to be that they are impervious to others. But Powell's people who do understand others are self-conscious. Perhaps he would say that other people must exist in Time, if one can truly be considered sensitive to them. (Their place, where they are, presence or absence, doesn't matter.) A speculation of this sort may give some clarification, at least, to Moreland's cryptic remark that "one might be said to be true to a woman in Time and unfaithful to her in Space" (CR 34). (In the case of Priscilla Tolland, with whom Moreland never went to bed—they couldn't ever seem to find a *place*—the remark turns out to be very poignant.)

We will go wrong if we try to carry Powell's distinctions here into the area of clear moral judgments. He is not separating sheep (Morelands: time-men) from goats (Barnbys: space-men). As Nick says of the aftermath of Barnby's affair with the waitress, "There was no ill feeling after Barnby had done with her; keeping on good terms with his former mistresses was one of his gifts" (CR 39.)*

Rather (though Powell might have conceived as sympathetic a book about *A Dash to the Guidon of Space*), the inference to

---

*Or take a completely space-identified man like Magnus Donners, amateur photographer. Despite his repulsive voyeurism in The Kindly Ones, we have had Matilda's word in the previous novel that Donners could be "generous—I mean morally generous. . . . One thing about Donners, he does not know what jealousy means" (CR 158).

draw is that time underrides space and makes its music heard, has
its dance. And once granting that the time-oriented men are
those really conscious of the existence of others, it becomes true
to say that mainly these "dance." In Poussin's portrait, the memory of which opens the whole novel, there are *figures* dancing,
not *a* figure; and there is no domination among the dancers: that
comes from outside, from Time's music. It seems therefore worth-
while to say that the directness (a spatial word) of Barnby has
little or nothing to do with shared sensuality, which seems for
Powell to be in good part a matter of the savoring of another
being, met halfway. About Barnby's technique in love Nick once
said there had to be, "on the part of the [other party], a depletion, if not entire abrogation, of 'the will' " (AW 24). We have
already heard (at the beginning of Chapter Four) about the potential sacrifice of sensuality that could be involved here, and
at the end of *The Kindly Ones* a funny anecdote rakes up this
old issue. Moreland tells Nick,

> "I once asked Barnby if he did not find most women extra-
> ordinarily unsensual. . . . Do you know what he answered?"
> "What?"
> "He said, 'I've never noticed.' "   (KO 248)

This wonderful reply does point to the fact I have been emphasizing about the "spatial" person not getting distracted from
his preoccupations by the imminence of another's personality.
But then a "dance" seems out of the question, since when the
"will" of a partner is abrogated, that partner becomes, primarily,
a counter in a game.

Still, crucial situations arise as often in life where the will of
one person does need to be energized and that of another abrogated, as when Conyers saved Billson or Widmerpool subdued
Stringham. Granting that "sharing" does not result from these
moments, we must observe that some other forms of good may
very well result. The danger is the danger of monstrosity—of
what might be called monstrous imposition of will—by which I
mean power administered knowingly over a period of time.

(That sort of thing would prevent the resumption of the "dance" —it would create a more or less permanent agent-and-patient status.) As a matter of fact Powell frequently finds one sort of power-figure approaching this dehumanized or monstrous state and another kind not doing so. The best pure examples, over the middle course of *The Music of Time,* would be Conyers, never dehumanized, and Donners, gradually seen to be less and less spontaneous until, in our latest glimpse of him, he is described as having "grown not so much older in appearance, as less like a human being. . . . Jerky movements, like those of a marionette . . . added to the impression of an outsize puppet that had somehow escaped from its box and begun to mix with real people . . ." (MP 206–207).

That glimpse came in *The Military Philosophers.* Since, in that book, Powell happens to compare two well-respected British commanders (Alanbrooke and Montgomery, though they are not named), I should like to advert to it for a moment. With these men, seen in passing as opposed to presiding figures like Donners and Conyers, Powell actually makes most clear the two views he holds of "spatial" will-imposers. We must repeat that he respects both—but one clearly more than the other, the force there represented being more wholesome (purely leagued with space, I would say—not making an ally of time as though to master space).

Nick has occasion to see at the War Office the Chief of the Imperial General Staff, and in Belgium the Field Marshal. "On the one hand," he records, there was

> the almost overpowering physical impact of the CIGS, that curious electric awareness felt down to the tips of one's fingers of a given presence imparting a sense of stimulation, also the consoling thought that someone of the sort was at the top. On the other hand, the Field-Marshal's outward personality offered what was perhaps even less usual, will-power, not so much natural, as developed to altogether exceptional lengths. . . . It was an immense, wiry, calculated, insistent hardness, rather than a force like champagne bursting from the bottle.
>
> (MP 183–184)

Arrested as he is by both, Powell responds more positively to the more ebullient variety. It seems for one thing more at home, humanly speaking, with itself; whereas the Field Marshal—this I take to be a crux—actually suggests "some mythical beast, say one of those encountered in *Alice in Wonderland . . .*" (MP 184). In other words, the rigorously developed will must sacrifice something in humanness, and respected though it might be, it could never bring about "consoling thoughts." Consoling thoughts do derive from the CIGS's kind of will-power, though the man is at the same time a pure power-figure.

The important thing in Powell is that only sometimes, with some people, does will-power become detrimental. Powell's attitude toward the will and power becomes impossible to clarify unless one of those words at least be given a set of qualifiers. It is not a simple problem, as critics have sometimes made it out to be—a nostalgic siding with men of grace, a grudging admission that power undoes grace. That is not essentially the picture distilled out of *The Music of Time*. Since in the long run Powell believes in the appropriateness of things that happen, and since power of some sort makes them happen, we have never been able to leap to conclusions about any despair he may feel in the face of power. Indeed, with these would-be admonitory remarks fresh in mind about the Generals, a last attempt to sound his classical view could perhaps best be approached through comparison with a romantic one.

When the Promethean Percy Shelley came to the despair of his late days, he wrote these words in *The Triumph of Life:*

> And much I grieved to think how power and will
> In opposition rule our mortal day,
>
> And why God made irreconcilable
> Good and the means of good. . . .[12]

In his poetry generally, and in these lines specifically, Shelley equates "will" with "good," that is, with the highest intentions. But he finds the best intentions here *opposed* by "power," so that the "means of good" (that is, power under the direction of enlightened will) cannot be realized. In Powell, who is as far removed from Shelley as anyone could be, a reversal is actually perceptible. It could be stated this way: "power" is good, but the "will" in the ordinary, struggling-and-striving, Shelleyan sense, is mischievous. This might be called "programmed" will, or perhaps wilfulness would be the right term. In Powell's early work and in *The Music of Time* this marred form of will does not succeed because it falls prey to chance—at least at length it does, for it cannot really make an ally of time. But there is another sort of will, which we might call "spontaneous" will, that leads to power because it is the ally of chance, and besides emanates from the basic sort of person one "chances" to be, rather than "plans" to be. Marcel Proust always condemned himself for lacking will; yet Powell concurs with Proust's best biographer that Proust had a "will of iron." In that dichotomy lies something of the difference between a frustrated or deranging program to exert will and the actual exertion of it, notwithstanding.[13] In someone like Widmerpool we have so many examples of the same double potential—the failure of his "program" for Mrs. Haycock versus his magical calling of a cab, for instance—that we are forced half the time to look at him as a villain-hero rather than a villain. Spontaneous will is the culprit that redeems him on those occasions.

A personage Shelley met in *The Triumph of Life*, sharing his despair, had asked him to "forbear/ To join the dance" of Life, and to "abate" his "thirst of knowledge."[14] The entire romantic rationale, the romantic agony, seems to work out to this. But the reverse and classical view of Powell sees the triumph of life as a good, and sees a mythic descent of good fortune should one be led into the steps and "join the dance." Poussin's *A Dance to the Music of Time,* the apparent germ of this novel, called up the cyclic truths that Powell seems to vouch for about human existence, and Poussin, as Powell said once, is the painter who follows the myths perfectly.[15] The actual men, at work round a street-corner excavation on a cold day, who reminded him of the Poussin, themselves appeared "as if performing a rite" as they fueled their skimpy fire. "For some reason," Powell wrote, "the sight of snow descending on fire makes me think of the ancient world—legionaries in sheepskin warming themselves at a brazier: mountain altars where offerings glow between wintry pillars: centaurs with torches cantering beside a frozen sea. . . . These classical projections, and something in the physical attitudes of the men themselves as they turned from the fire, suddenly suggested Poussin's scene . . ." (QU 1–2). It is a diversified sacramental view of life that registers here at the start of *The Music of Time,* comparable to the aware and sensuous view of life the Greeks had, to which Powell recurs often in his writing outside of fiction. The picture in front of Nick, calling up the imagined past, above all lacks abstraction. In each of the images, the present one and those of the past, there is a sense of adversity but none of dread. The aesthetic critic Wilhelm Worringer, who related the healthiness of the Greeks to their sense of at-homeness in natural environment, has said of non-naturalistic (especially Gothic) art forms which differ from those of the Greeks that their "urge to abstraction is the outcome of a great inner unrest inspired in man by the phenomena of the outside world. . . . We might describe this state as an immense spiritual dread of space."[16]

It would be speculative, at best, to try to make any direct connection between this idea and the main idea informing Powell's masterpiece. It is nevertheless apparent that most of the formidable space-oriented figures in *The Music of Time* seem actuated by a need to change or mold or hold things in a certain way, and that this might stem from their dread of the contiguity of all things which would make themselves in each case one of the things included. The terrible irony is that out of fear of becoming a thing, one may approach becoming just that—a mechanical robot, a cultivator of abstractions—touched with Gothic monstrosity. So it may have been with Donners in the world of action (a voyeuristic photographer—could not the origin of all photography be laid to a restless dread of space?), or even with Trelawney in the world of imagination (a drug reliant). Even their evolutions in character, however, deserve extenuation because these are forthcoming out of the kind of people they chanced to be. Powell can accept Trelawney and Donners and their like. Such unrest as theirs Powell had found to be a short-coming in men like Huxley and Orwell—who had to get the better of things so that things would not get the better of them—and who could settle down in no acceptance world essentially because of this. (But Orwell was a friend for whom Powell had much fondness.) Poussin's inspiration, conversely, and the Greeks' equanimity in space, perhaps do suggest a germinating idea for *The Music of Time,* which does offer a classical at-one-ness with the world through an overriding faith in Time. In this regard it is at least interesting that when Powell reviewed another Worringer work, he noted with strong approval how one of Worringer's seminal propositions was "the Greek lack of interest in space."[17]

·····◄ᴥ► 6 ◄ᴥ►·····

THE MUSIC OF TIME:
War

VAMPING TILL READY

A superficial first comment about *The Valley of Bones* and *The Soldier's Art*, when they came out, would have been that Powell seemed to have started a sextet rather than a trilogy about the 1939–1945 war. Each of these books covered only about a year's time, *The Valley of Bones* ending at the June 1940 occupation of Paris, and *The Soldier's Art* at the German invasion of Russia in June of 1941. This left four more years of war to go. With the arrival of *The Military Philosophers*, however, things accelerated. A five-part novel, this installment moved from year to year in brisk sections: 1942 (marked by the fall of Singapore) in the first; 1943 (and Stalingrad) in the second; 1944 (after D Day) in the third; and 1945, after the Bomb, in the fifth and last. One interlude was thus permitted; but whereas in the first two war volumes the interlude would bring Nick Jenkins back to former associations on periods of leave, in the fourth section of *The Military Philosophers* there is an excursion to recent battlefields of France, Belgium, and Holland. It is a fitting testimony to new mobility, undertaken almost in vacation spirit. Nick, as liaison officer, is chaperoning a group of Allied military attachés, some of them setting foot on their own native soils for the first time since the war began. This sense of motion and change cluttering the end volume of the trilogy does raise the question of disproportionate treatment—but only superficially, for the first two volumes really contain their own answer to it. Clearly, the psychological strain undergone while the Germans had the initiative is what Powell remembers as *the* collective ordeal of the British in the war: the first two years deserve the attenuation they get because they collect the weight of decades as decisive action remains postponed.

Where *The Valley of Bones,* full of the echo of religious and martial songs, registers almost a gratefulness that there is time to get an army ready for war *during* war, a major metaphorical shift occurs in *The Soldier's Art.* All through that book imagery of the theatre casts aspersions on the whole rigmarole of "readiness"; for entering yet a second year of priming after war's declaration has begun to make all effort look specious. "It's a tailor's war, anyway," says Nick at the end of *The Soldier's Art,* on catching sight of a civilian vest under the tunic of a certain Mobile Laundry officer (SA 224); in the first scene Nick had himself purchased an army greatcoat from an outfitter's in the theatre district, and been mistaken for an actor. How disgruntling this conviction of sham war can get is shown in the opening sentences of part two of the novel:

> Sullen reverberations of one kind or another—blitz in England, withdrawal in Greece—had been providing the most recent noises-off in rehearsals that never seemed to end, breeding a wish that the billed performance would at last ring up its curtain, whatever form that took. However, the date of the opening night rested in hands other than our own; meanwhile nobody could doubt that more rehearsing, plenty more rehearsing, was going to be needed for a long time to come.   (SA 88)

There is a good petulant bite in that "plenty more rehearsing," and the root of the petulance is that in 1940 and 1941 all the levers for curtain-raising "rested in hands other than our own. . . ." It is probably no accident that even the brief Commando-style forays, assuaging the morale of the British in those early years, were referred to as *shows*—convenient for Powell's motif at any rate. "This show I was in—"says a young officer called Odo Stevens, freshly returned to London with a medal. Even more pertinent, in *The Soldier's Art* this same Stevens recites an after-dinner poem of his own devising, and reveals a melodramatic and gloomy streak hitherto unguessed because of his usual "aggressive cheerfulness" (SA 148).

I have intended to mention this theatrical motif only in passing, to give a quick view of the shifted atmosphere of the second war novel. Actually, the departure thus made from *The Valley of Bones* can be seen as a variant of the commencement-opposition pattern distinguishing the other trilogies. Of this, more will be said later. For the moment, it is worth remarking that on no less than ten occasions songs sung by the men in Nick's regiment are transcribed in *The Valley of Bones*. It is a Welsh regiment and Welshmen are notorious singers: just the same, no songs are sung in *The Soldier's Art*. Odo Stevens's verses and one other poem appear in fact to be deliberate substitutions for them— until, in the last two divisions of *The Military Philosophers,* there is a wholesale return to hymns and poems to mark the synthesis effect of that third volume. What follows here will be an attempt to sketch the first two (antithetical) movements of the war trilogy, the whole pattern of which might be said to develop according to this triad: act without thinking; think before acting; at last, think and act simultaneously.

In *The Valley of Bones,* as the title (from Ezekiel) implies,* songs operate as a means of bypassing individuality, which needs to be bypassed if separate men are ever to make a start toward forming "an exceeding great army." But something altogether different is on tap in *The Soldier's Art*. Here the two poems

---

*A chaplain uses the text in an exhortation : "And [the Lord] said unto me, Son of man, can these bones live? ... Again he said unto me, Prophesy upon these bones, and say unto them, O ye dry bones, hear the word of the Lord. ... So I prophesied as he commanded me, and the breath came unto them and they lived, and stood up upon their feet, an exceeding great army ..." (VB 37–38).

mentioned above *recall* individuality. The second of them is really programmatic—a passage from Browning's "Childe Roland to the Dark Tower Came." Quoted by Stringham, who reappears in this volume, it gives the novel its title through the line, "Think first, fight afterwards—the soldier's art" (SA 221).

In a word, the burden of *The Valley of Bones* enjoins soldiers not to think, while its sequel gives them a wearying stretch of time during which they are obliged to recommence thinking.

These are the very broad lines on which the two novels move. Each has a section in which Nick, on leave, picks up several threads of the past by now familiar to us. He really does need to reach for these threads, because his army activity has become a sort of waking and imperative dream: from the first pages of the two novels on we can hear him referring to this or that portion of the past as "another existence, an earlier, less demanding incarnation" (VB 1)—to the bottle of wine he and Moreland once flushed down the toilet as having been bought "centuries before" (SA 4)—and so on.

The four sections of *The Valley of Bones* carry Nick through his first days with his regiment in Wales, their move to a training site in the North of Ireland, a spell of leave for Nick near London, and his return to duty at a castle in Ulster, headquarters of an anti-gas school, a place steeped in false feudalism. Powell reveres Wales and detests Ireland, and the decline that has been gone through comes in focus when part one and part four are compared. As Nick sniffs the Welsh air and considers his own bloodline, intimations of a genuine feudalism are given off. Nick's mind is cast back (as by the figures round the brazier in *A Question of Upbringing*) to warlike men "at once measurably historical, yet at the same time mythically heroic . . ." (VB 3). But part four in Ireland shows conformity to the growing "phoniness" of the war by disclosing the phoniness of the "sham fortress" called Castlemallock. This place does provide much military hubbub, but the makers of it are a group of misfits like "the seedy Anti-Gas instructors, sloughed off at this golden opportunity by their regiments" (VB 172). From here Nick will also quit his own regiment, not being exactly sloughed off, but requisitioned by Major Widmerpool to serve in the latter's office at Divisional Headquarters. This is the point at which *The Soldier's Art* begins.

Coming under Widmerpool's control will prove temporarily stagnating for Nick. In *The Valley of Bones,* at the fairly intimate level of regimental soldiering, Nick had sensed the onsetting mood of surrendered personality, whereas now, at the ten times more impersonal level of Divisional Staff, the disposition to "think first, fight afterwards" begins to gain ground. The time for real fighting, for applying one's own best leverage in action, has not arrived. (It is rather the time for finding that leverage.) This in spite of all kinds of in-fighting on the part of various majors and colonels, Widmerpool and Sunny Farebrother among them; for what Powell has done, through the figure of the Divisional Commander, General Liddament, and a few others like him, is reverse the cliché of the stupidity of ranking officers, so tediously encountered in modern war fiction. We might have anticipated this shift because of the admirable General Conyers of the previous trilogy. (Sceptics of course could lay any fair treatment of general officers to Powell's military predilections.)

In *The Soldier's Art,* Liddament's perceptiveness will work itself into the story because it is he who spots the "reader" in Nick and recognizes his possibilities in another line of work. Nick, attached to a platoon that sees to the security of Liddament's staff, chances to get into a literary talk with the General, who drops the wondrous comment, "You've been very patient with us here" (SA 49). The essential point is that through the General's scrutiny Nick will be pried away from duties under Widmerpool that have little bearing on his character—duties that stifle him from "thinking first," and have even less application to a "fight afterwards."

The three sections of *The Soldier's Art* turn on this notion of Nick's Divisional Commander, leading to a contact with Free-French liaison officers in part two when Nick gets to London on leave. But when he fails his French language test, compounding his disgrace by seeming "to let down the General too" (SA 103), he perforce must return to headquarters in Northern Ireland, later to discover that his name has gone in to the War Office, to

which he is posted as the novel ends. Someone appears still to
have an inkling of something for him to do commensurate with
his own identity.

He certainly has not flourished as regimental or staff officer
and seems on the way to becoming the oldest lieutenant in the
army. Because of this customary slowness off the mark, it may
be that Powell intended the army greatcoat scene as an indication that Nick himself, no less than the army as a whole, has
been "vamping till ready." Nick does not so much perform duties
as go through walk-throughs of them (never shirkingly though).
He may need to go over a rope bridge to reconnoitre land on the
other side of a canal:

> I started to make the transit, falling in after about three or
> four yards. The water might have been colder for the time of
> year. I swam the rest of the way, reaching the far bank not
> greatly wetter than the rain had left me. There I wandered
> about for a time, making notes of matters to be regarded as im-
> portant in the circumstances.   (VB 84)

As usual, style tells the story. Note the reverse subordination
in the first, third, and fourth sentences, devaluating each main
event to the status of a trailing phrase. Note also the depressed
comparatives ("might have been colder," "not greatly wetter"),
by which Powell can convey that this was a soaking and chilling
experience, but that Nick isn't to pass for one of Rogers's
Rangers, after all. Nick's training, the regiment's training, the
division's training, amount to the same thing. Pressures build
up, pressures are released (as in the several air raids described, or
as when some tea and chocolate refit Nick for action after his
inundation). But one "operation" over, the patient has to look
forward to another. The whole monolithic army seems anesthe-
tized, or rather (to return to the stage idiom) a vast kind of cap-
tive audience. Lord Haw-Haw comes through on the wireless, or
else there are provided such repeatedly insular transitions as,
"We returned from the exercise to find Germany had invaded
Norway and Denmark" (VB 98).

The aftertaste of every operation in *The Valley of Bones* is
a reminder that something bad, not yet experienced, is in the

offing. So the anti-gas training at Castlemallock goes on and on—
a sterling touch, for the gas masks of the English proved to be
symbolic (in never having to be used), pointing to the way that,
over the time-span of these novels, every soldier and civilian
waited for Hitler's never-to-be-mounted invasion of Britain.

All that waiting carried right on into a second volume understandably gets minds thinking again, and there are many upwell-
ings of self-interest, "equally unattractive in outer guise and
inner essence," as Nick says, yet necessary "for individual sur-
vival" (SA 190). He is talking here as one member of the audience who doesn't know his own next assignment (Widmerpool,
ready to move on, has made no provision for him). Nick and the
whole audience are unexpectedly released by the event that fittingly ends *The Soldier's Art*. It can occasion now a remark
apropos of the other important English trilogy about World
War II, Evelyn Waugh's. Nick hears the news from one of his
superiors:

> . . . "Haven't you seen a paper or heard the wireless this
> morning? Germany's invaded Russia."
> An immediate, overpowering, almost mystic sense of relief
> took shape within me. I felt suddenly sure everything was going
> to be all right.   (SA 226–227)

Of all comparisons that might be made between Anthony
Powell and Evelyn Waugh, I believe the one best founded must
rest on the last two sentences quoted. The second volume of
Waugh's trilogy also happens to pivot on the German invasion
of Russia, only in a revealingly opposite way. The breach of
faith between Germany and Russia *destroys* Guy Crouchback's
vision of a holy war against Fascism and Communism. Now the
detestable Communists must become allies. Nothing could demonstrate more powerfully the unideological basis of Powell's
writing, for though Waugh's splendid book does go on to vindi-
cate Crouchback's last and surest-held conviction—"that no good
comes from public causes; only private causes of the soul"[1]—
Powell too must be acknowledged as a hater of Communism. And
yet Nick feels only this great mystical *expediency* at the news of

the 1941 climacteric. His reaction is completely un-mental—that is crucial. It is something like the notification one feels as a member of an audience when the final scene of a film has arrived—the stir experienced all around one, visceral or vertebral as it may be, before the words "THE END" are themselves ready to arrive on the screen. The wave of passive relief seems rightly representative of the mass of Englishmen caught in the waiting war. (Guy Crouchback, on the other hand, *had* done some fighting—had been in a raid at Dakar, and in the evacuation of Crete.)

Mostly, however, to return to the un-mental reaction, it doubles on what Nick has been describing most of the way through both novels: the life of a soldier as a completely physical life. I do not so much mean to insist that other Englishmen would *en masse* have the same opinion of the luckiness of the German move to the east as I mean to emphasize the order of Nick's impression. That simple phrase "everything was going to be all right" is only on a par with many other of the plainest sorts of reactions, void of idea-content, such as one resulting when Nick's company commander, having done him an ugly turn and sent him off dinnerless, arrives at a bivouac with an apology and some chocolate. "I felt this a handsome apology, a confession that did Gwatkin credit. Even so, his words were nothing to the chocolate. There were still a few remains clinging to my mouth. I licked them from the back of my teeth" (VB 87).

Even the slightly curter style of the war novels, as compared to the earlier trilogies, owes something to this type of reaction. And I think I am right in saying that most readers will feel a return to more complex responses—to a renewed interest in very fine shadings—in the much different third volume of the trilogy, which provides for contributive movement and some release from this physicalness.

MEPHISTOPHELES AND MITHRAS

The "Gwatkin" of the last quotation is Rowland Gwatkin, Nick's company commander in the Welsh Territorial Battalion, an officer with a dream and a vulnerable flair for glory not unlike those of Captain Hudson in *What's Become of Waring*. These men are engaging because there is a difference between their dream and their flair for glory. The latter fault is personal, based on credulousness: Hudson's emulation of the Boy Scout standards of T. T. Waring, Gwatkin's belief that a chivalric pursuit of honor has opened up to him as he leaves his bank official's post for uniformed service. But their dreams are legal because each at his best will reduce himself for the good of something else he has at heart, without making much of the pains he might have to endure in performance of his job. (Captain Hudson is of course not embarked for war but for biography, and so the two cannot profitably be compared further.)

Most salient in Gwatkin is a tragic quality which invites comparison, more than to any other in my experience, with the fire captain Pye in Henry Green's *Caught*. Gwatkin and Pye try, how misguidedly they try, to handle with more than usual conscientiousness the authority with which they have been charged (though Gwatkin as bank official comes from a higher social station than Pye). A passage like the following, written about Gwatkin, goes to the heart of the problem of both of them:

> He seemed half aware that this intense keenness was not, in final result, what was required; at least not without more understanding on his own part. . . . The fact was Gwatkin lacked in his own nature that grasp of "system" for which he possessed such admiration. This deficiency was perhaps connected in some way with a kind of poetry within him, a poetry which had somehow become a handicap in its efforts to find an outlet.
>
> (VB 48–49)

It is even true that Gwatkin and Pye become unable to abide by their own revered regulations when woman-complications arise (Gwatkin forgets code words, Pye fails to keep account of the personnel in his station)—but the main purpose of drawing a comparison is the attribution of "a kind of poetry within" which links these "fairly coarse-grained" types, and perhaps can serve to illuminate theme- as well as character-realization in *The Valley of Bones*.

What the two are able to do best is *exhort;* self-consciousness
and too great a fear of failure blunt and mar their action. They
really have warmth for their men. Here is a specimen of Gwatkin's exhortation on the subject of care of one's rifle:

> . . . "The Commanding Officer has ordered me to tell you
> once again you must all take care of your rifles, for a man's rifle
> is his best friend in time of war, and a soldier is no longer a sol-
> dier when his weapon is gone from him. He is like a man who
> has had that removed which makes him a man, something
> sadder, more useless, than a miner who has lost his lamp, or a
> farmer his plough. . . . That is no funny matter, losing a rifle,
> not like long hair nor a dirty button. There is a place at Alder-
> shot called the Glasshouse, where men who have not taken
> proper care of their rifles do not like to visit a second time.
> Nevertheless, I would not threaten you. That is not how I wish
> to lead you. It is for the honour of the Regiment that you
> should guard your rifles, like you would guard your wife or your
> little sister. . . . You Corporals, you Lance-Corporals, consider
> these things in your hearts. . . ."
>
> I was impressed by the speech, though there were moments
> when I thought Gwatkin's listeners might deride the images he
> conjured up, such as a man losing what made him a man, or
> little sisters who had to be protected. On the contrary, the Com-
> pany listened spellbound. . . .   (VB 66–67)

Albert Pye's nearly identical harangues to his firemen also turn
on phrases like "A man's sister is sacred to 'im,"[2] or, making the
appeal from the other side,

> "The man who loses his mental faculties is the one to get left.
> What's left of him will be his axe and spanner, and the buckle
> of his belt. I'm not telling you a story, there's the museum at
> Headquarters, you've only to ask the bastards there, and if
> you're lucky, very, they'll let you in. You'll find the label with
> his name on they got from the number stamped on 'is axe."[3]

The annealed sentiments of both men are caught as their language (differing slightly) is caught: Pye's awe of Headquarters
worked into his description; Gwatkin veering into a form of

metronomic baby-talk to appeal directly as he thinks to his men.
If self-consciousness inhibits their action, it does not hinder them
from losing themselves in their speech—whence the poetry. The-
matically, they as well as their men become "spellbound," the
whole drive of Powell's novel (Green's as well) being to bring
men out of the valley of separateness into concerted, monolithic
life.

This is not a simplistic or fully realizable drive (perhaps being
more realizable on the German side), and there is a tension in
The Valley of Bones as Nick contrasts officers who are more
efficient in an all-around sense to Gwatkin. Odo Stevens, for
example—to be observed sleeping after lectures, "upright on a
hard wooden chair, while everyone else was clattering from the
lecture room, [suggesting] considerable powers of self-seclusion"
(VB 122). Or Idwal Kedward, who succeeds his captain upon
Gwatkin's dismissal from the company, and who "did not deal
in dreams, military or otherwise" (VB 13). Then there is Widmerpool, compared to Gwatkin more than once in *The Valley of
Bones* and *The Soldier's Art*. With Gwatkin manifestly less realistic than Widmerpool or those younger lieutenants, the tension
that arises amounts to this: which is the sounder way to get an
army ready or to get men actually led, the Widmerpool-Ked-
ward-Stevens way or the Gwatkin way? The reader's sympathies
are with Gwatkin (as with Pye); but where are Powell's thoughts?

The answer is, I think, with Gwatkin. To the others, in different ways, the army organizations are stepping-stones to their
own advancement; to Gwatkin, the army organizations are rev-
erential and his whole crusade has for context the service of
which he is part, *it* reaping the rewards of his ambition. Gwatkin's mythic approach to war is thus tempered by the fact that
he is not the center of his own myth. Kedward (whose promotion
means he can marry—he is a long-range planner), Stevens (who
aims to realize individualistic dreams of glory), and Widmerpool
the master intriguer, are, after all, myth-makers too; more successful only because conservative (even Stevens's sleep is a con-
servation of energy). They are using the army while spinning
webs from their own centers. But the rub is that *all* webs break,

even Widmerpool's master web in *The Soldier's Art*. " 'Honour
and Wit, fore-damned they sit,' " as that book intones (SA 4); but
the fact that Gwatkin's modicum is pledged in advance to something larger than himself will make the issue less harsh for him
when "honor and wit" are faulted. Where there is more dedication there is apt to be less need for plan, and therefore, though
he falls hard in *The Valley of Bones*, Gwatkin is motivated by
more realizable ideals than the realists'. His personality having
been sublimated (or suppressed—it doesn't matter, neither is
true of the planners), he has truer reserves for recovering from
shocks. This is why, at the end of the book, when Gwatkin has
his professional setback capped by a personal one, he can laugh
in the teeth of his own credulousness (with a certain Hudson-like
toughness) and cause Nick to say, "That was one of the moments
when I felt I had not been wrong in thinking there was some
style about him" (VB 230).

All of this accords with the theme of leaving oneself open to
chance—though Gwatkin would not rationalize it that way—per-
vading the whole of *The Music of Time*. To take Kedward for
the moment and prove him as sedulously myth-ridden as Gwatkin (though pinched in because of wariness), here is evidence of
a talisman of his, which he wouldn't dream of associating with
the war effort (but what then is its use?)—

> . . . "My dad was in this battalion in the last war and got sent
> to the Holy Land. He brought me back a prayer-book bound in
> wood from the Cedars of Lebanon. I wasn't born then, of
> course, but he got the prayer-book for his son, if he had
> one. . . ."
> "Do you use it every Sunday?"
> "Not in the army. Not bloody likely. Somebody would pinch
> it. I want to hand it on to my own son, you see, when I have
> one."   (VB 15)

In relation to the sermons and hymns treated seriously by
Powell in *The Valley of Bones*, this amounts to defection. So
much so, that when Nick meets Kedward on the battlefield in
The Military Philosophers, and learns that Kedward is the

father of two children, he asks, "What sex?" "Girls," says Kedward, "—that's what I wanted" (MP 175). This is the way the
secret planners are retaliated against—funny, but part of the
cosmic theme of *The Music of Time*. We realize Nick must have
remembered Kedward's boast about reserving his exotic prayer-
book for his son, because of the quickness of that question, "What
sex?" Now if Gwatkin had had that prayer-book, he would have
had it in his kit-bag. In fact he has something else there, imper-
fectly understood, but something that presents an alternative for
him when his star sinks. It is a copy of Kipling's *Puck of Pook's
Hill*. He and Nick discuss a story about a Roman centurion
which begins with a hymn to Mithras. This poem becomes a
referent when Gwatkin's entanglement with a girl causes him
to forget his duties and lose his company. (She is simply an Irish
barmaid but to him it is a bar of heaven she leans on like the
blessed damosel.)

The really interesting thing about the Mithraic motif—including the line "keep us pure till the dawn"—is that this soldiers'
religion is essentially practical rather than mystical: the prayer
(like the cult) designed for efficacy at the immediate level of fitness for the march or the fight. Powell's phrase about a "monk
of war" (VB 218) does not involve consecration beyond the
limits of war, and the continence itself that comes to be invoked
is a practical rather than an absolute chastity.

Powell may take a guarded enough approach to the subject of
promiscuity in war, yet it remains true, as *The Kindly Ones* fore-
told, that one of the great causes of the waste valley of bones was
sexual license. And war certainly opens some new avenues for
this. Gwatkin's adventure amounted only to a brush with it, yet
opened Nick's eyes to dangers as we shall see; as the war wears
on, the incidence of promiscuity increases. By far the most disastrous creature in the war trilogy is its most beautiful woman,
Pamela Flitton. This girl achieves mythic proportions in *The
Military Philosophers* as one who persecutes men—especially
about their incapacities in bed, especially men past their middle
thirties—and she is responsible for driving several to desperate
war-game heroics in order to recover the manhood she has

siphoned from them. Peter Templer is the most notable of Pamela's victims. In reaction against her sexual contempt, he volunteers, although still a civilian, for a secret mission in the Balkans and is killed in sordid circumstances: "dying in the service of what he himself would certainly regard as a Musical Comedy country, on account of a Musical Comedy love affair" (MP 222). As Nick's account implies, it seems all wrong. When Pamela and some other sexually rampant figures are found gravitating to wartime jobs associated with secrecy, they help build toward the creation of the trilogy's major symbol.

We have already touched on this symbol. Rowland Gwatkin's commitment to regulations, as opposed to Widmerpool's or Stevens's or Farebrother's penchant for secret military conniving, leads to the juxtaposition of an impersonal, Mithraic devotion to duty against a self-indulgent—also sexually indulgent—inclination to dabble with people's lives in the interests of personal power. Templer walking into a death trap, Odo Stevens's impatient cloak-and-dagger life, and the promise that Widmerpool will be tortured by his bride Pamela Flitton, all point to the eternal restlessness in store for the self when it is pushed by covert ambitions to control. The interests these types show in secret war activity is the symbol of their natures: or as Mrs. Erdleigh put it, referring to Pamela, "You do not understand enough her type's love of secrecy, her own unwillingness to give herself" (MP 136).

Alive to this duplicity and the sexuality that often marks it, Powell still makes no doctrinaire case for the opposite life style. Gwatkin, for example, considers himself invulnerable to temptations away from his duties because he is married. That ought to guarantee access to the Mithraic virtue of purity. But Powell never undersells the power of sex, as Maureen the barmaid proves to Gwatkin. "This business of Maureen," says Nick, "could be regarded only as a judgment on Gwatkin. . . . Now, he had himself been struck down by Aphrodite for his pride in refusing incense at her altars" (VB 198). Two sharp complications keep this from being the straight object lesson it sounds. Maureen having been the one to cause Gwatkin to forget code words, the scene of his military undoing in a night alarm is treated with ruthless sexual allusion.* The second complication involves Nick. Nick had first made Gwatkin consider Maureen as available for bed. It may have been only a man-of-the-world's mistake, yet Nick was misreading Gwatkin's character when he advised him to "Tell [Maureen] by all means" about being married and see what developed.

> He looked at me astonished. I felt a shade uncomfortable, rather like Mephistopheles unexpectedly receiving a hopelessly negative reaction from Faust. Such an incident in opera, I thought, might suggest a good basis for an aria.   (VB 191)

Drifting into the musical reflection seems to call up an old streak of Nick's: a tendency to vapidness, induced by the arts, that still needs some exorcism: and as a Mephisto or Pandarus here he is falling short again of considered loyalty. At least I think this is why Powell uses the quick Faustian allusion (if my remarks do not sound too priggish). Never does a question of adultery come up with respect to Isobel in *The Music of Time:* not yet, anyway, though Nick is stirred up some by Pamela Flitton in *The Military Philosophers.* In this instance with Gwatkin, however, his error seems that of mistaking his man through general laxity. Gwatkin will soon be thanking Nick for putting the idea of seduction in his head. And for this, Gwatkin is undone.

Where this culpability will be paid for is in *The Soldier's Art.* Then, once Nick's loyalty is relocated on sure orthodox lines, it will be retested in *The Military Philosophers.* (However, the story in those two places will not be directly related to Gwatkin, but rather to Odo Stevens, so my next section will deal with that aspect of the theme of purity slowly fashioned by Powell.) Meanwhile in *The Valley of Bones* Powell shadows Nick with

---

"Gwatkin stepped quickly out of bed. His pyjama trousers fell from him, revealing sexual parts and hairy brown thighs. The legs were small and boney, well made, their nakedness suggesting something savage and untaught, yet congruous to his nature. He grabbed the garments to him and held them there, standing scratching his head with the other hand" (VB 208).

a character reminiscent of Uncle Giles, called Bithel—a fellow
with false teeth and a false past, a subscriber to sexual digests—a
vague stand-in who may be thought of as concentrating the worst
of Nick's softness. In the officers' mess at Castlemallock, Bithel in
his cups had appeared to make advances to a private soldier
tending bar. Gwatkin made a dramatic arrest of him then, but
forgot to dispose of his case—this error providing a last link for
the dismissal of Gwatkin from his post. After their superiors have
seen fit to hush up the Bithel case, Nick has a brief talk with
Gwatkin which seems to fuse the laxity just spoken about into
the main theme of *The Valley of Bones*. Nick says:

> "Probably just as well to drop the whole affair."
> Gwatkin sighed.
> "Do you think that too, Nick?"
> "I do."
> "Then you really don't care about discipline either," said
> Gwatkin. "That's what it means. You're like the rest. Well, well,
> few officers seem to these days—or even decent behaviour."
>
> (VB 215)

Those are Gwatkin's last words as company commander. But a
final event with Maureen is to follow, and through its impact
Nick seems to shed *his* Mephistophelic uniform. It is an eaves-
dropping scene, and its conclusion brings on the laughter that
breaks up Gwatkin's infatuation. Maureen and a well-known
philanderer named Corporal Gwylt are discovered spread-eagled
on a bench in one of Castlemallock's more remote glades. Nick
is speechless; Gwatkin nevertheless hammers at him to say something. The reply thus startled out of Nick ought not to be taken
ironically or lightly, at the risk of misreading Powell gravely.
Powell's sense of mythic circularness, and of moments when polite
surprise will not suffice to insulate Nick Jenkins, is at stake.

> "Well, say something."
> "Gwylt ought to pray more to Mithras."
> "What do you mean?"
> "You know—the Kipling poem—'keep us pure till the dawn.' "
> "My God," said Gwatkin, "you're bloody right."
>
> (VB 230)

Much has been founded in these foregoing remarks on Nick's relationship with Gwatkin, and the moral residue it leaves, because Gwatkin, though an enormously important character, drops right out of *The Music of Time* after this. He is replaced in *The Military Philosophers* by Nick's last chief, Lieutenant Colonel Lysander Finn—another Celt, one gathers from his name, but a man who combines all of Gwatkin's amiable quixotic characteristics with much greater stability. For one thing, Finn has earned the Victoria Cross in the previous war. He may therefore become a paragon of orthodoxy without any restlessness about failing to make his mark; and we shall see that he is a synthesis-figure. In the middle volume, Widmerpool was Nick's chief; that was when the return to "thinking first" was warranted, rather than "serving first." Under Finn it will be a workable combination of thinking and serving that evolves (as the war gets won).

Though the prayer to Mithras is not repeated after *The Valley of Bones,* it is paralleled there and afterwards by a book of Alfred de Vigny's: *Servitude et Grandeur Militaire.* When Powell reviewed this book in 1953, he wrote: "Vigny's thesis is briefly this: that it is not so much a soldier's courage on the field of battle that makes him a person of a special sort, but the tedious life he has to endure to make him a fit person for his courage to be used. . . . The nobility and saintliness of a soldier's life, if properly lived—so Vigny indicates—is in his capacity to submit to the dullness, futility and servitude which are the unavoidable accompaniments of military routine."[4] A man Nick meets on a train, David Pennistone, shows him this book, and Vigny's subject becomes thematic thenceforward: "losing the man in the soldier—what he calls the warrior's abnegation," as Pennistone explains it (VB 108). Pennistone, who works for Finn, will become Nick's mentor in the war trilogy, in the sense that Barnby and Moreland were in the other ones—his "military philosopher."

As for Vigny's code, Nick has been working along this track himself, though as I have implied, "vamping" along it. In the section of *The Valley of Bones* covering his leave, he runs into the old fire-eater Dicky Umfraville (a nightclub owner met earlier in *The Music of Time*). It is important that Umfraville gives him another Frenchman's view of the art of soldiering—Marshal Lyautey's. "Do you know what Lyautey said was the first essential of an officer? Gaiety. That was what Lyautey thought, and he knew his business" (VB 152).

So again an idea of balance comes up, Powell again edging clear of a doctrinaire position. Unquestionably, sheer gaiety, near bravado, represents an alternative way of making "these bones live." All the same, for Nick the line of abnegation is the one being played out. A paragraph composed on his return from leave marks this conclusion:

> At Castlemallock I knew despair. . . . Like a million others, I missed my wife, wearied of the officers and men round me, grew to loathe a post wanting even the consolation that one was required to be brave. . . . Here, indeed, was the negation of Lyautey's ideal, though food enough for the military resignation of Vigny.   (VB 171–172)

In brief, Powell's view is broad enough to embrace opposite doctrines, but to understand as well the more consistent applicability of the second, Vigny's. "Like a million others. . . ." There are not many Umfravilles; nor are there many like Pennistone, a man who can actually combine the Vigny and Lyautey ideals. (He brings real joy to unglamorous liaison work. "Though absolutely dedicated to his duties with the Poles, he also liked getting as much amusement out of the job as possible" [MP 33].) Rather, there are more like Gwatkin, whose intentions are good but who become too far weighed down by events. Vigny and Mithras remain for them, providing their imaginations can have access to such doctrines. Failing this, disaster can result. As though to mirror Gwatkin's potential despair, Powell gives in each volume of the trilogy an account of a suicide. In the first book it is Sergeant Pendry who succumbs, strictly because of marital problems; in the second, Captain Biggs takes his life because of combined marital and military oppression; in the third, an officer named Stebbings has been invalided out of the army and has gassed himself. "Felt as browned off out of the army as in it," as someone informs Nick (MP 199). We recall that Albert Pye too, of *Caught*, gassed himself. And in *The Military Philosophers* we are to learn that Gwatkin has been invalided out of the army to return to a difficult domestic situation. Yet there is no hint at all that he will be borne under, a suicide, no matter what his disappointments, and they are great:

> The thought of Gwatkin and his mother-in-law had some-
> times haunted me; the memory of his combined horror and res-
> ignation in face of this threatened affliction. To have his dreams
> of military glory totally shattered as well seemed, as so often in
> what happens to human beings, out of all proportion to what
> he had deserved, even if these dreams had, in truth, been im-
> practicable for one of his capacity.   (MP 176)

No, not even on the heels of this do we assume Gwatkin may take the way out of Pendry, Biggs, and Stebbings. There is a different order of toughness I think we can count on. If Gwatkin aspired once to the gallantry of Kiplingesque heroes, it was Kipling himself who had quoted the Mithraic alternative. And *The Valley of Bones* has shown that the consolation of dedication beyond the self remains, offering the broadest context—extending even to an officer now returned to a bank job in war—after the demanding Lyautey ideal of gaiety may have proved inapplicable.

EMBARRASSMENT

Aside from the fact that Widmerpool enters at the end of *The Valley of Bones* to commandeer Nick, and that Bithel and Pennistone drift into both novels to provide moments of embarrassment and reassurance, there is not much in the story line to help connect *The Valley of Bones* and *The Soldier's Art*. (Gwatkin's failure to appear after the first book is a case in point.) What does secure the strongest continuity is the doubling of the home leave sections. In the first leave, some love affairs among Nick's in-laws the Tollands come to light on a visit Nick pays to Isobel (soon to have a baby). His staid sister-in-law Frederica, a widow, has become almost giddy over her engagement to Umfraville, now back in uniform. Gaiety, his recipe for facing a war, has clearly infected her. But her brother Robert Tolland conducts a very subdued love affair with Flavia Wisebite, of the luckless Stringham family. These two affairs offer a momentary little replica of the Lyautey-Vigny alternatives. Robert has volunteered for an overseas posting, and in leaving Flavia he is on his way to his death at Dunkirk. Nick ponders on the sense of precognition Robert seemed to have, his apparent submission to "a destiny that required him to fall in France; or was Flavia's luck so irredeemably bad," Nick wonders, "that her association with him was sufficient . . . [to dominate] the issue of life and death? Robert could even have died to escape her" (VB 196–197).

The mention of the shadow of Flavia's bad luck pushes forward toward the second and third books of the trilogy because Flavia, survivor of two wretched marriages, is Charles Stringham's sister and Pamela Flitton's mother. In due course Nick will meet Private Stringham—Childe Stringham, as Charles will have it—and once again submission, but this time with great clarity, will be the order of the day. The long and thoughtful passage on Robert Tolland's death (Robert had barely been glimpsed before in *The Music of Time*) is one of the best instances of Powell's moody and comprehensive thoughtfulness about individuals and their destinies—it being inconceivable for Powell to be in any way susceptible to thoughts about mass death. Meanwhile, a new couple have pitched into the musical chairs game at Frederica's house, and the strongest link between *The Valley of Bones* and *The Soldier's Art* is forged as a result of them. For, as was said before, Nick's error in *The Valley of Bones*—his failure to think and his lax advice to Gwatkin—turns round on him in the sequel because of his own family. He makes the same error again at Frederica's. He has been chauffeured there by Odo Stevens, whom he introduces to his sister-in-law Priscilla (staying with Frederica while her husband Chips is in the marines). Nick is no one's moral guardian, of course, and cannot be expected to sheer his comrades of the moment off from sanctified premises if the comrades happen to be confirmed sexual interlopers like Stevens. But his own error of not noticing (more of a mental fogginess than when he had turned his head from the Moreland-Priscilla affair) brings him to a condition of remorseful dutifulness in *The Soldier's Art*. There Priscilla has run off with Stevens. It is virtually a symbol in *The Valley of Bones* that Nick and Stevens have to rush back to their base at just the point when Isobel gives notice of her first labor pains. Nick's baby is born but Nick has got to be scurrying off with Stevens, in retreat as it were, for the folly of having compromised his family.

At the Café Royal, in the central section of *The Soldier's Art,* Nick has to face the accusation of Chips Lovell, who says to him, "It would interest me to hear more of this fellow Stevens. You seem to be mainly responsible for bringing him into our lives, Nick" (SA 107). The two phenomenal coincidences that are now about to occur bring Nick to bar as part of the prevailing *Music of Time* leitmotiv. He is impelled into loyalty, without a chance to draw breath, and when he tries to retard the pull of responsibility on him he is only yanked along by it. There is first of all the arrival of Priscilla and Stevens at the restaurant Chips Lovell has just quitted. As the couple join Nick's group (he is with Moreland and Mrs. Maclintick), the phrase that guides his behavior becomes "where Lovell's interests were in question" (SA 131). He even gets set to declare himself with the phrase that had marked the climax of the first sextet: "It was now or never." With this he painfully announces his position as Chips's advocate to Priscilla—an embarrassment of some magnitude in these circumstances.

The second coincidence is a daring one for Powell to have perpetrated, yet inescapable given his belief in the interlocking of events as finally corresponding with character, no matter what the scale of action. Priscilla, notably quiet as the group converse (perhaps chastened by not having received any sanction from Nick), thinks she hears a blitz in progress. She proves right: her husband Chips is killed at this instant, victim, with a whole party at the Madrid, of a single bomb dropped by a single bomber. Some unwelcome secret grasp of this turns Priscilla sour suddenly, to the degree that she abandons Stevens and Nick's group and returns to Lady Molly's, where she is staying. When

Nick learns later at Moreland's that Chips has been killed and it devolves on him to get the news to Priscilla, for the second time an unwillingness to be forcibly implicated in others' tragedies makes him want to evade. He does not telephone Molly's immediately. "In a cowardly way, I delayed action until Mrs Maclintick had returned with the tea" (SA 158). When he does finally telephone there is no line to the Jeavonses' that will work. Nick has to make his way there through London blackout, to find waiting for him an ugly double dose for his cowardice. Molly and Priscilla are both dead, the house bombed, as the Madrid had been, by a single plane.

This has been real cowardice, the curse of embarrassment. As Moreland had been saying a couple of hours before, "I have an impression of acute embarrassment when bombed. That rather than gross physical fear—at present anyway" (SA 138). Nick gives unqualified assent. Indeed, the whole question of action, of coming under fire, has been handled in *The Soldier's Art* as being directly complementary to being involved in crises demanding moral or even social courage.*

In effect what Powell does in the war novels is normalize the fear problem—reversing once again a time-honored technique of war reportage, with its emphasis on depicting to non-initiates "A Way You'll Never Be." The "action" war novel fragmentates and particularizes experience of war, but Powell's variation normalizes and generalizes. After an air raid at the beginning of *The Soldier's Art*, Nick reveals his own thoughts on the matter. He considers fear to be the result of tenuous rather than imminent pressures. The cliché thus overthrown (in terms of this trilogy's treatment of army life) is that seeing action and finding out about

---

*An interesting comparison, and one having relevance to the theme of "a tailor's war," can be drawn from Wyndham Lewis's memoirs: "When the first shell would come over, I would roll swiftly out of the flea-bag and pull on my trenchboots. That is really all I worried about. I think the whole of his feet are man's 'Achilles heel.' I would hate to face a firing squad in my stocking feet! Clothing and its part in the psychology of war is a neglected subject. I would have braved an eleven-inch shell in my trenchboots, but would have declined an encounter with a pipsqueak in my bare feet." (Blasting and Bombardiering [London, 1937], p. 127.)

one's personal bravery are matters of accident in war, and not nearly so relevant as *serving where one serves:* that it simply doesn't matter whether Gwatkin, for example, or Widmerpool or Stringham, will see action for no test ultimately resides there. Character as modified by war does not depend on coming under fire. Embarrassment at the source covers *all* forms of fear with a wide blanket—though the fear-graph might well "rise steeply" should physical danger become inordinately intensified, Powell is careful to add (SA 16). Hence the reflection on Nick's moral courage—the uncanny coincidence of the deaths of Priscilla and Chips—Nick's twisting about to gain time, either when Priscilla is approaching his table or when he is dodging, with a sip of tea, the imminent duty of dialling a telephone. These are none other than direct complements of soldiering, of doing or avoiding the brave thing in war, of going through war.

There is lastly the problem of human limits, and of strange reversals waiting when these are reached, treated by Powell through the civilian casualty at the Jeavonses'. At the house itself is Eleanor Walpole-Wilson, daughter of Sir Gavin, an annoying, barely half-explained character from the earlier novels, met here in the difficult role of having to give help and consolation. Nick's finding her here leads to a very Powellian inclusion, a brief expansion (like expanding a photo) of her character. Eleanor explains how she once came to take a flat with Norah Tolland— and much of what seemed a Lesbian mystery comes prosaically clear as a simple escape from boredom, her seizing of a chance to move to town from the country. Nick even kisses Eleanor. The quietness of these aftermath-of-shock reactions, which reveal only plainness at the base of a rather outré character, proves right to the bombing circumstances, where the weight of the loss cannot be taken directly and where, therefore, concerns of the living force their way uppermost.

And for Nick to kiss this mannish girl, "which I had never done before" (SA 165), is almost an atonement for having, in his inadvertent way, fouled his past by being the agent to have come between Chips and Priscilla. Perhaps this is saying too much. At least it is true that kissing her in the demolished drawing room of Lady Molly's, a house never known for tidiness or correctness anyway—the place where Chips had met Priscilla, by the way—is a gesture of compassion that releases Nick from the millstone of embarrassment.

Direct expression of emotion does seem the only release in many cases when disaster is faced, and in *The Military Philosophers* there are two occasions in particular which are reminiscent of the bombed out scene at Lady Molly's. That is, the two episodes give a sense of limits finally being reached. In each case, though celebration is in order now because of victory, there remains the sense of an outlet-valve having to work, and of a man needing to turn to the living.

The first occurs in Normandy. Nick, with the touring liaison officers, passes through recently liberated territory with many relics of recent fighting strewn about.

> In one of these secluded pastoral tracts . . . an overturned staff-car, wheels in the air, lay sunk in long grass. The camouflaged bodywork was already eaten away by rust, giving an impression of abandonment by that brook decades before. High up in the branches of one of the poplars, positioned like a cunningly contrived scarecrow, the tatters of a field-grey tunic, black-and-white collar patches just discernible, fluttered in the faint breeze and hard cold sunlight. The isolation of the two entities, car and uniform, was complete. There seemed no explanation of why either had come to rest where it was.
>
> At that moment, an old and bearded Frenchman appeared plodding along the road. He was wearing a beret, and, like many of the local population, cloaked in the olive green rubber of a British army anti-gas cape. As our convoy passed, he stopped and waved a greeting. He looked absolutely delighted, like a peasant in a fairy story who has found the treasure. For some reason it was all too much. A gigantic release seemed to have taken place. The surroundings had suddenly become overwhelming. I was briefly in tears.   (MP 157–158)

Here, for the first and only time in *The Music of Time,* Nick weeps. Of course the release comes partly because of the old peasant's delight, but part of the effect is sprung by the peasant's turning up on the spot when a shift to the living needed to be made. Most significant is that it is a German tunic up there so incomprehensibly in the tree—and perhaps it is a German car. Here is the place where Nick responds in the widest sense to the whole affliction, and all of the loss, that was the war.

The other episode occurs in a scene set after the war: the decoration of a French officer who had spent the duration as a clerk and later assistant attaché in the Free–French mission in London. Since liaison work came under "Intelligence," citations for decorations had to be kept secret, although in fact this Captain Kernével was being given an MBE for superior desk work over six years of war.

The irony is that the general—the new CIGS in fact—has become case-hardened to operational decorations awarded for exploits performed in the field. He has just awarded several of these and is unable, in the judgment of Nick who is there as guest, to come up to the appropriate pitch in view of the fact that these are truly heroic men in front of him. Then comes Kernével.

> "Captain Kernével," announced the MS officer.
> He paused for a second, then slightly changed his tone of voice.
> "Citation withheld for security reasons."
> For a moment I was taken by surprise, almost immediately grasping that a technicality of procedure was involved. . . . However, the CIGS heard the words with quite other reactions. . . . These chronicles of the brave had not galvanized him into being in the least garrulous. Now, at last, his face changed and softened. He was deeply moved. He took a step forward. A giant of a man, towering above Kernével, he put his hand round his shoulder.
> "You people were the real heroes of that war," he said.
>
> (MP 240–241)

This scene could have been ironic to the point of sacrilege in the hands of a writer with a different theme. The CIGS is deeply moved, however, on the behalf of many who could not come back from undercover activity in occupied territory—as he turns to this living one, so he supposes, this survivor whose deeds can never be disclosed. But Powell's theme is that the deeds do not make the difference so much as the serving where one serves does. Kernével warrants the show of emotion—on his own behalf and on the behalf of all the desk-sitters and stay-at-homes, Vigny men and Lyautey men combined. This second, positive irony cancels the first, conclusively and incontrovertibly. As Nick leaves with this embarrassed hero—and a most likeable man he is—he assuages Kernével by saying that, after all, if he had been dispatched to the continent and had fallen into the hands of the Vichy government, it could have gone terrible with him. And Kernével agrees that, yes, that could have been embarrassing.

CHILDE STRINGHAM TO THE DARK TOWER CAME

In their last interview Chips Lovell had asked Nick to be his executor; Priscilla had later left the same café as though under compulsion of a presentiment. Their single deaths, in the wake of virtual premonitions, return us to the title and the final theme of *The Soldier's Art*. The hint is that Priscilla and Lovell, even if obscurely, have come to take decisions based on knowledge: Lovell's, to move toward reunion with his wife (but without much hope), Priscilla's, to take a course that seems to pull her into sharing death with her husband.

The idea of decision based on knowledge prevails at last in *The Soldier's Art*. The title could be controversial in one sense, however. This would involve the plausible assumption that Browning's line about thinking first and fighting afterwards is to be taken ironically instead of seriously. All through this book I have of course emphasized the serious intentions of Powell and perhaps have almost dismally scanted his humor. Now the ironic occasion arises again. The reason would have been apparent if I had given anything like a plot instead of thematic summary of the novel, for at the former level it is Widmerpool's book and his exercising of "the soldier's art" is ironic beyond dispute. If the title applies to him then we have a scandal on our hands, no less than a travesty of poor Browning. Coercion and double-

dealing and ferreting skeletons out of closets are all part of
Widmerpool's strategy, but unfortunately the enemy amounts to
other majors and colonels at Divisional Headquarters. Widmerpool, for example, is working to have a protégé installed as chief
of a new Reconnaissance Battalion; he is foiled in the end by
his "opposite number at Command" (SA 22), Major Sunny Farebrother; but the "ineffable, unstemmable smoothness" (SA 196)
of this officer makes him only more slippery than Widmerpool,
not more admirable in their war of wits. And as far as Widmerpool's more immediate enemy is concerned—a colonel who has
his own candidate for the Reconnaissance command—there is no
doubt that Widmerpool does the army a service in uncovering
the military embezzlement carried out by this colonel's pet warrant officer, Diplock. Finally,

> One thing at least was certain: whomsoever [Widmerpool] had
> been trying to jockey into the position of commanding the
> Recce Unit would have done the job as well, if not better, than
> anyone else likely to be appointed. . . . That had to be said in
> fairness to Widmerpool's methods. . . .   (SA 206)

Well, *The Music of Time* has always been amply fair to Widmerpool and his methods: the whole plot of this installment
(especially the Diplock affair) being fairly devoted to them. The
final rub, however, which makes it impossible for the title of
The Soldier's Art to bear heavily in the end on Widmerpool, is
that Kenneth sings two tunes. He *does* make personalities count,
sizes up or tracks down individuals, but those personalities do
not make for anything constructive beyond Widmerpool's own
range (as they do when General Liddament singles them out).
Meanwhile, Widmerpool *forever professes that he never operates
with any individualistic forethought.* He "never tired of repeating the undeniable truth that the army is an institution directed
not towards the convenience of the individual, but to the production of the most effective organisation for an instrument designed to win wars" (SA 44).

With a sentence like this one, we have in a trice the main
theme of *The Valley of Bones* cancelled, for Widmerpool is par-
roting that theme now (for his own convenience) and it is thus,

as though at a signal, that the theme serves notice of needing to be abandoned. Consider that when General Liddament singled Nick out as filling a misfit role, Nick remarked, "He was also, it occurred to me, acting in contrast with Widmerpool's often propagated doctrines regarding the individual in relation to the army" (SA 49). The switch from "commencement" to "opposition" should be clear.

This is to say no less than the following: that the Judaic-Christian myth of Ezekiel, the classical-pagan myth of Mithras, the modern-logical myth of Vigny, even the camaraderie induced by popular song—all these converging motifs of anti-individualism may be carried only a certain distance, a turning point arriving when the ear catches the false echoes of such sentiments being pressed into service by the Widmerpools. For heartlessness can terribly easily supplant the submissiveness that is at the core of them. Widmerpool's impersonal heartlessness probably reaches its limit in *The Military Philosophers*. When the Polish mission in London makes a formal protest against the now-Allied Russians (who had committed mass murder on Polish officers in 1939), Widmerpool is again vexed that anything verging on personal or even national grievances should get in the way of smooth cooperation among the Allies. "They are rocking the boat in the most deplorable manner," he says of the aggrieved Poles (MP 105).

In *The Soldier's Art* the scale is smaller, but connivance at murder is not so far out of the picture as it might appear to be. Nick himself does not realize these possibilities and even at the end of the book, when Widmerpool has Charles Stringham transferred from his waiter's job to the Division Mobile Laundry, Nick believes Widmerpool has done Stringham a favor for "old school's sake." Not a bit of it: Widmerpool has acted *im*personally and is simply sweeping a bug under a rug. Stringham, entirely innocently, had helped Nick and Widmerpool carry the drunken Bithel back to his quarters one night, and this was too unsavory (Stringham being only an "other rank") for Widmerpool to countenance. "Nicholas, have you heard of the word discipline?" is the excuse employed by Widmerpool, who knows that Stringham's laundry unit will be shipped off to the Far East in short order (SA 190). That way no one need be embarrassed by Stringham's knowledge of a post officer's squalid behavior. And when Widmerpool simultaneously has Bithel administratively removed from that same Mobile Laundry and from the army as well, the awful deadweight involved in the "principled" or impersonal approach comes over as clearly as anywhere in Powell's work. Says Widmerpool off-handedly of Bithel,

> "Tears poured down his cheeks."
> "He was upset?"
> "So it appeared."
> The episode plainly struck Widmerpool as of negative interest. That he should feel no pity for Bithel was reasonable enough, but it was a mark of his absolute lack of interest in human beings, as such, that the several implications of the interview—its sheer physical grotesqueness, for example, in the light of what Bithel must have drunk the night before—had made no impression on him he thought worth repeating.
> (SA 187)

The implications are that he has saved Bithel's life and cost Stringham his, but range of this sort simply does not come into the question because Widmerpool deals about him with that "absolute lack of interest." And so, paradoxically, where a man could have been eased to safety and no harm done, Bithel instead is crushed, Powell introducing a lethal metaphor to characterize the Bithel-Widmerpool interview: "there was no melodrama; only effective disposal of the body" (SA 188).

Yet the sources of Powell's titles in the first two war novels, the Bible and the Browning poem, *are* melodramatic, since melodrama seems a giveaway to the presence of the human heart.

"I shut my eyes and turned them on my heart"—this is the first line quoted by Stringham from "Childe Roland" (SA 221). Such a condition rules Widmerpool out from participation in the real meaning of "the soldier's art." I think, in view of the commencement—opposition antithesis, that the earlier theme should be considered, in retrospect, as a means of getting a soldier into *condition:* into a different mental and physical state from what independent civilian life had produced. The idea is that one can't make the transition straight—must be dipped like a novitiate into the service, be "translated from a relaxed system to a far more stringent one," as Wyndham Lewis once put it, and his mutational verb is an excellent choice.[5] But once this is done—as say in the simple anonymity of the Officer Training Corps or basic training—there comes the time for the new application of once more becoming individual. This pattern is demonstrably not followed by Widmerpool.* Rather, it is followed by his archantagonist in *The Music of Time,* and possibly its greatest individual, Stringham, through whom the Browning title is marked out once for all as unironical.

Widmerpool "couldn't have done me a better turn," says Stringham when informed by Nick that the Far East is the destination of the Mobile Laundry. Then Stringham begins to read:

> "I shut my eyes and turned them on my heart.
> As a man calls for wine before he fights,
> I asked one draught of earlier, happier sights
> Ere fitly I could hope to play my part.
> Think first, fight afterwards—the soldier's art;
> One taste of the old time sets all to rights."
>
> (SA 221)

Inside the lines there may be ironies—Stringham thinks back bitterly to "old times" when he was under the thumb of Miss Weedon (Tuffy), as in *Casanova's Chinese Restaurant*—but these are realistic pointers which clarify Stringham's picture of his own past. If Miss Weedon left to go to the challenge of shoring up an aging soldier (Conyers), she seems unknowingly to have left a forming soldier behind her: her will operating negatively now, because Stringham is kicking off the traces of its once necessary oppression. Strange as Stringham may have grown as a standoffish messboy laundryman, he is on a road to reclaiming self-respect as well. There is almost a phoenix type of symbolism

---

"Although Widmerpool prided himself on his own grasp of army life, he had not been able wholly to jettison the more civilian approach, that you are paid to give advice to your superiors . . . that such advice should be presented in the plainest, most forceful terms" (SA 60).

working, Lady Molly's having been destroyed: where Stringham "used to live in that top floor flat with Tuffy looking after me— where I learnt to be sober. Where Tuffy used to read Browning. Is it all in ashes?" (SA 222).

All of this centers on Stringham's accepting his new life *with clarity,* and Powell ultimately puts so much leverage into this idea that he springs it three times, causing Stringham's first enunciation of a quest for clarity to echo twice more in *The Soldier's Art.* This is an intention that Robert Morris observed also.[6] Civilian and military alternates, as they might be called, relay the theme. And the characters are among Powell's wisest: stabler than Stringham, and able to amplify what he begins when he confides to Nick long before the Browning episode, "My great amusement now is trying to get things straight in my own mind" (SA 82). The soldier Pennistone is the second to promote the theme of thinking things through.

> When I came to know him better, I found what mattered to Pennistone was what went on in his head. . . . While other people lived for money, power, women, the arts, domesticity, Pennistone liked merely thinking about things, arranging his mind. . . . It was the aim Stringham had announced now as his own, though Pennistone was a very different sort of person from Stringham, and better equipped for perfecting the process. I only found out these things about him at a later stage.
>
> (SA 105–106)

This deliberate flash forward is then matched on the civilian side by Moreland at the Café Royal:

> "Since war prevents any serious work," he said, "I have been trying to think out a few things. Make my lymphatic brain function a little. All part of my retreat from perfectionism. . . . I find war clears the mind in a few respects. At least that can be said for it."
>
> I was reminded how Stringham, too, had remarked that he was thinking things out. . . .   (SA 121)

The most hopeful feature of this reiterated mental activity is that it runs counter, in its way, to the staleness effected by the second year of inactivity in war. Thus *The Soldier's Art* becomes a book of tension, with a positive as well as a negative element to be discovered in its basically static circumstances. There has been ample time to make a retreat from perfectionism, to reduce egotism: this may be the very thing that can set a man's mind straight. Certainly it is a classical precept and certainly it can lead to clear-eyed action or submission, as the tempo of the time may demand. One thing it assuredly does not posit is *compulsive* sacrifice. (Sacrifice, yes.) We should be at peace and understand that we are reading *Stringham* straight because of something *Moreland* says of the war (reversing the apathetic drive of Guy Crouchback, by the way): " 'I seem to have neutralised the death-wish for the moment,' he said. 'Raids are a great help in that' " (SA 114).

If there is any death-wish in this novel, it is that fulfilled by suicide on the last page by the clownish tormentor of Stringham, Captain Biggs, a kind of dragon felled to clear the way for Childe Stringham.* Of course Widmerpool is a bigger, deadlier dragon and is actually characterized that way, seen in his lair below ground in the Cabinet Offices, on many macabre occasions in *The Military Philosophers.* And Stringham's being shipped off to the Far East, just in time to fall into Japanese hands at Singapore, seems to have fulfilled his own joking prophecy about Widmerpool made all the way back in *A Question of Upbringing:* "That boy will be the death of me" (QU 49).

Stringham, listed as missing in the first section of *The Military Philosophers,* is pronounced as unequivocally dead by Widmerpool in the fifth. From the reader's point of view, one recognizes the difficulty Powell must have had to manage the demise of Stringham, whose hold on readers is so palpable. It seems that Powell almost permits the reader to set his will against the probability, while gradually acceding to the likelihood that Charles is dead. In a strange way, Powell creates shock waves around the death of Stringham by announcing the sudden death of other

---

*Robert Morris says perceptively of Biggs that he is the kind that "fights first and thinks afterwards," a complete impediment to the positive theme of the novel. (The Novels of Anthony Powell, p. 241.)

long-endeared figures of *The Music of Time*. Coming to sudden notice late in the book, the unexpected end of Peter Templer muffles the impact of gradually consolidating information about Stringham. Before that, as the middle section opened, Nick had looked at a building Barnby had once helped to decorate, and from out of nowhere had revealed that "Barnby was no longer available to repaint his frescoes. Death had undone him. It looked as if death might have undone Stringham too" (MP 113). The reader has a straw to hold onto here: reacting to the unstinted news about Barnby, he sees how the report on Stringham is less than final. The effect is no less than to make the reader believe, even after Widmerpool's fairly strong but still hearsay evidence, that Stringham remains alive.

That, I think, is very lifelike. But I do not mean that it is emotionally necessary. Powell is not assuaging the reader. One can accept the death of Stringham. Powell causes Nick to reflect several times on qualities of Stringham which show Charles always could have been satisfied with this early death. He remembers Stringham's addiction to the imagery of hymns, for example (MP 221); and he remembers his early and weary clairvoyance, while at school, about inadequacies of life and love—which once disrupted a class of Le Bas' when Stringham quietly read aloud these lines from a Victorian poem:

> "Love is abolished; well that that is so;
>   We know him best as Pain.
> The gods are all cast out, and let them go!
>   Who ever found them gain?"   (MP 63)

Stringham perished in the hands of the Japanese. There is a famous photograph from World War II, showing a kneeling Australian airman about to be beheaded by a Japanese, and the composure of that man's face contains, I think, something of what Powell was able to convey about the unreluctance of Stringham to meet death, however and wherever it would be dealt. Like that airman, he turned out to be a fit monk of war.

Nevertheless Stringham was in effect, though at long range, murdered by Widmerpool. And Widmerpool will marry his victim's niece, on whom Stringham's assets were settled by a will. A savage twofold irony will rectify this wrong. Pamela Flitton is the niece, and it was she who had sent Peter Templer so off his head that he had volunteered for hazardous secret duty in the Balkans. But Pamela blames *Widmerpool* for Peter's death. In an utterly ferocious scene she attacks her new fiancé and calls him, to his face and at a public gathering, a murderer. But it is clear that, despite his callousness, he was not responsible for the abandonment of Templer. "As for not getting Templer out, as you call it, how could I possibly have anything to do with the action, right or wrong, for which the Operational people on the spot are responsible?" (MP 212). The enraged Widmerpool cannot be faulted here; Pamela herself was a more culpable deserter of Peter than he. Yet we realize that Pamela will never let this case rest and that she will hound her husband, perhaps to his death. She has already begun to flay his thick skin worse than a whole corps of Gypsy Joneses could have done, and all on a trumped-up charge.

That is the first irony, and it becomes twofold when we recognize that it is Stringham's legatee who will keep the albatross of murder fast round her husband's neck. The question is not whether Widmerpool will weather the attack in volumes to come —that we cannot know; the man's essential resilience demands that we keep an open mind. The issue is rather that the accuser of murder is Stringham's kinswoman, and that while apparently attacking on behalf of Peter Templer, she will be the proper one to keep the wound green; because, after all, murder indeed is what occurred, and her uncle Charles has been the victim.

THE WINNING COMBINATION

Aside from the new disclosures of such magnitude about *Music of Time* characters, there are two themes developed to great fullness in *The Military Philosophers,* one of which, the synthesis of action and thought, has been suggested already in that it completes the structure of the trilogy. As for the other, it presents something new, which, to my knowledge, has not been tried in the literature of World War II. This is the attempt to appraise the contribution of the minor Allies in the war effort—to see the final years at least from their point of view: Poles, Dutch, Free French, Belgians, Yugoslavs, Czechs, Brazilians, Norwegians, Arabs, Indians. There are characters from all these nationalities and more in the book: characters duly given their idiosyncrasies, faithfully summed up in terms of their commercial or military pasts, felt as real presences interacting, and combined at last into a sort of great spearhead of dedicated wishfulness. What these groups actually contributed was not momentous; yet Powell relegates the two major parties, the Americans and Russians, to the wings. He does, democratically, include a liaison officer from each of these powers in the action—and he includes a Chinaman too ("the vainest people on earth," says a Belgian attaché [MP 155]). But Nick in his liaison section at the War Office does not deal with attachés from other than the minor powers. The result is a widening of the angle of approach almost beyond the point of daring, in that a novelist should decide to bring in such a variety of new characters. But the result becomes very moving, especially since these fighter-diplomats based in England are almost to a man displaced people, representing displaced governments, adumbrating a displaced world.

Powell's success in working them into the novel can hardly be judged critically, it is so much a matter of texture; of his convincing us continuously—in corridors, on staircases, at various headquarters spotted around London, or at benefit concerts or transients' apartment houses—that all these people are functioning as persons but also pulling infinitesimal oars of war. As Nick advances in his job, through the novel's sections, one national group can without confusion replace another. There is a tendency to dwell a bit more on men and types from the countries Nick gets to visit, France, Belgium, and Holland. At least this is true in a way that matters a great deal. To Nick, these types summon up historical, often classical resemblances, and at the same time make him revert to his own bloodline as he had done when in Wales at the commencement of *The Valley of Bones.*

The importance is that the war becomes historically placed. There is less chance for rancor when, for example, the Low

Countries are seen as "designed by Nature for a battlefield, over which armies had immemorially campaigned" (MP 172). The enduring types from these places stretch right through the past, to Nick's practiced eye.

> On the whole, a march-past of Belgian troops summoned up the Middle Ages or the Renaissance, emaciated, Memling-like men-at-arms on their way to supervise the Crucifixion or some lesser martyrdom, while beside them tramped the clowns of Teniers or Brouwer, round rubicund countenances, haled away from carousing to be mustered in the ranks. These latter types were even more to be associated with the Netherlands contingent. . . .   (MP 88)

Their leaders—the attachés with whom Nick is friendly—evoke the same responses: Kucherman "seemed to belong to the eighteenth-century, the latter half"; "Van der Voort's air had something faintly classical about it too . . ." (MP 88, 89). By way of a Breton figure, Kernével, Powell carries the idea across to his own Welsh kind. "It was tempting," he has Nick reflect, "to look for characteristics of my old Regiment in these specimens of Romano-Celtic stock emigrated to Gaul under pressure from Teutons, Scandinavians and non-Roman Celts" (MP 139). And when Nick comes into the sound of cannon fire, near Roermond which the Germans still hold, he senses no less than a geological homecoming: he has encountered members of his and Gwatkin's old regiment, and hears them sing one of their old hymns before they pass out of sight, "to move eastward towards the urnfields of their Bronze Age home" (MP 177).

All of this counter-resistance to the aggressive Teutons marks a vast theme, carried well beyond England of course, of the to-and-fro movements of generations upon generations of men. The individuals we have been mentioning are meanwhile men close to Nick's heart. It is Kernével, as we have seen, who is to receive the MBE and be named among the real heroes of the war; it is Kucherman to whom Nick gives advice at the end—his own personal contribution, a combination of thinking and acting—that will enable many Belgians to be evacuated to England at a most opportune time.

One more Belgian, Clanwaert, also figures very pointedly in the story. Because of the color of the trousers this man once wore into battle, Powell presents a startling symbol of another universal factor—the connection of sex and war—and again the angle has been kept very wide, a minor foreign figure being suddenly revelatory of a theme already well worked into the trilogy.

Commenting on Clanwaert's amaranth trousers—part of the uniform of a 1914 Belgian unit—Nick indicates that the amaranth is a flower "supposed to be unfading in legend. The other name for it in English is Love-lies-bleeding" (MP 94). With this amaranth comes an accidental verbal doubling: the idea of unfading loyalty, the idea of love faded out. Precisely the same connection can be made here as when Nick read the French officer's translation of *The Arab Art of Love,* where the pull of duty overshadowed the treacherous pull of love. It repeats the biggest message offered in *The Music of Time* through the three quarters of its length to now: the invitation to the English, in *The Kindly Ones,* to find their relief in turning to more austere dedications, having seen or participated in the failure of love. It explains again the tension pushing Gwatkin in the first war novel, Stringham in the second, Templer in the third: the rush-into-danger or the controlled acceptance of monasticism. And that this idea is now offered in a wider perspective can be proved by the fact that this same Clanwaert, because "a love affair went wrong" in decadent Brussels (MP 90), left Europe, after the first war, for Congo service. "For a long time, if you believe me," he tells Nick, "I was Elephant Officer. Something to hold the attention" (MP 95). That Clanwaert proves to be one of the few officers in *The Military Philosophers* who can react coolly to Pamela Flitton is another tribute to the role of the unregretful austerity he represents.

In the light of all this, one may wonder why the duty complex of the war trilogy needed any leavening at all. Pamela Flitton and other secretive characters seem to generate such divisive effects that it would seem natural to endorse a theme radically opposed to her own abandoned program. For, of all the men she snares in England, Pamela's name is most closely associated with that of a character never met, a certain Szymanski. He is an undercover agent, always employed on some knife-in-the-back mission: but when he returns to London (where various foreign missions disclaim him) he always makes trouble. He is a lord of misrule, "one of those professional scourges of authority that appear sporadically in all armies . . ." (MP 83). Even that most circumspect of all officers, Sunny Farebrother, actually loses his job as a result of getting Szymanski out of jail on one occasion of underhandedness.

The question returns—why does the theme of the trilogy not brand the presence of Pamela and Szymanski anathema and settle for aboveboard behavior alone as the criterion for prosecuting a war? The answer is that Powell, for all his affinity for order, goes close to acknowledging that the whole abstraction for which the English are fighting is an unclean one after all. What happens at the bottom happens, or is condoned, at the top too. The British Government itself is no different from any other. With no taste himself for the "military bohemianism of the most raffish sort," to which he finds the British leaders willing enough to resort, Powell is not stiffish and can have Nick reflect with fairness, "It was just another view as to how the war should be won; perhaps the right one" (MP 93).

By all means Powell prefers the opposite view of his hero Colonel Finn; but he will not dogmatize and this preference becomes registered only *as* a preference. Finn is devoted to the whole war effort, but his first commitment is to those with whom he is serving, and their preservation of mutual confidence. This is close to the theme of friendship in *The Music of Time*. To Finn, inordinate appetite for secret trafficking undermines confidence, and he would just as soon let all that part of war alone.

> Secret machinations of the most outlandish kind might be demanded by total war; they were all the same to be avoided— from the security point of view and every other—by those doing a different sort of job. That was Finn's view. You could take it or leave it as a theory.   (MP 10)

We can see from these two competing views why Powell called his novel *The Military Philosophers*. By tracing Finn through three brief sequences—the first, middle, and final moments of contact with him—we shall also be able to see him revere the abstraction of Government Regulations and then be delivered from *unqualified* reverence of it—which is all that matters.

On the second page of the novel Finn is caught sight of "heavily descending the stairs with the tread of Regulus returning to Carthage"—a humorous allusion nevertheless matching him up with perhaps the most regular hero of all time, one who honored a Carthaginian parole and returned voluntarily to be tortured to death. It is an appropriate label for Finn, sticking to him till the end.

Of all his brisk responses to the call of duty, the best is reserved for France. Finn, too, is chaperoning the Allied attachés on their battleground tour, and has one large worry—that his charges not stumble on the top-secret logistics operation called Pluto, Pipe Line Under The Ocean. However, a call of nature causes the motorcade of officers to stop once near certain excavated ground.

> The convoy halted at last to allow the military attachés to relieve themselves. Out of the corner of my eye, I saw the worst had happened. We had blundered on a kind of junction of Plutonic equipment. Finn must have instantaneously seen that too. He rushed towards the installation, as if unable to contain himself—perhaps no simulation—taking up his stand in such a place that it would have been doubtful manners to pass in front of him. On the way back to the cars he caught me up.
>
> "I don't think they noticed Pluto," he whispered.
>
> (MP 158)

There can be but few other cases on record of the male organ being put to use in service of military security. That it has been used to the disruption of security has of course long been known; this has been one of the sub-themes for Powell all along—involvement in or betrayal of war secrets has always been paired with sexual shadiness, from the time poor Gwatkin forgot the code words till Widmerpool, on a secret jaunt to Egypt, met and became engaged to Pamela Flitton.

Funny as it is—and it vies with the funniest moments in *The Music of Time*—this paragraph must not be underestimated in importance. It is an anticipation, in the purest possible form, of Nick's own rapid analysis of a situation and his immediate action, which at the end of this fourth section gets many restive Belgians delivered out of harm's way to England. That is the clue: action along with analysis, the synthesis of the two antithetical themes of *The Valley of Bones* and *The Soldier's Art;* the fusion (rather than having either take precedence) of action and thought. "Finn must have instantaneously *seen. . . .* He *rushed. . . .*" And what is the ultimate proof of the moment's significance is that Finn discharges simultaneously both a military and a personal feat: again the parallel themes of the first and second war novels. The phrase "taking up his stand" is half military and half urinary. There is no gainsaying that. The scene is not the climax of the trilogy but is the very next thing to it and the epitomizing symbol of it.

Only when the war is over does Finn relax his standards. He and Nick are in charge of the foreign contingents—Neutrals and Allies—present at the Victory Day service at St. Paul's. Finn uses the liaison section's car to collect a salmon sent to him from Scotland (Regulus turns in his grave). This act precipitates Nick himself back into civilian life because, walking instead of riding home from the ceremony, he falls in with a Neutral attaché who offers him a lift. It is the Argentine officer who married Jean Duport in Buenos Aires, and Jean and her daughter are in the car. No reunion could have possibly brought back the pre-war world with such force as this one. What it may signify the future will show.

But I intend to end not looking forward but rather back, and back immediately to Finn. When Finn made his break with Regulations the war was over; but all the time before that he had remained something of a martinet—so much so that Nick needed to bypass him, when engaged in his own small bit of intrigue to get his Belgians out of Brussels. Finn would have remained firm about protocol at that time, and the Belgians might have meanwhile gotten decimated by friendly liberating forces. Yet Finn's Regulus-like inflexibility is never disparaged. The reason for this might be put this way: Finn is a Celtic type. There is enough volatile potential in this single fact to make it all well and good that he should advocate and practice such austerity. His behavior holds a rein on volatility and quixotry—the best possible pattern for character-realization under tension. (That is just what Powell said too, about writing, when he likened it to jumping horses along a ribbon with just the right amount of effort.)

But the English at large are as much Teutonic as they are Celtic. The Bretons Nick had referred to had been pushed out of England after all by Teutons. And this other plain fact elicits one of Powell's most sweeping admissions. He locates, in what might be called English cant about discipline, and in a certain surliness displayed by their officer class, qualities which positively require that no hundred per cent dutifulness be forthcoming. Kind as he is toward the quirks of generals, he is not averse to showing them at their worst. In one such unflattering scene Nick observes a surly, relatively high-placed general transgress on a senior general's sanctuary and be given a horrendous dressing down. The junior general immediately grovels, a reaction which "was disturbing to me," says Nick (MP 143); his description of the transgression is equally disturbing.

> . . . This reckless incursion produced a really alarming result. Somebody—if it were, indeed, a human being—let out a frightful roar. Whoever it was seemed to have lost all control of himself.
> *"I thought I told you to wait outside—get out . . ."*
> (MP 142)

If this sounds Hitlerish, it ought to. The intelligent Belgian Kucherman trumps this scene only two pages later by causing Nick to take back some words about the "caving in of the German military caste" (MP 145)—a remark made apropos of the German generals' plot against Hitler. Nick had felt German militarism to have been something unique to that country. "That's something you always exaggerate over here," he is told by the Belgian.

> "I don't mean what you say isn't true of the Germans," he said. "Of course it is—anyway up to a point, even in the last

twenty years. What you underestimate is the same element in
your own country."
"Not to any comparable degree."
Kucherman remained obdurate.
"I speak of something I have thought about and noticed," he
said. "Your fathers were in the War Office too."
(MP 145–146)

Kucherman is speaking more or less figuratively in his final
sentence; nevertheless Nick is rather floored by this line of attack.
And it is immensely generous of Powell, whose father was, after
all, in the "War Office" too, to accept the barb. After two wars,
the men of Powell's generation—especially conservative men, especially soldierly men—have found it virtually impossible to forgive
the Germans. A likeness such as that drawn by Kucherman is
bitterly hard to accept. But truth has to come first, and it is
always a tribute to *The Music of Time*—especially at the trilogy-
enders, *The Acceptance World*, *The Kindly Ones*, and now *The
Military Philosophers*—that Nick, intelligent as he is, is increasingly enlightened by unpalatable truths which indicate how he
has been content to go along a little smugly on this or that "con-
ventional enough summary of [a] situation . . ." (MP 145).

That is why, to the major input of austerity and discipline,
there must be added a minor input of subversive individualism,
to prevent any fixed attitude from jelling and to bring this
trilogy, like the others, into balance. Again it is a balance that
includes but suppresses one of the antithetical factors, allowing
the other to predominate. The "calls to order" sounded in the
war trilogy are rather continuous. But at the same time, all along
the way, there is sporadic acceptance of the irregular—a factor
that prevents the theme from advocating sheer dutifulness. Dedication to the war effort is strong, but as was observable even in
The Valley of Bones, "the individual still counts . . ." (VB 109).
Together these made a very winning combination.

NOTES

1. ORTHODOX ORIGINALITY

1. Anthony Powell, "The Worthies of Wales," London *Daily Telegraph*, June 26, 1959, p. 14.
2. Lady Violet Powell gives an engaging account of her life as next-to-youngest of the Earl of Longford's children in *Five Out of Six* (London, 1960).
3. Powell, "The Wat'ry Glade," in *The Old School: Essays by Divers Hands*, ed. Graham Greene (London, 1934), pp. 147–162; "Anthony Powell: Some Questions Answered," *Anglo-Welsh Review*, XIV (1964), 77–79. Powell also contributed a questionnaire response to *Twentieth Century Authors*, First Supplement, ed. Stanley J. Kunitz (New York, 1955), pp. 789–790. And recently Powell has written brief memoirs of his friends George Orwell and Evelyn Waugh: in *The Atlantic*, CCXX (Oct., 1967), 62–68; and in *Adam*, XXXI (1966), 7–9.
4. Quoted by Frederick J. Stopp, *Evelyn Waugh: Portrait of an Artist* (London, 1958), p. 24.
5. David Garnett, rev. of *Party Going*, *New Statesman and Nation*, XVIII (Oct. 7, 1939), 489.
6. Interview with the author, August 1965.
7. *Ibid.*
8. "Music of Time," *New Yorker*, XLI (July 3, 1965), 18.
9. "The Wat'ry Glade," pp. 147–148.
10. Harold Acton, *Memoirs of an Aesthete* (London, 1948), p. 93.
11. Henry Green, *Pack My Bag* (London, 1940), pp. 210–211.
12. Interview with the author, August 1965.
13. He once rated Jack London's treatment of violence and spartan achievement as much inferior to Kipling's, "who never undertook a hundredth part of London's adventurous doings. . . ." ("The Violent American," London *Daily Telegraph*, June 21, 1963, p. 20.)

226

14. Powell, rev. of *Marcel Proust: Letters to His Mother, Punch,* CCXXXII (Jan. 2, 1957), 78. In a review dealing with Aubrey Beardsley, Powell quotes a description of the same stamp, Beardsley's record of a conversation with a French priest: "He asked me if I had completed my military service in England, and I felt quite ashamed to confess that we were not expected ever to do anything at all for our country." ("Pierrot of the Minute," *Times Literary Supplement,* March 19, 1949, p. 184.)

15. Interview with the author, August 1965.

16. Powell, rev. of Kenneth Allsop, *The Angry Decade, Punch,* CCXXXIV (June 4, 1958), 755.

17. "The Wat'ry Glade," p. 162.

18. Kunitz, *Twentieth Century Authors,* p. 790.

19. G. U. Ellis, *Twilight on Parnassus* (London, 1939), p. 385.

20. Interview with the author, August 1965.

21. Francis Wyndham, "Novels," *Encounter,* XIX (Sept., 1963), 76.

22. "Work-in-Progress," *Newsweek,* LIX (Jan. 22, 1962), 82.

23. V. S. Pritchett, "Books in General," *New Statesman and Nation,* XLIII (June 28, 1952), 772. Richard J. Voorhees pointed out this same retracing-effect when he observed "how much pathos and tragedy may be revealed by a second look at a comic or farcical situation." ("Anthony Powell: The First Phase," *Prairie Schooner,* XXVIII [Winter, 1954], 341.)

24. Anthony West, "Wry Humor," *New Yorker,* XXVIII (Dec. 13, 1952), 150.

25. Singling out the "conflicting forces of Will and Chance" in Powell, W. D. Quesenbery, Jr., looks back to *Waring* as, "in this respect, a first draft of *The Music of Time:* the chain of coincidence . . . chance acquaintanceship and casual meetings lead eventually to *Waring* where logic has failed." ("Anthony Powell: The Anatomy of Decay," *Critique,* VII [Spring, 1964], 11.)

26. Kingsley Amis, "Afternoon World," *Spectator,* CXCIV (May 13, 1955), 619.

27. Ralph Waldo Emerson, *The Complete Works,* II (Boston, 1903), 58.

28. Interview with the author, August 1965.

29. For example, the phrase is quoted by Arthur Mizener, "A Dance to the Music of Time: The Novels of Anthony Powell," *Kenyon Review,* XXII (Winter, 1960), 80; and by Richard J. Voorhees,

"*The Music of Time:* Themes and Variations," *Dalhousie Review,* XLII (Autumn, 1962), 315.

30. James Hall, *The Tragic Comedians* (Bloomington, 1963), p. 162.
31. Interview with the author, August 1965.
32. The fairly recondite choices of Struwwelpeter and Caracalla bear out Richard Voorhees's remarks about "the cultural superstructure of the series, which," he goes on, "is altogether different from a Huxley novel. Huxley meets his readers halfway by alluding more often than not to major figures (Blake, Renoir, Bach), but Powell is inclined to cite minor and obscure ones (Webster, Pannini, Lortzing)." ("*The Music of Time:* Themes and Variations," p. 316.)
33. Evelyn Waugh, *A Little Learning* (Boston, 1964), p. 201.
34. Interview with the author, August 1965.
35. Norman Shrapnel, "The Artful Rambler," Manchester *Guardian,* July 1, 1960, p. 7.
36. Matthew Arnold, "The Buried Life," lines 30–40, in *The Poems of Matthew Arnold,* ed. Kenneth Allott (London, 1965), p. 272.
37. Wyndham, p. 37.
38. Emerson once wrote: "Men go through the world each musing on a great fable, dramatically pictured and rehearsed before him. If you speak to the man, he turns his eyes from his own scene, and slower or faster endeavors to comprehend what you say. When you have done speaking, he returns to his private music. Men generally attempt early in life to make their brothers first, afterwards their wives, acquainted with what is going forward in their private theatre, but . . . all parties acquiesce at last in a private box with the whole play performed before himself *solus.*" (*Journals of Ralph Waldo Emerson,* VII [Boston, 1912], 75.)
39. Jocelyn Brooke, "From Wauchop to Widmerpool," *London Magazine,* VII (Sept., 1960), 62.
40. Marcel Proust, *Remembrance of Things Past,* tr. C. K. Scott Moncrieff and Frederick A. Blossom (New York, 1934), II, 1123.
41. For example, as early as *Swann's Way* he would say of ordinary memory that "the facts which I should then have recalled would have been prompted only by an exercise of the will, by my intellectual memory, and . . . the pictures which that kind of memory shews us of the past preserve nothing of the past itself. . . ." (*Ibid.,* I, 33.)
42. *Ibid.,* II, 433, 518, 887.

43. *Ibid.*, II, 732.

44. *Ibid.*, II, 995.

45. Gene W. Ruoff, "Social Mobility and the Artist in *Manhattan Transfer* and *The Music of Time,*" *Wisconsin Studies in Contemporary Literature*, V (Winter-Spring, 1964), 75.

46. Proust, II, 293.

47. *Ibid.*, II, 375.

48. Powell, "Lewisite," *Punch*, CCXXXIII (July 10, 1957), 52. The phrase was leveling suspicion at, of all writers, Wyndham Lewis.

49. Lawrence Durrell, *Balthazar* (London, 1958), p. 23. The whole mystique of flux and fever in Durrell and Proust can be seen if one compares Durrell's epigraph to *Clea* with a Proustian passage. The epigraph is taken from Sade: "The Primary and most beautiful of Nature's qualities is motion, which agitates her at all times, but this motion is simply the perpetual consequence of crimes, it is conserved by means of crimes alone." Proust maintains the same thing in getting at the heart of the narrator's fascination for Albertine: "Even when you hold them in your hands, these people are fugitives. To understand the emotions which they arouse, and which other people, even better looking, do not arouse, we must take into account that they are not immobile but in motion, and add to their person a sign corresponding to what in physics is the sign that indicates velocity." (II, 441.)

50. *Ibid.*, pp. 90–91.

51. Durrell, *Clea* (New York, 1960), p. 249.

52. *Ibid.*, p. 251.

53. Proust, II, 164.

54. Durrell, *Balthazar*, p. 148.

55. Powell, rev. of George Gissing, *New Grub Street*, *Punch*, CCXXXV (July 30, 1958), 149.

56. Powell, rev. of Aldous Huxley, *The Doors of Perception*, *Punch*, CCXXVI (Feb. 17, 1954), 243.

57. Powell, "Orwell," *Punch*, CCXXV (July 15, 1953), 100.

58. [Powell], "Marcel Proust," *Times Literary Supplement*, Aug. 18, 1950, p. 516.

59. Durrell, *Balthazar*, p. 15; *Clea*, p. 70.

60. Powell, rev. of *The Diary of John Evelyn*, *Punch*, CCXXX (Feb. 8, 1956), 212.

61. Powell, rev. of *The Private Diaries of Stendhal*, *Punch*, CCXXVIII (June 1, 1955), 688.

62. [Powell], "West African Rock," *Times Literary Supplement,* May 29, 1948, p. 302; "Power Without Glory," *Times Literary Supplement,* Jan. 20, 1950, p. 40.

63. Pamela Hansford Johnson, "Literature," in *The Baldwin Age,* ed. John Raymond (London, 1960), p. 182. Powell would agree, having said with respect to *A Writer's Diary,* "The fact was, so we feel as we read on, Virginia Woolf had not the smallest idea how the rest of the world lived: even in the case of those quite close to her." ("Window in Bloomsbury," *Punch,* CCXXV [Nov. 18, 1953], 614.)

64. William Van O'Connor, *The New University Wits* (Carbondale, 1963), p. 155. Rubin Rabinovitz devotes a whole book to this issue, *The Reaction Against Experiment in the English Novel 1950–1960* (New York, 1967), but he does not make a really searching or enlightened study of it.

65. David Lodge, *Language of Fiction* (London, 1966), p. 245.

66. John Wain, *Essays on Literature and Ideas* (London, 1963), p. 43; Amis, "Afternoon World," p. 619; John Braine, quoted in *Isis,* No. 1507 (Feb. 23, 1966), p. 9.

67. Powell, rev. of Patricia Hutchins, *James Joyce's World, Punch,* CCXXXII (March 27, 1957), 424.

68. Lodge, pp. 259–260.

69. Powell, "D-Day 1066," *Punch,* CCXXXIII (Sept. 11, 1957), 306.

70. Powell, "Ruinenlust," *Punch,* CCXXV (Dec. 23, 1953), 768.

71. Powell, "Idolised Aviator," London *Daily Telegraph,* Sept. 23, 1960, p. 18.

72. Bernard Bergonzi, "Anthony Powell: 9/12," *Critical Quarterly,* XI (Spring, 1969), 81.

2. QUINTET FROM THE THIRTIES

1. Powell mentioned this visit in a review of *The Memoirs of Marshal Mannerheim, Punch,* CCXXVI (Feb. 3, 1954), 187. Invited to "the triennial ball of the nobility of Finland"—his father having had a military post there—he undoubtedly got some of the material for the ball which closes out the action of *Venusberg.*

2. Fyodor Dostoevsky, *Notes from Underground,* tr. R. E. Matlaw (New York, 1960), p. 6.

3. "From a Chase to a View," *Times Literary Supplement,* Feb. 16, 1951, p. 100.

4. Robert K. Morris, *The Novels of Anthony Powell* (Pittsburgh, 1968), pp. 39–40. Morris has also rightly seen the Venusberg title as deriving from the Tannhäuser myth, but where "Tannhäuser recoils sated from the lure of Venus," Lushington yields to Ortrud. (*Ibid.*, p. 37.) The reversed analogy could be taken farther by indicating that just so far as Lushington is not a knight, so is Ortrud not a temptress. His eventual recoil from her being fastidious, she is the one who has all the "knight-shine."

5. Morris, "The Early Novels of Anthony Powell: A Thematic Study," unpub. diss. (U. of Wisconsin, 1964), p. 179. Morris asked these questions not in his book on Powell, but in this partial early version of it.

6. Geoffrey Wagner, *Wyndham Lewis: A Portrait of the Artist as the Enemy* (New Haven, 1957), p. 271.

7. Roger Ascham, *The Scholemaster*, in *English Works*, ed. William Aldis Wright (Cambridge, 1904), p. 215.

8. Christopher Isherwood, *The Berlin Stories* (New York, 1945), p. 46.

9. Robert Browning, "Waring," lines 83–84, in *The Works of Robert Browning* (London, 1912), III, 320.

3. TWO DISTINCTIVE STYLES

1. Susan Sontag, "On Style," *Partisan Review*, XXXII (Fall, 1965), 546.

2. [Powell], "Satire in the Twenties," *Times Literary Supplement*, Sept. 13, 1947, p. 464.

3. George Orwell, "Politics and the English Language," in *Shooting an Elephant and Other Essays* (New York, 1950), p. 90n. Said Orwell, "One can cure oneself of the *not un-* formation by memorizing this sentence: *A not unblack dog was chasing a not unsmall rabbit across a not ungreen field.*" One of Powell's critics became testy on this same issue and cited Orwell in exasperation. (James Stern, rev. of *At Lady Molly's*, New York *Times Book Review*, July 27, 1958, p. 12.)

4. *The Maxims of the Duc de la Rochefoucauld*, tr. Constantine Fitz-Gibbon (London, 1957), p. 151.

5. Peter Quennell, *The Sign of the Fish* (New York, 1960), p. 95.

6. "From a Chase to a View," *Times Literary Supplement*, Feb. 16, 1951, p. 100.

7. Kingsley Amis, "Afternoon World," *Spectator*, CXCIV (May 13, 1955), 619.
8. Interview with the author, August 1965.
9. Cyril Connolly, "The Novel Addict's Cupboard," in *The Condemned Playground* (New York, 1946), p. 116.
10. G. U. Ellis, *Twilight on Parnassus* (London, 1939), p. 385.
11. *Ibid.*, p. 389.
12. R. P. Blackmur, *The Double Agent* (New York, 1935), p. 83. One of the Eliot passages excerpted by Blackmur was itself about abstract time, from *The Waste Land:* "The awful daring of a moment's surrender / Which an age of prudence can never retract."
13. The phrase is Jocelyn Brooke's, in "From Wauchop to Widmerpool," *London Magazine*, VII (Sept., 1960), 62.
14. Mentioning Pope calls to mind V. S. Pritchett's critique of the sugar episode: "The fantasy lies in the brutal thoroughness of the narration. . . . The labyrinth of Proust is connected up with the mock heroic that has run from Fielding to Wodehouse." ("Books in General," *New Statesman and Nation*, XLIII [June 28, 1952], 775.) The point is that a temporary shading over into the mock heroic does not lock the style once for all in that mode.

4. *The Music of Time:* FIRST MOVEMENT

1. E. M. Forster, *A Passage to India* (New York, 1952), p. 76.
2. Robert K. Morris, *The Novels of Anthony Powell* (Pittsburgh, 1968), p. 115.
3. Forster, p. 76.
4. William Butler Yeats, "Ego Dominus Tuus," line 48, in *The Collected Poems of W. B. Yeats* (New York, 1955), p. 159. The connection between dissipation and reality is made explicitly and unironically in *Afternoon Men* when the hangover-ridden Atwater is interrupted in a train of thought by a telephone call. "The secret of life had seemed at that moment not far away. A few more minutes and absolute reality might have been grasped. . . . Years of thought, years of labour, years of dissipation might never bring the conception so near again" (AM 43).
5. Reviewing *Casanova's Chinese Restaurant*, Pritchett said that "What began as a panorama begins to sound like a gossip column. . . . The characters exchange too much hearsay." ("The

Bored Barbarians," *New Statesman and Nation,* LIX [June 25, 1960], 947.)

6. James Hall, *The Tragic Comedians* (Bloomington, 1963), p. 135.

7. [Powell], "Pierrot of the Minute," *Times Literary Supplement,* March 19, 1949, p. 184.

8. Powell, "The Wat'ry Glade," in *The Old School,* ed. Graham Greene (London, 1934), p. 152.

9. James Ward Lee, "The Novels of Anthony Powell," unpub. diss. (Auburn University, 1964), p. 51.

10. F. Scott Fitzgerald, *The Great Gatsby* (New York, 1953), p. 1. While Powell has denied that he named his protagonist after his other Nick, the two are nearly identical in their way of observing life and in their slow approach to loyalty. And Powell considers *Gatsby* to be the best American novel of this century.

11. The phrase is David Williams's, from his review of *At Lady Molly's,* Manchester *Guardian,* Nov. 5, 1957, p. 4.

12. Arthur Mizener, "A Dance to the Music of Time: The Novels of Anthony Powell," *Kenyon Review,* XXII (Winter, 1960), 86.

13. Morris, p. 139.

5. *The Music of Time:* SECOND MOVEMENT

1. Robert K. Morris, *The Novels of Anthony Powell* (Pittsburgh, 1968), p. 171.

2. "Time Marches On," *Times Literary Supplement,* Nov. 1, 1957, p. 653.

3. James Hall, *The Tragic Comedians* (Bloomington, 1963), p. 144.

4. William Butler Yeats, "Under Ben Bulben," lines 33–36, in *The Collected Poems of W. B. Yeats* (New York, 1955), p. 342.

5. Hall, p. 146.

6. Arthur Mizener, rev. of *Casanova's Chinese Restaurant,* New York *Times Book Review,* Oct. 9, 1960, p. 5.

7. Evelyn Waugh, "Marriage à la Mode—1936," *Spectator,* CCIV (June 24, 1960), 919.

8. F. Scott Fitzgerald, letter of September, 1935, in *The Letters of F. Scott Fitzgerald,* ed. Andrew Turnbull (New York, 1963), p. 530.

9. Richard Lister, "The Strange Case of Mr. Powell," *New Statesman and Nation,* XLIX (May 28, 1955), 754.

10. Melvin Maddocks, "Poise Among Shadows," *Christian Science Monitor*, Sept. 27, 1962, p. 11.
11. Wyndham Lewis, *Time and Western Man* (New York, 1928), p. 428.
12. Percy Bysshe Shelley, "The Triumph of Life," lines 228–231, in *The Complete Works of Percy Bysshe Shelley*, ed. Roger Ingpen and Walter E. Peck (New York, 1965), IV, 174.
13. Powell, rev. of George D. Painter, *Marcel Proust*, Vol. I, London *Daily Telegraph*, Sept. 18, 1959, p. 14.
14. Shelley, "The Triumph of Life," lines 188–189, 194.
15. Powell, rev. of Michael Grant, *Myths of the Greeks and Romans*, London *Daily Telegraph*, Dec. 28, 1962, p. 13. Said Powell of the book under review, "This is really the final impact of Mr. Grant's work: the intense reality and importance of these myths to contemporary life, the way in which they form a coherent pattern which can at the same time be endlessly varied."
16. Wilhelm Worringer, *Abstraction and Empathy*, tr. Michael Bullock (London, 1963), p. 15. In his 1948 preface to that 1908 work, Worringer said a very Powellian thing: "I am sacrificing to the god in which I believe most deeply, the *deo ignoto* of chance. . . ." (*Ibid.*, p. xii.)
17. Powell, rev. of Wilhelm Worringer, *Form in Gothic*, *Punch*, CCXXXIII (July 17, 1957), 79.

6. *The Music of Time:* WAR

1. Quoted by Frederick J. Stopp, *Evelyn Waugh: Portrait of an Artist* (London, 1958), p. 46.
2. Henry Green, *Caught* (New York, 1950), p. 77.
3. *Ibid.*, p. 22.
4. Powell, rev. of Alfred de Vigny, *The Military Necessity*, *Punch*, CCXXIV (March 18, 1953), 360.
5. Wyndham Lewis, *Blasting and Bombardiering* (London, 1937), p. 30. "In a word, this existence—that of a soldier—was another existence: not the same one, continued, in a change of scene and circumstances merely." (*Ibid.*, p. 26.)
6. Robert K. Morris, *The Novels of Anthony Powell* (Pittsburgh, 1968), p. 242.

INDEX